Advances in social theory and methodology

Advances in social theory and methodology

Toward an integration of micro- and macro-sociologies

Edited by
K. Knorr-Cetina and *A. V. Cicourel*

Routledge & Kegan Paul
Boston, London and Henley

First published in 1981
by Routledge & Kegan Paul Ltd
9 Park Street, Boston, Mass. 02108, USA
39 Store Street, London WC1E 7DD, and
Broadway House, Newtown Road,
Henley-on-Thames, Oxon RG9 1EN
Photoset in 10 on 12 Baskerville by
Kelly Typesetting Ltd, Bradford-on-Avon, Wiltshire
and printed in the United States of America

Library of Congress Cataloging in Publication Data

Advances in social theory and methodology.

Includes index.
Contents: The micro-sociological challenge
of macro-sociology / K. Knorr-Cetina – Notes
on the integration of micro- and macro-levels
of analysis / A. V. Cicourel – Micro-translation
as a theory-building strategy / R. Collins – [etc.]
1. Sociology–Methodology–Addresses, essays,
lectures. 2. Microsociology–Addresses, essays,
lectures. 3. Macrosociology–Addresses, essays,
lectures. I. Knorr-Cetina, K. II. Cicourel, A. V.
HM24.A33   301   81–8695

ISBN 0-7100-0946-1   AACR2
ISBN 0-7100-0947-X (pbk.)

Contents

Notes on contributors

Pierre Bourdieu is Professor of Sociology at the Ecole des Hautes Etudes en Sciences Sociales in Paris. He began his career as an anthropologist in Algeria (cf. *The Algerians* (1962), *Outline of a Theory of Practice* (1977), and *Algeria 1960* (1979)). Later, he turned to the sociology of culture and education (*The Inheritors* (1979) and *La Distinction*, (English translation forthcoming)). From his widely diverse empirical work on education, intellectuals, literature, art and power, particularly of the ruling class, he developed a systematic theory of the social world founded upon the fundamental concepts of the 'field' and the 'habitus'.

Michel Callon originally completed his studies as an Ingénieur des Mines before turning to sociology and economics. His interest in the policies of great industrial enterprises led to his work on the modalities of the social construction and success of scientific objects, of which a first translation into English appeared in the *Sociology of the Sciences Yearbook Vol 4* on *The Social Process of Scientific Investigation* (1980). He is currently Maître de Recherche at the Centre de Sociologie de l'Innovation at the Ecole des Mines in Paris, where he teaches sociology of science and technique.

Aaron Victor Cicourel received his PhD in sociology from Cornell University. He has taught at various branches of the University of California for the past 21 years. He is a Professor of Sociology in the School of Medicine and the Department of Sociology at the University of California, San Diego. Among his best known works are *Method and Measurement in Sociology* (1964), *The Social Organization of Juvenile*

Justice (1968), *Cognitive Sociology: Language and Meaning in Social Inter-action* (1973) and *Theory and Method in a Study of Argentine Fertility* (1974).

Randall Collins is Professor of Sociology and Member of the Center for Advanced Studies at the University of Virginia. He is the author of *Conflict Sociology: Towards an Explanatory Science* (1975), *The Credential Society* (1979), and *Sociology since Midcentury: Essays in Theory Cumulation* (1981), as well as of a number of papers on both micro- and macro-historical aspects of sociology. He is also co-editor of the newly founded journal of the American Sociological Association, *Sociological Theory*.

Troy Duster is currently Professor of Sociology and Director of the Institute for the Study of Social Change, at the University of California, Berkeley. He is the recipient of a number of research fellowships including awards from the Swedish Government (1962), Guggenheim (1971) and Ford Foundation (1979). He has been a member of the Assembly of Behavioural and Social Sciences of the National Academy of Sciences. He is the author of *The Legislation of Morality* and of a variety of articles including works on theory and methods in the *American Sociologist*, and he is now completing a mono-graph on the social and political issues in the new technology in microbiology.

Gilles Fauconnier is Professor of Linguistics at the University of Paris VIII and the Ecole des Hautes Etudes en Sciences Sociales. His research centres on the syntax and logic of natural language, including work on anaphora, polarity, scalar phenomena, speech acts, pragmatic functions, and mental spaces, on which he lectured at universities in Europe, Africa, the USA and Canada. He is the author of *La conference: syntaxe ou semantique?*, *Theoretical Implications of Some Global Phenomena in Syntax*, *Aspects de la quantification et de l'anaphore* and articles in *Language, Linguistic Inquiry, Theoretical Linguistics, Actes de la Recherche en Sciences Sociales*, etc.

Anthony Giddens is a Fellow of King's College and Lecturer in Sociology at Cambridge University. He is the author of several works in the fields of social theory and political sociology including

Capitalism and Modern Social Theory (1971); *The Class Structure of the Advanced Societies* (1973); *New Rules of Sociological Method* (1976); *Studies in Social and Political Theory* (1977); *Central Problems in Social Theory* (1979). His latest book is *A Contemporary Critique of Historical Materialism* (1981).

Jürgen Habermas, born in 1929, was Professor of Philosophy in Heidelberg (1961–64), and of Philosophy and Sociology in Frankfurt (1964–71). From 1971 to 1981 he was Director of the Max-Planck Research Institute in Starnberg, Germany. He intends to return to a German University. Most of his major works (not, however, *Strukturwandel der Öffentlichkeit*) have been translated into English (see the detailed bibliography in Thomas A. McCarthy, *Critical Theory of Jürgen Habermas*). The title of his forthcoming book represents his main field of interest: *A Theory of Communicative Competence*.

Rom Harré was educated in engineering, mathematics and philosophy, and lectured at the Universities of Punjab, Birmingham and Leicester before he moved to Oxford as a University Lecturer in the Philosophy of Science. He is Fellow of Linacre College, Oxford, has been Visiting Professor at several American and European universities, and is Regular Adjunct Professor in the History and Philosophy of the Social and Behavioural Sciences at Suny, Binghampton. Rom Harré is the founder (with P. F. Secord) of the *Journal for the Theory of Social Behaviour* and author of numerous books and articles including *Social Being, The Principles of Scientific Thinking* (1970), *Causal Powers* (with E. H. Madden, 1975), *The Explanation of Social Behaviour* (with P. F. Secord, 1976).

Karin D. Knorr-Cetina is Associate Professor of Sociology currently visiting at the University of Pennsylvania and Privatdozent at the University of Bielefeld, Germany. A member of the Institute for Advanced Studies, Vienna, and Lecturer at the University of Vienna, she went as a Ford Fellow to the University of California, Berkeley, to work on an empirically/anthropologically founded epistemology of knowledge. In addition to articles in *Theory and Society, Knowledge, Social Science Information, Social Studies of Science*, she is the author of *The Manufacture of Knowledge* (1981) and co-editor of the *Sociology of the Sciences Yearbook 1980*.

Bruno Latour is currently at the Centre Science, Technologie et Société in the Conservatoire National des Arts et Métiers, Paris, where he teaches sociology of science. After studies in exegesis and philosophy, he obtained his 'agregation' in 1971 and his PhD in 1975. He then carried out a sociological study in the Ivory Coast before embarking on a two-year anthropological study of brain science at the Salk Institute in San Diego. He is the author (with Steve Woolgar) of *Laboratory Life: The Social Construction of Scientific Facts* (1979) as well as of a variety of articles on this subject in *Fundamenta Scientiae*, the *Sociology of the Sciences Yearbook 1980*. He is also an editor of the science and technics bulletin, *Pandore*.

Victor Lidz was educated at Harvard University, from which he received both BA and PhD degrees. A student principally of the late Talcott Parsons, he has worked on a variety of problems in the theory of action, with the development of generative theories of process being a major interest. He is co-editor of and contributor to *Explorations in General Theory in Social Science* (1976) and author of several technical papers in the theory of action that have appeared in *Sociological Inquiry*, including essays on law and on secular moral culture.

Niklas Luhmann is Professor of Sociology at the University of Bielefeld, Germany, since 1968. After the war, he originally studied law and worked for some time in public administration. He has published widely in sociology of law and sociological theory, including *Soziologische Aufklärung* I and II (1970 and 1975), and (with Jürgen Habermas) *Theorie der Gesellschaft oder Sozialtechnologie* (1971). Translations of his work into English include *Trust and Power* (1979) and *Differentiation of Society* (forthcoming).

Preface

In the last two decades, we have witnessed a widening gap between micro- and macro-social theory and methodology. This book is an attempt to begin bridging the gap. As argued in the Introduction, micro-sociological developments have challenged traditional macro-sociological approaches to social reality for quite some time. In addition, some authors have now begun to reconstruct macro-sociological phenomena based upon a micro-sociological foundation. On the other hand, new macro-social perspectives such as neo-functionalism or neo-Marxism prominently address and incorporate micro-level phenomena. In short we believe that the time is ripe for re-examining the problems that underlie the micro-macro question, based upon the advances in social theory and methodology that have been made since the 1950s.

We have invited a series of authors to present and discuss their theoretical and methodological version of the relation between micro- and macro-social phenomena, starting from the advances in theory and method to which they often have contributed. The book is a collection of original essays addressed to this topic, with the exception of the paper by Habermas which has appeared elsewhere in English. We count as our audience those working on (or interested in) social theory and methodology, and those who are advanced students of social science disciplines. The original idea for the book was born during an extended observation study which made it plain that if we want to give adequate accounts of the social reality observed, we need to integrate systematically notions of macro- and micro-research. The book seeks to provide conceptual models and observational dimensions for prospective researchers who recognize the need for an integration of macro- and micro-levels of theory and research.

The editors wish to thank the Foundation for the Advancement of Scientific Research, Vienna, for financing part of the theoretical work involved in preparing this volume, and the departments of sociology at the University of California, San Diego, and the University of Pennsylvania, Philadelphia, for facilitating the work. The Institute for the Study of Social Change at the University of California, Berkeley, provided the environment which led to the initiation of the book, and we have drawn from the ideas and critical comments provided by colleagues at many other places over the last years.

Above all we would like to express our appreciation to the contributors to the book who responded with enthusiasm and with almost no delay in writing and reviewing their papers, and to the patience and support of our families.

Editors' note

Each contribution is prefaced with an introduction by the editors.

Introduction:
The micro-sociological challenge of macro-sociology: towards a reconstruction of social theory and methodology

Karin D. Knorr-Cetina

In the last 20 years, we have witnessed an upsurge of social theories and methodologies which are characteristically concerned with micro-processes of social life, such as with face-to-face interaction, with everyday routines and classifications, with strips of conversation, or with definitions of the self and of situations. I have in mind specifically approaches such as symbolic interactionism, cognitive sociology, ethnomethodology, social phenomenology, ethogenics in sociology and the ethnography of speaking and ethnoscience in anthropology.[1] It goes almost without saying that these approaches differ markedly in theoretical background and substantive interest. For example, while today's symbolic interactionism appears to be an outgrowth of Herbert Blumer's reconception of the theories of Mead and Cooley, ethnomethodologists have linked their concerns to Wittgenstein, Heidegger, and most recently Merleau-Ponty, and social phenomenology has obvious roots in the works of Schutz and Husserl.[2] While cognitive sociology has stressed the role of language and memory in the cognitive processing of information in everyday settings, ethnomethodology has focused on the organizational features of 'practical reasoning', and ethogenics and symbolic interactionism, though also concerned with symbolic communication, have described the rules and resources which underlie social accounts on the one hand and the negotiation and management of meaning in interaction on the other hand.

One result of these varying pursuits, which I will refer to as *micro-sociologies*, has been a challenge of established theories and methods in sociology, and particularly of macro-sociological orientations. Macro-sociology is commonly understood as the study of society, of social institutions and of socio-cultural change on an aggregate level.[3] A macro-sociological approach can entail both the use of theoretical concepts on a system level and the use of aggregate data derived from individual micro-level responses to characterize social collectivities. The micro-sociological challenge of such endeavours can best be illustrated by two distinctive but interlocking developments: the move from a normative notion of social order to that of a *cognitive order*, and the rejection of both methodological collectivism *and* individualism in favour of *methodological situationalism*. Both developments have called into question the dimensions in terms of which the micro-macro problem has traditionally been posed, such as the juxtaposition of individual and collectivity or of individual action and social structure. And both developments point in the end towards a reconstruction of macro-social theory and methodology based upon a micro-sociological foundation, or at least based upon an integration of micro-sociological results. I will first present the *cognitive turn* which sociology (and other social sciences) have experienced since the 1950s, and then proceed to discuss methodological situationalism and the consequences of micro-social research for a renewed conception of the micro-macro problem and for a reconstruction of macro-social theory and methodology.

1   From the normative order to the cognitive order

According to Dahrendorf's prominent exposition of modern social thought, two conceptions of social order have ruled Western social philosophy since its beginnings. One is the *integration theory of society* which conceives of social structure as a functionally integrated system regulated by normative consensus. The other he calls the *coercion theory of society* which views social structure as a form of organization held together by force and constraint transcended in an unending process of change.[4] The source of the conflict model of social order is commonly sought in Marx, while the founders of the normative-functional integration model are of course seen to be Durkheim and Parsons.[5] Needless to say, in the American tradition of sociological thought in which most recent micro-sociological approaches have originated, the normative model of social order has dominated the scene. Hence the upsurge of recent micro-sociological orientations must be seen against the contrast of the normative model of order, and not against the contrast of a conflict model informed by Marx.

Discussions of the merits and particularly of the shortcomings of normative functionalism have haunted sociological theorizing for so long that they need not be repeated here. Suffice it to recall the role played by moral obligations in these models and their treatment of human agents. Durkheim, as we know, tended to identify social facts primarily as moral obligations.[6] He recognized moral diversity as concomitant to the division of labour and organic solidarity which he held to characterize modern society. He also assumed that the social being of an individual depends upon internalized norms which are usually seen as a condition for the freedom of action. Yet his emphasis on the 'external' nature of social institutions which impose themselves upon the individual as facts that are 'independent of his individual will', and his crusade against methodological individualism (see below), left no room for conscious social action. With Parsons, on the other hand, individual conduct is explicitly integrated into society through internalized need dispositions, which establish the harmony between individual motivations and the social whole. Parsons took as his starting-point the 'Hobbesian problem of order' which he defined as the problem of how society can exist in a stable way in face of individual interests, the war of all against all.[7] He sought the answer in the notion of common values which, if properly internalized by individual actors as need-dispositions, guarantee that the individual wants what s/he should want, and acts as s/he should act.[8] Yet as critics have pointed out,[9] despite the elaborate 'action frame of reference' social action with Parsons remains a residual category: it is conceived as not more than the execution of a normatively pre-established harmony through individual agents who, in contrast to Durkheim, are seen as internally (rather than externally) controlled by society. The normative conception of order is at the same time a macro-level conception of order. Society is integrated by shared values and obligations. When mediated through an individual's ties to the occupational group (Durkheim) or through reciprocal sets of expectations structured as roles (Parsons), these values and obligations determine individual conduct.

Compared with the normative conception of order, the cognitive turn which I have attributed to micro-sociological approaches is marked by a shift of interest towards language use and cognitive processes that represent and interpret the relevance of values and obligations. It is a move which gives primary consideration to the agents' practical reasoning and which is unconcerned with the causes that allegedly operate behind one's back, a move which posits a *knowing, active* subject as the source of human conduct.[10] Depending on whether the emphasis is placed on 'knowing' or on 'active' in this compound, different research traditions result. In the first case, the knowledge attributed to agents is thought to account for their conduct: participants act in terms of tacit knowledge and rules which they know how to apply in specific situations, but which they may not be able to explicate. It is the task of the social scientist to identify the rules and tacit resources which underlie everyday activities (see Harré and Giddens, below).

The difference between the cognitive rules postulated by this model and the normative obligations invoked in the previous conceptions becomes clear when we spell out the analogy to linguistics drawn upon by many authors (see the summary of Lidz, below). Like the rules of syntax identified in transformational grammar, the rules of conduct sought after in some micro-sociologies are analogous to a level of deep structure of human behaviour, acquired by the individual through socialization. They are not socially codified in a public sense like legal rules or culturally entrenched value-orientations, and their disregard will result in questioning a person's competence or in his or her disqualification as a knowledgeable member of society rather than in legal or moral retaliation. The theory of social action relevant here is a *competence* theory. An explicit version is represented by anthropological ethnoscience.

Ethnoscience deals with what Goodenough once called the ideational order: it attempts to specify explicitly what native speakers have to know (implicitly) about their culture in order to function adequately as competent members of the respective society:[11]

A society's culture consists of whatever it is one has to know or believe in order to operate in a manner acceptable to its members, and to do so in any role that they accept for any one of themselves. . . . It is the forms of things that people have in mind, their models of perceiving, relating and otherwise interpreting them. . . . Ethnographic description, then, requires methods of processing observed phenomena such that we can inductively construct a theory of how our informants have organized the same phenomena.

Research in ethnoscience has mostly concentrated on native terminological systems, by which it hopes to discern 'how people construe their world of experience from the way they talk about it'.[12] Its ultimate goal has variably been described as a 'cultural grammar', an ethnology of knowledge or a descriptive epistemology.[13] While some micro-sociologists might agree with such a broadly defined goal, micro-sociological research practice has differed sharply from that of ethnoscience. Symbolic interactionism, for example, has been described as seeking the solution to the problem of social order in the assumption that society is possible because interacting selves share the same basic symbolic order of meanings, definitions and situations.[14] The analyst's task, similar to that proposed for ethogenics (see Harré, below), is to discover how members' conceptions are organized such as to produce the orderly patterns of behaviour that s/he observed. Yet research by symbolic interactionists has illustrated how meanings, situations, objects, selves and events are continually being defined and negotiated, presented in front of an audience and dramatically enacted.[15] In other words, it has shown the cognitive order to be an emergent order with a particular dynamics of its own. Thus, in practice it has *blurred* the distinction between the levels of competence and performance so prominent with Chomskyan theory of language, and made little progress towards a systematic description of the rules presumed to govern symbolic interaction.

Promising new steps towards a competence-based theory of social conduct have been taken in cognitive sociology (see the summary by Lidz, below) and in ethogenics (see Harré, below), and Lidz has proposed a normative functionalism reconstructed on the basis of the model of transformational grammar. However, the ambitious programme itself is not likely to meet with fewer difficulties in sociology or anthropology than it has met in linguistics.[16] By its own definition, most of micro-sociology deals with meaning rather than with formal (syntactical) structure, and the systems of knowledge said to generate social conduct appear to be far more variable, more rapidly changing, and less entrenched than the rules of grammars. It is clear that the search for relevant cognitive structures will continue in different directions with renewed appeal, best exemplified perhaps by Cicourel's exploration of memory mechanisms,[17] by Goffman's frame analysis,[18] or by Giddens's theory of structuration (see

below). On the other hand one might submit that not only in interactionism, but also in other micro-sociological approaches research
has been most successful to date in pointing out the accomplished,
constructed and continually negotiated character of symbolic order.
Thus it is not only a knowing subject, but a knowing and *active* subject
which is posited in this research. Not only has order become a
cognitive (including linguistic) rather than a normative phenomenon, it has also become a man-made rather than a man-coercing
matter: it is produced, contested, repaired, organized and displayed
in concrete situations whose definition become the subject of continual accomplishment and interruption.

To a degree micro-sociological approaches can be seen as torn
between a predilection for a competence theory of action in which
conduct appears to be controlled by similar cognitive processes, and a
skilful display of human subjects as actively engaged in working out,
interfering with, and persuading others of the meanings, rules and
definitions which presumably they share. This conflict is perhaps
most apparent from the stance taken by ethnomethodology which has
renounced any interest in *explaining* social order as the product of
actors' cognitive orientation to and compliance with shared rules and
meanings. The orderliness and coherence of social activities is seen
not as a fact to be explained by sociology, but as an appearance
produced, for example, 'by and through such procedures as analyzing
an event as an instance of compliance (or noncompliance) with a
rule'.[19] It follows, then, that interaction must be analysed with respect
to the methods and procedures by which members make their daily
activities recognizable and accountable to themselves and to others,
thereby acquiring and conveying a *sense* of orderliness and structure.
For example, conversation analysis has found orderliness to derive
from the sequential organization of members' utterances through the
taking of turns.[20]

Cicourel has suggested that devices such as these may be regarded
as transformational procedures for sustaining a sense of social structure in face of the innumerable differences actors encounter in
concrete situations.[21] In general, however, ethnomethodologists have
not attempted to reconcile the apparently accomplished, negotiated
'orderliness' of everyday life with the assumption of an underlying
stability of social practice rooted in shared cognitive rules. Instead
they have suspended the assumption of stable social conduct alto-

gether in favour of a search for the practices through which persons see, describe, and act as if social action were stable. The problem of social order has come a long way from being defined as a factual problem of social integration whose answer was sought in shared normative obligations. Instead of a society integrated by common values and moral constraints, it is the *cognitive order of sense making and describing* which emerges from microscopic studies of social life. Instead of being seen as a monolithic system which regulates individual action, order comes to be seen as an upshot of concrete, communicative interaction. In a sense, the problem of social order is redefined by turning the traditional approach to social order on its head. Social order is not that which holds society together by somehow controlling individual wills, but that which comes about in the mundane but relentless transactions of these wills. The problem of social order has not only turned into a problem of cognitive order; it has also turned from a macro-level problem to a *micro-problem* of social action.

2 From methodological individualism and collectivism to methodological situationalism

The cognitive turn mentioned above is not limited to the microscopic approaches discussed here. Influenced by linguistics, logical structuralism (Lévi-Strauss), psychoanalysis as reinterpreted by Lacan, and even Marxism (Althusser) have all experienced such a shift.[22] The distinctive feature of micro-sociological approaches is not only their preoccupation with members' cognitive processes, meanings, and accounting procedures, but also the privileged status they accord to the analysis of small-scale social situations. Most micro-sociologies appear to be founded on the assumption that 'the only valid and reliable (or hard, scientific) evidence concerning socially meaningful phenomena we can possibly have is that based ultimately on systematic observations and analyses of everyday life.'[23] The ultra-detailed observation of what people do and say *in situ* is not only considered a prerequisite for any sociologically relevant understanding of social life, but concrete social interactions may also be considered the building blocks for *macro*-sociological conceptions (see Collins, below). This specific, methodological stance of micro-sociologies challenges macro-sociological theory-building as well as macro-sociological research based upon aggregate data. In its radical version, it claims nothing less than that macro-social phenomena are *unknown* and *unknowable* unless they can be based upon knowledge derived from the analysis of micro-social situations.

The methodological stance of micro-sociological approaches has a precedence in the defence of *methodological individualism* by Popper, Hajek and W. J. N. Watkins in the 1960s. It is crucial to see, however, that micro-sociological methodology constitutes in fact a rejection of the principle of methodological individualism *as well as* of the doctrine of methodological collectivism which is usually set up against it as the only alternative. To illustrate the dichotomy, let me quote a passage from Watkins's exposition of methodological individualism:[24]

> If social events like inflation, political revolution, 'the disappearance of the middle classes', etc., are brought about by people, then they must be explained in terms of people; in terms of the situations people confront and the ambitions, fears and ideas which activate them. In short, *large scale social phenomena must be accounted for by the situations, dispositions and beliefs of individuals.* This I call methodological individualism.
>
> You may complain that this is commonsensical and hardly needed saying. The trouble is that some philosophers of history have made the opposite assumption . . . In the secularized version of (their) theory it is the social whole which so determines matters for the individual that he cannot avoid (or would be foolish to try to avoid; the determinism may be a little loose) fulfilling his function within the whole system. On this view, the social behaviour of individuals should be explained in terms of the position or functions of these individuals and of the laws which govern the system. These laws must be regarded as *sui generis, applying to the whole as such and not derivable from individualistic principles.* This I call methodological holism [my italics].

Methodological individualism demands that all of the concepts used in social theory be analysable in terms of the interests, activities, etc., of individual human beings, since ultimately only individuals are responsible, purposive human actors. Micro-sociologies, on the other hand, do not turn to individuals, but to *interaction in social situations* as the relevant methodological 'units'. As Goffman pointed out in an article called 'The Neglected Situation', the implication of most social research has been that 'social situations do not have properties and a structure of their own, but merely mark, as it were, the geometric intersection of actors making talk and actors bearing particular social attributes.'[25] For example, survey research based on attitude data generally rests upon the assumption that human conduct can be described and predicted from variables which characterize individual actors. In contrast, most micro-sociological approaches conceive of social situations as a reality *sui generis* which entails a dynamics and organization of its own that we *cannot* predict from knowledge of the attributes of single actors.

Strictly speaking, the argument as to a reality *sui generis* of social situations refers to two distinctive features of social action. It requires us to see the outcome of social action as tied to particular *occasions* and to *other participants* in the situation. The second aspect can be referred to as 'interactionism' in contrast to individualism, and it follows from the fact that social conduct displays itself as contingent upon the conduct of others. Hence, while it might be correct that only individuals are intentional actors, social action arises from the interlocking of intentionalities rather than from their singular existence. An eloquent statement of this interactional basis of social action derives from Simmel:[26]

> Society exists where a number of individuals enter into interaction. This interaction always arises on the basis of certain drives or for the sake of certain purposes. Erotic, religious, or merely associative impulses; and purposes of defense, attack, play, gain, aid, or instruction – these and countless others cause man to live with other men, to act for them, with them, against them, and thus to correlate his condition with theirs. In brief, he influences and is influenced by them. The significance of these interactions among men lies in the fact that it is because of them that the individuals, in whom these driving impulses and purposes are lodged, form a unity, that is a society.

Human conduct appears to be interlocked not only through the forming of interpersonal ties, but also through individuals' *taking account* of others. Consequently, the individual has come to be seen as part of an *interactive process* in which the perspective of others partly constitute the self. Simmel, for example states that

All of us are fragments, not only of general man, but also of ourselves. We are outlines not only of the types 'man', 'good' 'bad', and the like, but also of the individuality and uniqueness of ourselves. Although this individuality cannot, on principle, be identified by any name, it surrounds our perceptible reality as if traced in ideal lines. It is supplemented by the other's view of us, which results in something that we never are purely and wholly. It is impossible for this view to see anything but juxtaposed fragments, which nevertheless are all that really exists. However, just as we compensate for a blind spot in our field of vision so we are no longer aware of it, *so a fragmentary structure is transformed by another's view into the completeness of an individuality* [my italics].[27]

There is implicit in this view a notion of the individual as a typified, discursive construction which bears some similarity to the later dissolution of the self as an unproblematic unit of action as found in George Herbert Mead. Mead's conception of the individual as a parliament of selves and his notion of interior audiences is relevant to the argument that men attribute motives to each other from the perspective of internalized reference groups.[28] Thus intentionality, though physically located in individual bodies, in principle always takes account of others, and must be construed as an interactive rather than as an individual concept. Furthermore to a certain extent 'individual motives' appear to be literally accomplished in communicative encounters with others, in the process of establishing interpretations and definitions of the situation.[29]

The conception of social behaviour as externally and internally contingent upon others thus entails the notion *interacts* rather than acts as the crucial observables of human conduct. It has also been adopted, in other areas of sociological theory, and has prompted the notion of triads which conceptually include 'the complicating other' (who could be an internal audience) as crucial to the understanding of social action.[30] Micro-sociologies have been more concerned with the additional element of the *context* in which interaction is embedded. As Goffman has noted, a student interested in the properties of speech may find himself having to look at the physical setting in which the speaker performs his gestures, simply because you cannot describe a gesture fully without reference to the extra-bodily environment in which it occurs. And someone interested in the linguistic correlates of social structure may find that he must attend to the social occasion when someone of given social attributes makes his appearance before others. Both kinds of students must therefore look at what we vaguely call the social situation.[31]

Micro-sociologies often define the social situation in terms of the immediate presence of face-to-face interaction in a particular setting. However, as argued by Cicourel (below), the notion of relevant context is itself problematic, as reflected in varying methodological practices of different micro-sociological orientations. Social situations may not have a natural beginning and an end, thus forcing the researcher to choose an arbitrary cutting point. When a short segment of conversation is carved out of an encounter between two or more persons for microscopic analysis, the situated character of the organizational properties of the talk, and certainly the content of the utterances, may be lost. Furthermore, it is clear that members themselves selectively organize and draw upon their 'environment'. Though much of the physical setting of an encounter may be *potentially* available for attention, most of it will remain unnoticed. Furthermore, circumstances of action which *transcend* the immediate situation are continually called upon by social actors. For example, while recent micro-sociological studies of scientific work consistently confirm the circumstances of laboratory action to be of crucial relevance in the process of knowledge production, they also illustrate that it is not their (physical) presence but their availability in the sense of an awareness of a phenomenon which makes it contextually relevant. In addition, actors can be seen to consciously manipulate contextual limitations and to increase their contextual knowledge or attention, if needed.[32]

The organized contextuality of social action has of course been dealt with extensively by Schutz: the environment, the context, the setting of social action emerge as something toward which action is directed, which is lived and reflected upon, rather than being 'external' to social action.[33] It is crucial to see that the settings and occasions emphasized in micro-sociological research, though they can be analytically distinguished from interaction, are not viewed as 'external environments' to which individuals 'adapt', but are themselves seen as (re)constructed in social action. Yet the question of contextuality of social action raises another issue which bears directly on the micro-sociological stance toward methodological collectivism. Participants not only routinely transcend the immediate setting by referring to occasions and phenomena at a different time and place, they also continually employ notions and engage in actions whose mutual intelligibility appears to be based upon their presupposition and knowledge of broader societal institutions. Since micro-sociological approaches generally conceive of social behaviour as an interpretative process, they too must rely on an analyst's presupposition of and recourse to societal institutions to make an observed stream of behaviour intelligible and accountable. As Mandelbaum has argued, if one wished to explain to a Trobriand Islander the act of cashing a cheque one could start by explaining the filling out of the withdrawal slip as a means to getting the teller to hand us some notes and coins.[34] One could then explain the significance we attach to these notes and coins by letting the Trobriander follow us and noting how our passing on of the notes to others leads them to give us goods. However, we would also have to inform the stranger that the slip could not be handed to just anyone we meet, and that one must have 'deposited' money before one can expect to be handed money in exchange for a slip. In short, we would have to explain at least the rudiments of a banking system to the Trobriander. The behaviour of clerks at the bank is unintelligible unless viewed in terms of their role and status, and these concepts in turn have to be interpreted in terms of organizational features of our society. If we try to explain these roles exclusively in terms of the behavioural expectations of others towards the persons occupying the roles, then the behaviour of these others remains unexplained.

The point is that micro-sociological approaches, in describing social encounters and in accounting for participants' behaviour, make reference to institutional concepts which may well be irreducible to interactional terms. As far as I can see most prominent authors in micro-sociological research have taken no notice of or no issue with this phenomenon. Thus the methodological situationalism of micro-sociologies has not been explicitly reductionist in the sense of methodological individualism, that is, in the sense of requiring that all concepts used and explanations given be ultimately translated into interactional terms. This reductionism seems to arise only with the very recent attempt of radical micro-sociological orientations *to reconstitute* macro-sociology on the basis of a micro-sociological foundation (see Collins, below).

In what sense, then, have micro-sociologies been opposed to methodological collectivism as claimed in the beginning? To begin with, methodological collectivism (or 'holism') is not a unified doctrine. It encompasses such views as the notion that society is a whole which is more than the sum of its parts; that society 'moulds' individuals in socialization so that they must be seen as dependent upon social institutions rather than as their active constituents; or that 'social facts' constrain and coerce individual conduct. The original micro-sociological attack against macro-sociological procedure was not directed to such assumptions. Rather, it implied that we may not be in a position to know anything about phenomena on a societal level, given the (however much ignored) problems of social science measurement procedure.

If we take as the cornerstone of the methodological challenge promoted by micro-sociologies to be Cicourel's influential study of 'Method and Measurement in Sociology', we can find this challenge to rest on at least two arguments.[35] First a critique of existing quantitative measurement in sociology which relies on mathematical measurement requirements such as properties of scales that are hardly ever fulfilled with variable of the type used by traditional sociology. Second, it advances a critique of the model of social action implied by the use of dominant sociological methods. These methods suggest that data which are, for example, collected in interviews can be taken at face value, except for measurement error and bias which can however be statistically remedied or at least be estimated. Micro-sociological research, on the other hand, sees such data as unspecified collaborative products created during the interview in accordance with the practical procedures and background assumptions of participating actors.

For example, any instance of classifying an observation or occurrence between interviewer and respondent must be seen as resulting from the working perspectives of participants as negotiated in a temporal sequence in which certain statements will be ignored while others will be reinterpreted within the respective everyday vocabularies. It is unwarranted to assume that the perspectives, vocabularies, etc., will match to such a degree as to make comparable the data-outcomes of interviewing various respondents. Studies of organizational records produced by mental health clinics, hospitals, police departments, juvenile courts – the statistics on which macrosociology relies in addition to interview data – have shown that members of any social organization develop perspectives for handling their clients which are sufficiently different from those of all other similar agencies to make comparisons problematic.[36] According to Denzin, these studies suggest that: (1) organizations perpetuate themselves through time by generating fictitious records; (2) comparable organizations differ in the meanings they assign to the same events (birth, death, mental illness, cure, etc.); (3) the production of organizational records is basically an interactional process based on rumours, gossip, overheard conversations, discrepant information, and biographically imperfect bookkeeping; (4) agencies routinely create documentation that a particular act has or has not occurred by piecing together conversations between the parties involved, and in piecing together these organizational reports routinely rely on open-ended categories of meaning and interpretation to classify recalcitrant and ambiguous cases.[37]

The conclusion to be drawn from such results is simple, but consequential. It says that the meaning of a social phenomenon like deviance cannot be read off from social acts but must be traced to the definitions, working perspectives, negotiations and translations which arise during interaction and which characterize bureaucratic procedure. Since the comparability of the outcomes of such situated procedures, perspectives and negotiations is highly problematic, the meaning of aggregate data and records thus generated will also be highly problematic. In other words, short of sufficient knowledge of *how* data, records and reports are generated interactionally and organizationally, we have no basis for unequivocally assessing the meaning of these outcomes, much less for assessing their validity. The methodological imperative for developing a macro-sociology that is grounded in empirical observation is therefore to study the situated social production of data and records microscopically across different types of organizations. The methodological challenge of macro-sociology promoted by micro-sociological orientations does not entail a rejection of macroscopic preoccupations. It does, however, entail the assumption that the process of data- and record-generation is highly relevant for the outcomes obtained, and cannot be simply ignored or rendered irrelevant through statistical cleaning operations.

To sum up this section, let me stress that the methodological situationalism promoted in micro-sociological research challenges methodological individualism for the simplifying assumption that the locus of social action is the individual human being, and it challenges methodological collectivism for the equally simplifying and presumably related assumption that interview responses, or data in the form of reports and organizational records, constitute direct, valid sources of macroscopic inferences. Methodological situationalism has replaced the model of the individual actor as the ultimate unit of social conduct by a conception which incorporates the reciprocity and the situated character of social action. It is of course precisely this model which at the same time renders problematic the macro-researcher's reliance on data and records about whose context-bound, and interactionally accomplished production s/he knows nothing. Yet methodological situationalism is not only tied to the critique of traditional sociological research practice. As argued in the first section, it is rooted in the shift of interest through which language and cognition have partly replaced a previous concern with normative social integration. To some this shift of interest has suggested a search for the order of rules and resources which presumably underlies (and generates) social conduct and which is to be identified through micro-sociological research. To others, it suggested a search for the practices through which members (re)produce and acquire a sense of order. In both cases, the result is a new form of theoretically informed empiricism and a body of data about everyday practical action which have reinforced the original methodological critique. For this empiricism, 'hard' data are by no means quantitative data. They can only result from a microscopic, sensitive methodology which successfully registers and preserves the characteristic traits of the field of study.

3 The dissolution of the micro-macro dimension

One consequence of research on the micro-processes of social life in sociology and related areas appears to be that many of the dimensions in terms of which the micro-macro problem has traditionally been couched will have to be reconsidered, if not abandoned. I have in mind distinctions such as that between the individual and the collectivity, between action and structure, between small-scale uniformity and large-scale complexity, or between the association of the micro-level with neutrality or powerlessness and of the macro-level with power. The above remarks suggest that the connection made between the various poles of such dimensions and the micro- versus macro-level may be a function of the observer's distance to the respective field of study rather than being inherent in the problem itself.

To expound the thesis, let me start with the conception of the individual as a micro- and the collectivity as a macro-phenomenon. To the degree to which this view searches for unity in the individual and sees the collectivity as a compound of these units it leads directly to methodological individualism which I have discussed before. As indicated, the thrust of certain areas of micro-level research has been to dissolve the notion of the self as consisting entirely of the willing consciousness of an individual organism, and to thereby challenge the conception of macro-phenomena as composed of the aggregated actions of individuals. The research initiated by William James and George Herbert Mead has distinguished the self, person, or individual from the physical organism with whose cognitive processes or behavioural repertoire it has often been identified.[38] At the same time it renounced a conception of the self as split from the environment and from other human beings, positing a multiplicity of selves constituted in communicative interaction. James, for example, distinguished between a social self (as perceived by others), a material self (the self of possessions and belongings) and a spiritual self (the psychological faculties), which were later to be elaborated in Mead's dialectic between the 'I' and the 'Me'. Today we are confronted with the notion of multiple identities which appear to be insulated rather than to be functionally integrated into just one person, or one individuality.[39]

The tremendous complexity which attempts to deal with the self, the individual or the person, arises out of two dimensions.[40] A person is capable of manifesting a multiplicity of personas of which some are seen to be role-based, while others appear situation-based or dramaturgical, and some take part in the inner dramatic productions which apparently are routinely enacted by individuals. A second dimension refers to the cycle of reflexivity by which persons are tied to the symbolic actions and reflections of others as well as of themselves, and by which they do in fact constitute their selves. Given these two dimensions, there appears to be no theoretical justification for taking the individual for granted as a simple, elementary unit of social action. At the same time of course the dichotomy between individual and collective becomes jeopardized, no longer serving to illuminate micro- and macro-levels of social analysis.

Now it could be argued that the more analytically relevant distinction is that between action and structure rather than that between individual and collectivity, and that regardless of any dissolution of the individual as a natural unit of the social world, the notion of purposeful, intentional action can be retained as a basic element out of which are built structures of patterned relationships between actors (not individuals!). However, such an argument would have to confront the phenomenon that for much of micro-social research, the act has become a complicated process composed of verbal and non-verbal elements and tied to cognitive structures such as 'frames', 'scripts' or 'plans'. Micro-sociologies have increasingly used tape- and video-recordings of observations which have made us acutely aware of a fine-grained structure of social action not normally noticed by the sociologist. Research in this tradition has suggested that the encoding and decoding of the meaning of social acts attends to composing features such as eye glances, body positions and body movements. In addition, since it has been recognized that verbal messages have performative functions and must be considered as speech *acts*,[41] a whole new repertoire of physical cues linked to linguistic utterances has been found to be relevant to action meaning. For example, there seems to be some consensus among linguists that tone-units are the organizational device the speaker employs for dividing discourse into message blocks, i.e. for conveying communicative acts. The speaker has a choice between rising and falling tone movements, and combinations thereof, to perform different acts with one and the same sequence of words.[42]

While linguists, sociologists and psychologists have thus displayed the behavioural complexity of what we commonly call an act, the new emerging discipline of 'cognitive science' has been concerned with conceptual representation and processing aspects which underlie the identification and interpretation of action in context. For example, a simple act like 'give' will be represented by a structural network (a schema) including different agents, objects and subschemata, analogous to a play with the internal structure of the schema corresponding to the script of the play.[43] Much mainstream research in micro-sociology, on the other hand, has paid less attention to the behavioural and cognitive processes underlying single social acts than to the interlocking turn-taking behaviour of different social actors in particular situations. Thus those most concerned with social action have either moved to the cognitive-linguistic level underlying social action, or to the level of situated interaction which I have outlined in connection with methodological situationalism. We can also say that they have moved to topics and concepts *below* or *above* the level of purposive, meaningful action.

Most sociologists today would probably subscribe to the assumption that the social sciences are interested in action, where 'action' according to the classical definition of Max Weber includes all human behaviour 'when and insofar as the acting individual attaches a subjective meaning to it'.[44] While authors such as Winch seem to have held that sociological explanations are exhausted by actors' explanations in terms of their intentions, the predominant view seems to draw more upon Schutz's two-stage model of sociological methodology. According to this model, actions must first be described, and understood in terms of actors' meanings after which they can be explained by concepts meaningful to the analyst and the audience.[45] Whatever explicit commitment micro-sociologies have to this programme, their research often testifies to a different practice. On the one hand it has illustrated the interactively and contextually accomplished character of actors' meanings. Thus it has not drawn upon actors' avowed intentions as the sociologist's resource and first step towards explanation, but rather shown that actors' meanings are themselves *constituted* within social relationships. On the other hand, directions such as ethnomethodology have proclaimed themselves uninterested in actors' intentions and have given most attention to the apparently *not* specifically motivated *routine* practices of everyday life.

In short, both directions have in fact replaced the classic concept of individually meaningful social action by some notion of situated interaction or practice, in a sense declaring individual purposeful action a derivative rather than a constituent of these larger structures. If there is today a social 'unit' emerging from micro-sociological research which is considered relevant to macro-social phenomena, it is the *episode of situated interaction* (including routine) which will have to be considered as a candidate. The point here is of course that in the process of looking at these larger units (or, for that matter, at the previously mentioned smaller units of a more basic and tacit structure of action), the dichotomy between action and structure has been dissolved as a theoretically significant dimension of the micro-macro problem.

Let me now turn to a third dichotomy which might easily lend itself to the present discussion. The notion of macro-social structures as a compound of individuals or of individually meaningful action entails that more complexity is attributed to the former than to the latter. In other words, it entails the assumption that *complexity* has something to do with size and scale, and that the distinction between complexity and uniformity (or simplicity) might allow us to distinguish between micro- and macro-social phenomena. This assumption does indeed have some tradition in sociology. One of the obvious features of the modern world is the increase in the scale of political units such as states and nations which are sometimes effectively united. Though there have of course been large empires in the past, their existence is said to be sociologically contingent, and many more small-scale communities seem to have existed.[46] For the social sciences, the term 'small-scale society' has become almost synonymous with anthropologists' 'native tribes'.

In information theory, complexity is measured in terms of variety, which means in terms of the number of different, constitutive elements of a system.[47] This notion, however, depends crucially on what is considered as a constitutive element, a choice left to the observer. In social theory complexity has usually meant functional differentiation, noteworthy specialization arising from the division of labour by which Durkheim distinguished modern from traditional societies. Neo-evolutionism postulates a general direction of development toward greater differentiation and hence greater interdependence and functional complementarity of societies. The ideal type of a folk society, Redfield writes, is isolated, non-literate, homogeneous and small, with a strong sense of group solidarity and ways of living conventionalized into a coherent culture.[48] From there we move to large size, density and heterogeneity of population, and functional differentiation.

So it seems that if we consider the functions performed by members of societies as their constitutive elements, we find a correlation between scale and complexity. On the other hand, at least some anthropologists have argued that, when measured by the concerns of their members, relatively small-scale societies are much more complex than we are led to expect.[49] For example, there often are many specialized crafts and groups specialized in particular ecologies or in mediating between and controlling access to other groups. There are specialized manufacturers, musicians and poets, warriors and genealogical experts. Hence it is entirely possible that when measured against the scale of the culture, there is no surplus of complexity associated with the larger size, even if we consider no other criterion than functional differentiation. If, on the other hand, we admit a different variety the picture may change even more drastically.

We need hardly remind ourselves that there is at least one tradition of theories of modern society which assert that our world is tending toward greater standardization, conformity and uniformity, in brief toward greater homogeneity rather than toward variety.[50] As many have cried out, the larger society is also the mass society, atomized and marked by a ruthless erosion of regional and group differentiations. The USA, for example, should also be more monocultural, ethnocentric and parochial than many smaller societies, a thesis not totally implausible to its enlightened inhabitants. The border conditions which in the large society imply that most of its members will have contact only with other members of the society, equality of education and a mass production economy can be seen to contribute to the homogeneity.[51]

The point here is of course not to hold theories which posit a development towards greater complexity against theories of mass society. Both theoretical traditions may even be compatible with each other. The point is to illustrate that any correlation between size and complexity depends on the choice of the element whose variety is considered. What is the relevance, for example, of functional diversity compared with a more massive economic, political or cultural unification which can presumably also be argued? But the correlation between size and complexity not only depends on the choice and definition of the element considered, it also depends on the *knowledge of the observer*. In information theory, the variety of a system is at the same time a measure of the information which we do not have, that is of our ignorance regarding the system.[52] However, this complexity becomes visible only in relation to an order which we have reasons to believe exists, or *which we search to identify*. We have seen that our notions of the individual and of social action have vastly increased in complexity as soon as they have become a focus of empirical studies. I assume that nobody would pretend that the problem of what constitutes a person or of what we are talking about when we refer to social acts has been resolved in micro-sociological research. However, this research has pointed out the *enormous complexity* of the micro-transactions of social life, and the drawbacks of a research tradition that proceeds to measure 'social reality' while largely ignoring this fine-grained structure.

Thus, complexity *per se* is not a distinctive characteristic of an increase in scale, and the dichotomy between complexity and uniformity seems of little help in distinguishing between micro- and macro-social phenomena. What if we now turn to the notion of power as a concept distinctively relevant to macro-level phenomena? Power has been called a notoriously contested concept which carries the load of long-standing and unresolved disputes in philosophy and in political and social theory.[53] However, many of the more prominent, empirically relevant conceptions have defined power in terms of a capacity to realize one's will (Weber), or the objective interests of a social class (Poulantzas) against the resistance of others.[54] They entail a notion of power which is measured by the *extent* of influence of an agent or a group, by the *reach* of personal or corporate action, by the *number* of those who are regulated and dominated by a source of power, or by the *volume* of resources and relationships which can be mobilized in a power struggle. Size thus becomes a correlate of power, as reflected in our everyday vocabulary which associates big with powerful and important, and small with insignificance. Can the dichotomy between power and powerlessness, or freedom of power, be used to get a grip on the micro-macro distinction?

In recent social theory power has not been linked to 'great' individuals, but rather to collectivities or to societal structures. Since the age of despots and princes has passed, it is political, ideological and professional elites interlocked in networks of transaction and communication which have caught our attention. Mills's analysis of power elites and studies of the 'military-industrial complex' which emerged in the USA after the Second World War provide examples

for this conception of power. The structuralist position is best represented in the recent Marxist discussion by Althusser and his succes-
sors. Structure here refers to an objective system of relations of
production, to social classes and the state. Power is 'an effect of the
ensemble of the structures' on the relation between social classes. The
state, repressive, indoctrinating, and external to a self-regulating
economy, according to Althusser, takes on a constitutive role in the
reproduction of the power relations between classes analysed by
Poulantzas. Both agree, however, in their ridicule of any humanism of
a Marxist or existential kind which grants freedom and creativity to
individual agency. Power remains inherently a large-scale, macro-
phenomenon irreducible to interpersonal relations or individual
action.[55]

Within the French discussion, Foucault has repeatedly attacked
the Marxist position for identifying power with the state, or with the
ensemble of institutions and the 'apparatus' which guarantee the
subordination of citizens in a given state. This tendency, which is of
course well entrenched in the history of political thought in general,
has contributed to our view of power as monolithic and repressive, as
a binary and global opposition between those who dominate and
those who are dominated. Against this conception Foucault has
argued that power emerges from local arenas of action. Power is
strictly relational and cannot exist other than as a function of multiple
points of resistance. The play of power relations is complex, instable,
self-transforming, and never definitely sure of a particular global
effect. The effects of power are not only repressive, but also productive, entailing positive results. In short Foucault has argued that
power must be analysed as a *microprocess* of social life, as an all-
pervading phenomenon which emerges everywhere out of the infin-
itesimal violences of concrete, local transactions.[56]

Foucault's programme can be linked to a variety of results arising
from microscopic analyses of social interactions. Though micro-
sociological studies have not, in general, employed the notion of
power as a topic or resource of their analyses, many of the results of
these studies can readily be seen to illuminate aspects of power in the
interplay of social action. For example, juvenile delinquents emerge
from Cicourel's extended observational study of law enforcement
agencies and of police and probation files as the collaborative product
of parents, arresting officers, counsellors, judges and others, of the

judgments and prejudgments they bring to bear in conversations selectively pieced together into official records, and of the resources juvenile suspects and their parents are able to mobilize and to insert into the process.[57] Thus, they emerge as the product of multiple forces and powers associated with strategic positions, of techniques of persuasion and tactical moves in conversations, of implicit alliances, and of interest affiliations. It is hardly difficult to translate the results of this and other studies of a similar nature into the language of power, if so desired.

The relevance microscopic studies can have for what Foucault has called the *micro-physics of power* is best exemplified in a tradition which explicitly incorporated a notion of micro-power. I am referring to the sociologically informed work on schizophrenia and the family, particularly by Ronald Laing and his followers.[58] Studies in this direction have displayed the family and other interpersonal institutions as a microcosm of potential hate, envy, fear and mutual self-destruction. In short, as the locus of a power struggle no less complicated than that of the larger political system. As Brittan has noted, 20 years ago it is unlikely that the following passage would have appeared in a standard sociological text:[59]

> The essential similarity between the family and more complex political systems is, that, in both, relations of dominance and submission rest in the last analysis on violence or threat of violence. Father can out-whack mother, who in turn can out-whack the children, at least until adolescence, when parental authority becomes challenged. Power is not automatically received and unquestioningly accepted. It is in the nature of power to be resented and challenged and defended by those who hold it. Violence, or the threat of violence, is the ultimate argument in a power contest. The average family is no more exempt from violence than the average state, though our ideology concerning the family makes us reluctant to accept the fact.

The point here is not whether the somewhat schematic derivation of power from violence in the above quote is appropriate to everyday transactions, but rather that the text refers to power as a routine component of close encounters, even though the respective relationships may be intended by agents to provide emotional security and love. Given the pervasiveness of relations of force in micro-social interaction, it is of course not clear why the notion of power should be reserved for a characterization of the body politic, or of structural class relations.

Micro-social research leads to the same conclusion in regard to the notion of power as it did in regard to the notion of complexity. Though both notions are conventionally employed as macro-level concepts, studies of the fine structure of social life display their theoretical relevance for an understanding of the microcosms of social practice. Unless they are restrictively tailored to entail a conceptual relationship with size, notions such as power and complexity need not be distinctively correlated with the larger scale.

To conclude this section we can perhaps say that microsocial research challenges any conception which identifies power and complexity with macro-level phenomena, and it challenges any conception which takes individuals or individually motivated action to be unproblematic units of which social phenomena are somehow composed. All that we have learned about the micro-processes of power, about the processes pertaining to the production and fragmentation of individuality, or about the behavioural, cognitive, and interactive structures which underlie any single, purposeful act, points to an unexplored depth and complexity of micro-level phenomena. It is plausible to assume that units presupposed by our natural language and present cultural universe will be replaced by more theoretically defined units in the process of analysing this complexity. As we shall see in the next section, present attempts to reconstruct macrosociology based upon micro-sociological results proceed methodologically by considering the micro-episode as a cosmos of its own, not to be divided any further for purposes of macroscopic analysis. In passing we might add that sociology is not the only and not the first discipline which has come to revise its theoretical and methodological conceptions upon discovering a whole new micro-order of events. I translate from Prigogine and Stengers's account of the metamorphosis of natural science, and particularly of physics today:[60]

> We can no longer take seriously the idea of a simplicity of the microscopic level; the elementary particles are not simple, not any simpler than the world of stars. The only objects whose behaviour is really simple belong to our world, to our macroscopic level of

scale; they are the first objects of Newtonian science, the planets, the heavy bodies, the pendulum. Classical science had carefully chosen its objects from this intermediary level. We know now that this simplicity is not an indicator of the fundamental, and that it cannot be attributed to the rest of world.

4 The micro-sociological reconstruction of macro-sociology: two hypotheses

If micro-social research has successfully challenged prevailing defini-tions of the micro-macro problem the following question arises: what substitutes has it to offer for the concepts it put into question? Phrased differently, where do we stand today and where are we to go from here? It is clear that there is no one 'micro-macro problem', and that the notion serves as no more than a catchword for what some might argue does not even exist in these terms. Most micro-sociologists, as well as most of their colleagues who defend a macroscopic view, have not addressed the problem explicitly, and their implicit versions are often far from clear. The lived experience of many social scientists is probably that micro- and macro-conceptions live next door to each other like hostile neighbours, mostly ignoring and occasionally picking at each other. Yet the work of those who have addressed the problem, like the contributors to this book, shows a series of over-lapping concerns as well as some major theoretical divisions. Several of the differences relate to long-standing disputes in sociology, such as that between centres of theorizing which have been strongly in-fluenced by Marxist thought and authors who promote a neo-systems theory of society. I do not, however, propose a discussion along the outworn lines of the divisions which separate schools of thought. Rather, I will focus on what I take to be the two newly emerging conceptions of macro-social phenomena implied in the present dis-cussion which are consistent with – or explicitly built upon – the theoretical and empirical results of microsocial research. I will refer to these conceptions as the 'aggregation hypothesis' and the 'hypothesis of unintended consequences'.

The aggregation hypothesis is explicitly and vigorously advanced in the work of Randall Collins, but is perhaps also implied, for example, by some of the proposals of Aaron Cicourel (see below).[61] In essence it says that macro-phenomena are made up of *aggregations* and *repetitions* of many similar micro-episodes. Micro-episodes, of course, refer to the situated social encounters described by micro-sociologies and discussed in detail earlier in the chapter. 'The stuff of social structure', as Brittan calls it, are the social situations in which we engage, the situated interactions which are partially structured by past definitions and yet at the same time 'always open' to reinterpretations.[62] Since by definition we cannot ever leave these micro-situations whether we do research or participate in practical action, all evidence regarding macroscopic phenomena must be aggregated from such micro-experiences. The proposal can, for example, bridge the gap between the notion of social class as a collective, macro-level phenomenon advanced by Marxist traditions and the notion of social class as a habitus (Bourdieu) or as an attribute of individuals surveyed in social research (see Harré, below).[63] If class relations are seen to consist of a multitude of situations in which those who dispose of the means of production confront and exploit those who do not, a social class can presumably be defined in accordance with the aggregation hypothesis as the sum total of individuals who engage in their working-life situations in similar relations of this kind. Along the same lines the notion of mobility can be traced down to, among other things, the classroom decisions of the school personnel who create official educational records which are later used selectively in specific situations to determine a student's career advancement (see Cicourel, below).

In defining the micro-elements of social reality, to include inter-action, relationships, internal environments, power, etc. – that is *all* sociologically interesting phenomena – macro-phenomena can be logically derived from micro-situations. The above proposal draws the micro-sociological 'revolution' to what is perhaps its most radical conclusion. Note that macro-phenomena emerge from this move as taxonomic properties in the sense of Harré (see below), that is as 'societal' properties derived from the formation of similarity classes based upon selected membership criteria. Though social strata or mobility rates thus defined may be said to characterize social 'structure', these notions do in fact refer to aggregate sets of similar episodes. We can also say that structure is seen as *internal* to the episodes themselves rather than to consist of patterns of interrelationships between episodes. And society is characterized by the (aggregated) properties derived from the analysis of these internal structures.

In contrast to the aggregation hypothesis, the hypothesis of unintended consequences does not relate macro-phenomena to that which visibly or knowingly happens in micro-situations. Rather, it postulates properties of a more global system which emerge by virtue of the *unintended* (in addition to the intended) consequences of micro-events. The hypothesis is suggested in this volume by the work of Harré and Giddens. Harré construes the macro-order in analogy to the physical and biological sciences which are accustomed to the idea of emergent properties manifested by a whole but not by its parts when these are considered independently. In the social sciences, it is the unintended consequences of action which correspond to such emergent properties not manifested (not intended) in the micro-episodes of social life. However, unlike the natural sciences the social sciences cannot hope to get to know the macro-order conceived in terms of emergent properties: they are methodologically bound to draw upon members' knowledge and accounts, yet ramifications of unintended consequences by definition cannot be part of social knowledge.

According to Harré, the relevance of unintended consequences of social action is that they constitute system properties which confront us as selection environments of future action, and which thereby exert a diffuse but significant influence upon the course of social events. For example, these environments determine (analogously to biological evolution) which mutations occurring in micro-social practices will 'take' and persist to create actual social change. Along similar lines Giddens argues that the long-term formation and transformation of social institutions must be seen in the light of the unintended consequences of social action through which the capability and knowledgeability of social actors is always bounded. These unintended consequences of social action work behind our back and implicate transformations which we have to distinguish from the continual and contingent reproduction of institutions in everyday life. Giddens holds that unintended consequences *condition* social reproduction and hence fundamentally determine the process of structuration through which systems are maintained and change over time. Social systems appear to exist and to be structured only 'in and through' their reproduction in micro-social interactions which are in turn limited and modalized through the unintended consequences of previous and parallel social action.

The hypothesis of unintended consequences transcends the purely micro-sociological perspective promoted by the aggregation hypothesis by acknowledging influences which operate behind the back of agents, and which therefore *cannot be found in micro-situations*. Yet the perspective advanced by the hypothesis of unintended consequences is no less radically micro-sociological than the one promoted by the aggregation model: it concludes that these macro-influences cannot be known through direct evidence, and that we can, at best, derive a proof of their *existence* from extremely simplified conditions. The micro-sociological reconstruction of macro-phenomena has remained consistent in and of itself. It has derived the macro-order from that which can be learned in micro-situations, and if and when a residuum of macro-social properties over and above the situation has been recognized, it has also been declared unknowable. What is there left to say on this position?

The theoretical model most conspicuously absent from the above conceptions is one which addresses the *interrelation* between situated social events, or one which refers to the *linkage* between the happenings of diverse micro-situations. Established sociological theories appear to have paid much attention to this phenomenon, conceiving of it, for example, in terms of the exchange of goods and services, or in terms of functional interdependence and role differentiation. It may not be surprising that the issue is most often raised in this volume by authors leaning toward a macroscopic view of social order. For example, when the macro is seen as a form of social integration whose historical locus for us is the political order (Habermas), reference is made to a particular institutional arrangement of organized (i.e. *interrelated*) action such as the state and its further interrelationships with those micro-social actions whose integration is at stake. Neo-systems theory (Luhmann) conceives of integration as no longer achieved through actual presence as in small-scale societies, but through (structural and functional) *interrelations* between social situations. In this connection, Lidz attributes particular importance to symbolic media which *circulate* information between different arenas of action – a precondition, it appears, for their unification and combination into societal subsystems of action. In contrast to functionalist and Marxist conceptions, Bourdieu has advanced the notion of a field as the locus of competitive struggles for the monopoly of symbolic capital among agents. Thus the field of Paris fashion or the fields of scientific disciplines can be seen as the battlegrounds on which designers and scientists respectively become *interrelated* through their competitive endeavours.[64]

All authors mentioned above hold different views of micro-level phenomena and their relation to macro-level questions. Bourdieu (see below) rejects distinctions such as those between the individual and the social (the collectivity), arguing instead in terms of the interaction of two histories – the past which is frozen and objectified in positions, laws, machines, etc., and the embodied history which makes up the habitus of a person. The micro-macro problem is projected here upon the problem of the interaction between agents' *disposition* and (institutional) *positions*. Habermas, on the other hand, postulates an evolutionary learning process which leads to new forms of social integration, and which crucially involves individual learning capacities. The learning of individuals in marginal groups may spread to the interpretative systems of other society members, thus creating a cognitively shared potential for reorganizing societal action systems. The process involves the *institutional embodiment* of individually acquired rationality structures and functions as a pacemaker for the development of productive forces. Finally, within neo-systems theory, face-to-face interaction is seen to play a crucial role in negotiating the boundaries and the locus of an interaction as belonging to a certain system, as when an issue is debated as a matter of morals versus a matter of the courts (Luhmann). And Lidz proposes the model of transformational grammar – which entails a view of the sociological actor as engaged in the *interactive transformation* of normative materials – to resolve the difference between the creative negotiation of social order on the micro-level and the presumably shared normative order which integrates society members on a macro-level.

Macro-sociologically inclined theories sampled in the present volume have incorporated many more micro-sociological concepts, as illustrated, for example, by Habermas's work on speech performances and distorted communication.[65] As noted before, they have also proposed mechanisms of interrelation between individuals or situations in connection with their macroscopic stance. On the most general level, one could say that it is a characteristic feature of macro-sociological approaches *to start from the assumption of such interrelationships*, and to attempt to describe and explain these interrelationships in their theoretical endeavours. Compared with the micro-sociological hypotheses outlined before, the macroscopic orientation can be described as based upon a hypothesis of inter-relation.

The question which interests us here is whether a microscopically reconstructed macro-sociology entailed by some of the contributions to this volume can avoid the issue of interrelationships between micro-social situations. Duster, for example, draws our attention to the transformations which occur routinely in social action, for example when a law is passed on from the legal context to different contexts of law 'application'. As he points out, to understand these transformations requires that we systematically study micro-situations which are related to each other, for example by the circulation of a law across different contexts of action. Obviously, the respective transformations cannot be examined, and might not even be noticed, when a study is restricted to a particular setting. Fauconnier in his chapter provides another, more linguistically and epistemologically oriented example, when he demonstrates that the notion of truth is socially relativized to rituals and contexts, and cannot be studied as an autonomous unit independent of social relationships and social interaction. Cicourel had already pointed out the need of expanding one's knowledge base about the immediate event examined, which includes the need of bringing to bear information from situations and contexts *related to* the event.

In its most extreme version, the demand for considering the context and interrelationships of micro-social episodes leads us to Waller-stein's 'world-system', a position which acknowledges only one clear-cut and inclusive system, the 'modern world'. Characteristically, Wallerstein arrives at this position in the struggle for delimiting units of analysis, that is contexts of interrelated historical events.[66] To such all-encompassing strategies of contextualization radical micro-socio-logical perspectives supply the antithesis of a *monadic* conception, which looks for the happenings of social life within micro-events considered in relative isolation.

5   The representation hypothesis

The arguments advanced in the last section leave us with a seeming contradiction between two obvious truths: the fact that all social action necessarily happens in micro-social situations upon which the radical micro-sociological perspectives promoted by Collins and

Harré have based their attack and reconstruction of macro-sociology; and the equally obvious fact that social events appear to be inter-related which has led authors such as Wallerstein to posit the 'world-system' as the only unit of analysis which justifiably constitutes an (all-inclusive) whole. One way out of the dilemma is to postulate levels of system formation and systems differentiation which start with interaction systems and end up with societal systems (see Luhmann, below). Thus neo-systems theory arrives at a hierarchy of more inclusive systems whose interrelationship is itself a topic of analysis.

But what if we insist, for methodological and ontological reasons, on the primacy of micro-social situations whatever the 'level' to which the respective action can be attributed? What if we attempt to carry the micro-sociological perspective as far as possible while at the same time attempting to avoid the pitfalls of Leibniz's monadism? I take this to mean that we start from the fact that transactions attributed to 'the state' no less than family transactions or private interlocutions with oneself arise in micro-situations *and* need to be studied in these situations. Yet at the same time we would have to recognize that micro-transactions always *in principle transcend* the immediate situation or, more radically speaking, we would have to concede that many micro-situations *appear only to exist in virtue of other such situations*. In the language of micro-perspectives this implies that many defini-tions of the situation are construed *relationally*, by reference to other imputed, projected or reconstructed situations and events. Thus another way out of the dilemma posed above may be to endorse the model of social reality as composed of micro-social situations, but at the same time to expand this model by taking into account the *macro-constructions endogenous to these situations*.

To expound the thesis, let me start by an example. I want to propose that the problem of unintended consequences which plays such a crucial role in one of the reconceptions of the macro-social order can be clarified, if not resolved, if the situationally construed representations through which agents map a field of interrelation-ships between scenes of action are not ignored. Consider a renowned historical account of a whole explosion of unforeseen effects, the history of the Thirty Years War by C. V. Wedgwood.[67] Historical accounts provide ready illustrations of unintended consequences, given that they usually cover a larger time span than sociological studies. According to Wedgwood, the Thirty Years War is itself the outstanding example of a meaningless conflict which nobody wanted, which proved economically destructive and socially degrading for most who engaged in it, and which solved no problem and left both the Catholics and Protestants involved unsatisfied:[68]

> The overwhelming majority in Europe, the overwhelming majority in Germany, wanted no war; powerless and voiceless, there was no need even to persuade them that they did. The decision was made without thought of them. Yet of those who, one by one, let themselves be drawn into the conflict, few were irresponsible and nearly all were genuinely anxious for an ultimate and better peace. Almost all – one excepts the King of Sweden – were actuated rather by fear than by lust of conquest or passion of faith. They wanted peace and they fought for thirty years to be sure of it.

How is it that not only those who had no voice but also those who ruled and had the power to decide for or against a war 'let themselves be drawn into the conflict', one by one? The first obvious thing to note is that no one of the leading politicians ever decided for 'the Thirty Years War'. They decided to locally intervene or to wait, to help out with troops or money, to curtail somebody's power or to seize upon an advantage. For at least 17 months after the date of 1618 traditionally assigned to the outbreak of the war, it was apparently not clear 'even to the leading men in the countries most deeply concerned', that the revolt of that date rather than any other incident in that stormy time had initiated a war.[69] How did the original incident which consisted of the overthrow of an unpopular Catholic government by rising Protestants in Prague grow into a conflict of that size and duration? The Elector Palatine of the upper Rhenish Palatinate became convinced that this was an occasion to break the Hapsburg succession to the imperial throne by wresting the crown of Bohemia from the Hapsburg family. His advisors may even have played a role in engineering the revolt. While the Elector Frederick busied himself in Prague, the Spaniards moved into his Palatinate which proved crucial in bringing the manpower of the north Italian plains into action in Flanders, by which they planned an attack after an earlier truce had expired. The Protestant princes of Germany had thought to end the war by sacrificing Frederick, but were moved to further action by the Spanish move. Equally, the Dutch moved against the Spanish plan by subsidizing Frederick in order that he regain the Palatinate on the Rhine, after he had lost Bohemia. The newly elected Hapsburg emperor renewed his coalition with Catholic German princes and proceeded against Frederick's plan. And so forth.

The above lines which hardly cover 3 years of the war can only indicate how futile it is to attempt to summarize a complicated sequence of events which involved virtually all European centres of power and their diplomatic and military schemes in a few sentences. They may however give us a sense of the interrelatedness and reciprocal interdependence of these events. The point I wish to make is first that we are dealing with events *chained together* by the mutual expectations, imputations of interests, misread communications, fears, grudges, and finally by the concrete projects of the parties involved with or against each other. And second, that there appears to be *nothing unintelligible* about this chain of events and its 'unintended' outcome if we take the trouble to look concretely at the relevant scenes of action and their interrelation, however complicated. If agents' intentions were continually frustrated in this war, it is, according to the historian, because they had been built upon assumptions about other relevant agents which did not hold water, and it is because other agents had moved against the respective intentions in an attempt to further their own interests. Our recourse to the notion of unintended consequences may become redundant, at least as far as social consequences are concerned, if the interrelation of scenes of action by and for agents construed through representations of mutual knowledge, intentions, projects, interests, etc., are given adequate consideration.

What exactly is involved in taking into account the *relational* character of agents' definitions of the situation? It seems that we can either adopt, not unlike agents themselves, a birdseye perspective and proceed to reconstruct the network of interrelated affairs which emerges from these definitions. This is the perspective which appears to underlie macroscopic orientations. Or we can take a step back and start from the representations by which agents and sociologists alike construe these interrelations. It has perhaps been the major thrust of Cicourel's work to document interactional and organizational accounting procedures and decision-making activities whereby situated events are routinely transformed into summary measures, aggregated distributions, bureaucratic records, and similar macro-information.[70] The macro emerges from such work not as the sum of unintended consequences of micro-episodes nor as their aggregate or network of interrelations, but rather as a summary representation actively constructed and pursued within micro-situations. In other words, the macro appears no longer as a *particular layer* of social reality *on top* of micro-episodes composed of their interrelation (macro-sociologies), their aggregation (aggregation hypothesis), or their unforeseen effects (hypothesis of unintended consequences). Rather, it is seen to reside *within* these micro-episodes where it results from the *structuring practices* of agents. The outcome of these practices are representations which thrive upon an alleged correspondence to that which they represent, but which at the same time can be seen as highly situated constructions which involve several levels of interpretation and selection. We can also say that agents routinely transform situated micro-events into summary representations by relying on practices through which they convince themselves of having achieved appropriate representation.

The constructed character of representations and the practices involved can perhaps best be illustrated in cases encompassing whole *technologies of representation*, for example in econometrics. Every few months, economists represent the state of national and supra national 'economies' by estimating – with the help of linear equation models and large-scale computers – the development of investments, exports, imports, private and public consumption, the gross national product and other economic indicators. Normally, the first prognosis is made in the autumn and refers to the subsequent year. It will be revised several times until, at the last revision, what is calculated is a representation of the economic situation of the year just passed. Calculations are based on input indicators prepared, for example, by statistical bureaus and other agencies.

However, the results of the first computer run of the model usually do not correspond to the expectations and desires of those who attempt to map the economic situation. Consequently, there will be many more runs, in which more plausible and justifiable values are generated through manipulations of the model, for which there are a variety of possibilities.[71] Thus, the representation of the economic situation which is finally published results from a complex process of construction and interpretation which furthermore includes several stages, since similar processes of construction and negotiation of meaning underlie the generation of the original data series which serves as an input for the econometric model. Compared with inter-actional accounting procedures, the process includes formalized techniques which do not, however, reduce the selectivity of the process, though they may well serve to better stabilize its results: particular formal procedures are themselves *decision-impregnated*, and their application *in situ* can be shown to involve continual further interpretations, translations, and selections.[72]

It should be noted in passing that technologies of representation are not, as one might expect, an invention of the social sciences. For example, history demonstrates that fourteenth-century Inquisitors used a kind of standardized questionnaire by which they interviewed suspected heretics. In the case of the so-called heresy of the Free Spirit, Grundmann has shown that the questionnaire contained literally those eight errors of 'an abominable sect of malignant men known as beghards and faithless women known as beguines in the Kingdom of Germany' condemned by the Pope at the Council of Vienne in 1311.[73] These 'heretic' doctrines were the questions posed to the suspects in Latin to test their faith. Yet not only the questions were standardized, the answers had also been predetermined – and, apparently, the answers given by the first heretic condemned as a Free Spirit quite literally served (after they had been translated into Latin) as response categories in future examinations. Answers by later 'heretics' were written down as much in accordance with the original formulation as possible, or else it was only particular deviations and additions to the original responses which were noted at all. Thus a heretic from Eichstatt and 77 years later a suspect interviewed in Mainz claim, by virtually the same words, that they had been penetrated during devotions by a terrible, agonizing sound from the top of the church, and that they had thereby been inspired by the Holy Spirit. Based upon the accordance which they thus identified, Inquisitors convinced themselves of the existence of a morally abhorrent sect of the 'Brothers and Sisters of the Free Spirit' (also beghards and beguines), and proceeded to eliminate its members. It is clear that their practice of prosecution resulted in ever new confirmations of the sect. Until very recently, historians too joined force with the Inquisitors in an attempt to reconstruct the heresy.[74] It is only a few years since a closer examination of the historical sources of these reconstructions showed that the heresies of the late Middle

Ages may actually have been generated by the methods Inquisitors used.[75]

The case of the heresy of the Free Spirit is interesting not only because it invokes certain analogies to the procedure of empirical social research, but also because we are alerted to the proximity – if not identity – between representation and *reification*. This proximity can also be demonstrated in the case of econometrics. For example, a comparison made between econometric prognoses for the years 1974–9, and actual economic development as measured by the variables which the models predict, shows for the first predictions a coefficient of determination – and consequently an explained variance – near zero.[76] The prognoses seem to be no better than chance predictions, and the accordance between different institutes engaged in econometric modelling is much higher ($R^2 > .60$) than between any single prognosis and later actual values of economic indicators. Matters improve only with the fourth revision which already draws upon actual data from the first few months of the year for which predictions are made. By the time of the last revision, we have an almost complete agreement. This is, however, hardly surprising given that the last revision retrospectively 'predicts' the economic situation of the year just passed and represented by 'real' input values in the model.

The correspondence or non-correspondence between the representing and the represented is not only a matter of epistemological reflection, but also an issue of everyday contestation among participants. In other words, not only are summary representations actively construed and pursued in everyday social interaction, the equivalence between these constructions and that which they represent must also be seen as actively negotiated, interpreted and constructed. On the one hand, this is simply part of the self-referential character of social life by which issues pursued may also become topics of thematization. On the other hand, such thematizations are part of a repertoire of social strategies by which claims connected to a particular summary representation can be challenged and replaced. What I want to suggest is that representations as understood here are not imaginary pictures of the world which belong to the realm of free-floating ideas. Summary representations are not only routinely and actively constructed in everyday life, they are also routinely invested with faith and interests, they are fought over and manipulated. As the study of science has shown, to construe a certain representation of the world is in principle always at the same time a matter of truth (correspondence, equivalence) *and* a matter of political strategy, that is of imposing one's say and of instituting certain consequences *with or against* others.

To illustrate this point let us turn, for a moment, to the story of Enoch Powell as recounted by F. G. Bailey.[77] Powell was a Conservative MP who, through only three formal speeches delivered in 1968, rose from an eccentric and minor member of the party's elite to a national figure who eclipsed the leaders of English public life. He did this by transforming the question of coloured immigrants from India, Pakistan, etc. from a matter of 'localized grumbling' and occasional disorders in some poor areas of industrial cities to a matter of national heritage and interest. Powell proceeded by presenting statistics on immigration and the relative size of the white and the coloured population. He also told many homely anecdotes of small and defenceless persons who hold high standards of decency and work ethic, but who are persecuted, molested and discriminated against by blacks. By the time of his third speech he had achieved an enormous mass following and considerably embarrassed his party, which felt that Powell's speeches went far beyond Conservative policies on race.

Powell's statements provoked three kinds of answers by critics. The first simply denied the 'facts' which Powell claimed to present; the second type of answer criticized Powell for making a mountain out of a mole-hill: and the third accused him of being a racist through denying the principle of common humanity which unites all men. Interestingly, it was the second type of response through which Powell was 'ditched' by one of his party colleagues – Quintin Hogg. Hogg dealt with the problem by making many feeble jokes and by relegating the 'race question' from the level of the nation and its heritage to that of housing and job opportunities in particular areas of particular towns, a level easy to deal with in local politics. By reducing the problem to one that had really nothing to do with race or culture or Britain, he also effectively reduced Powell as a spokesman of 'the people', and reaffirmed the party establishment. The story illustrates the practical negotiations of the scale of a problem, and alludes to the investments and strategies by which an issue comes to be defined as of micro- or of macro-scale.

Powell did, of course, not only promote a macro-description of what was in the interest of the decent majority of the country, he also promoted himself as a defender of those interests. According to Callon and Latour (see below), micro-actors blow themselves up to a macro-size by what could be called 'the Powell strategy', that is by making themselves the spokesmen of many others whose following they enlist. Callon and Latour offer the example of a corporate actor like Renault who attempts to enrol the public for its purpose of increasing or sustaining growth by translating the will of the public (regarding private cars). In this sense, summarizing the interests of many can be equivalent to collecting their support, and thereby to 'embody' a large number of people. Political representation is such embodied representation, in which the represented and the representing are both agents rather than events. The sociologically interesting phenomenon here is of course that actors come to stand for others *in virtue of* summary representations which are themselves, as we have seen, highly internally constructed, and which become the issue of processes of intervention, dissolution and substitution.

As Bailey has argued, an increase in scale goes along with a simplification of the perceptual clues for interaction: by simplifying one's message, one enlarges the scale of one's congregation.[78] A political leader may seek anonymity not only for reasons of privacy, but also because this removes his or her rounded humanity from other people's perception, and allows for acceptance by a wider audience. Macro-information by definition will be more general, more abstract and more simplified than the micro-information it represents. Yet entropy decreases as scale increases only *in relation to* the original level of scale. The 'state' as circumscribed by a particular constitution can be seen as a highly simplified, large-scale abstraction. However, the concrete enactment of this abstraction, the 'state' as a level of political–administrative action, involves nothing larger in scale (*or simpler in structure*) than the situated *micro*-interactions of members of congress and parliament, or of the people who frequent such localized government sites as the White House or 10 Downing Street.

The issue is complicated by the fact that we tend to conceive of the affairs of the 'state' as matters more complex than those of micro-social action, as indicated before,[79] while at the same time reducing them by way of aggregate measurement to a level *less* complex than that of everyday practical action. The assumption that higher order levels of social life must also be more complex seems to be derived from the assumption that they somehow *subsume* levels of smaller scale, which in turn seems to be related to the idea that macro-structures effectively *control* micro-events. However, we may remind ourselves that the degree, desirability and effectivity of such control is a continual matter of controversy and struggle in social life. Indeed, we might just as plausibly assume that micro-social interactions evolve parallel to, and partially independent of, activities qualified as belonging to a higher hierarchical level. For example, Braudel, in his study of economic development in pre-industrial Europe, distinguishes between at least three different economies: the market economy which governs our statistics; an informal, self-sufficient infra-economy of short-distance exchanges of goods and services; and a transnational economy of privileged actors such as the big merchants of Amsterdam who engaged in 'world'-wide trade and played complicated credit games.[80] It is clear that none of these economies simply subsumed the others, though there may have been influences and cross-references. Similarly, Wedgwood describes the peasantry and indeed the 'great majority' of the people in Europe during the period of the Thirty Years War not only as ignorant of but also as indifferent to the dynastic ambitions which governed the political and diplomatic relations. Of course it was the latter which brought about and sustained a prolonged war. Yet except for the actual districts of fighting, the civilian population is said to have remained undisturbed by wars fought largely by professional armies, at least until the need for money caused an exceptional levy on their wealth.[81]

It follows that there may be no difference in scale nor in consequentiality between the mutually related actions of statesmen, diplomats and business multinationals, on the one hand, and the locally inter-related actions of peasants and townsfolk, on the other. Both versions of interaction are equally microscopic *in structure*, though they obviously involve significantly different distances in space. The direct and indirect influence may be as great as the effects of politicians' actions on the former, for example by means of taxation. It should also be noted that whatever effects there do exist will become reconstructed, reinterpreted and modified through local practices. These are the transformations to which Duster (see below) refers when he illustrates the changes a law undergoes as it moves from congressional hearings to local enforcement agencies and to those concerned by the bill.

However, there can be no doubt in regard to the above examples that there has been a difference of voice and visibility, and of the macro-claims associated with the representations construed in different arenas of action. As a result, it is the dynasties of Europe which populate our history books, and it is a certain level of market exchange which dominates our economic statistics. In principle, we may achieve more by studying the production of such claims in their micro-social environment rather than to take them at face value. This is not to ignore or neglect the issue of power which hides beneath everyday differentiations between 'big' and 'small' actors. It is, however, to relocate and redress questions of power, as I have suggested before.

6   Conclusion

Macro-social theories and methodologies have generally focused their interest on the interrelationship of social action. They have promoted conceptions of (macro) social order which start from an interrelation hypothesis and employed notions such as social system and social structure to deal with this interrelation. In contrast, micro-social theories and methodologies favour conceptions which start from the ontological and methodological primacy of micro-social situations. While this has resulted in a long-standing challenge of macro-approaches to social reality, attempts to *reconstruct* macro-sociology from a microsociological perspective are new. I have outlined the aggregation hypothesis advanced by Collins and the hypothesis of unintended consequences which I have identified with the work of Harré and (partly) Giddens as two major attempts in this direction. In addition, I have promoted a representation hypothesis as supported by much of the work of Cicourel and his students, and (despite their macroscopic stance) by some of the theses of Callon and Latour in this volume. The main difference between the representation hypothesis and the other two hypotheses is perhaps that it conceives of the macro as actively construed and pursued *within* micro-social action, while the aggregation hypothesis and the hypothesis of unintended consequences regard the macro-order as an *emergent* phenomenon composed of the sum or the unintended effects of micro-events. Pushed to its extreme, the representation hypothesis would have to deny the existence of a macro-order *apart from* the macro-representations which are routinely accomplished in micro-social action. Note that according to the representation hypothesis, we expect to find macro-structuring practices not only in big politics of big business, but also within the more homespun spheres of everyday life. Note also that it is these practices through which agents presumably convince themselves of achieving equivalence between the representing and the represented, and of legitimately substituting the former for the latter. In this context reification can be seen as defined by such substitutions which conceal the 'decision-ladenness' of the processes through which representations are actively negotiated and constructed, challenged and deconstructed.

It is clear that all three hypotheses outlined here do not yet go far enough in their attempt to reconceive of the 'macro-order' from the perspective of micro-social theory and methodology. Specifically, assertions which imply a dissolution of our received notions of the macro-order by declaring such an order as non-existent, unknowable, or as nothing but aggregated micro-episodes may raise a series of angry questions none of which has been addressed sufficiently yet. At least some of what is said in this volume which bears on the three hypotheses sketched may directly contradict learned sociological intuitions and the rhetoric of everyday life. We need to do a lot more work on the process of reification in micro-social situations, and on the issue of interrelationships between micro-situations.

The problem of social order is of course as old as social theory, yet in the past two decades it often appeared quietly forgotten in the struggle and the widening gap between micro- and macro-social theories and methodologies. Happily, the authors of this book have set about rethinking and researching the problem based upon the theoretical and methodological developments of recent years, and their results suggest that the issue has gained much potential and appeal in its slumber. We are now not only in a new position to raise the question of the relation between micro- and macro-social theory and methodology, but also to point out new directions in which to search for a resolution. Quite obviously I think that this direction will be heavily informed (but not bounded) by advances in the more microscopic approaches, for it is there that most theoretical and methodological developments have taken place. I also believe in the seeming paradox that it is through *micro*-social approaches that we will learn most about the macro-order, for it is these approaches which through their unashamed empiricism afford us a glimpse of the reality about which we speak. Certainly, we will not get a grasp of whatever is the whole of the matter by a microscopic recording of face-to-face interaction. However, it may be enough to begin with if we can – for the first time – hear the macro-order tick.

Notes

1 For a by now classical formulation of symbolic interactionism see H. Blumer, *Symbolic Interactionism* (Englewood Cliffs, NJ: Prentice Hall, 1969); for cognitive sociology see A. Cicourel, *Cognitive Sociology: Language and Meaning in Social Interaction* (Harmondsworth: Penguin, 1973); for ethnomethodology see H. Garfinkel, *Studies in Ethnomethodology* (Englewood Cliffs: Prentice Hall, 1967); recent social phenomenology is best described by P. Berger and T. Luckman, *The Social Construction of Reality* (London: Allen Lane, 1967); and ethogenics has been proposed by R. Harré and P. Secord, *The Explanation of Social Behaviour* (Oxford: Basil Blackwell, 1972). For a codification of the ethnography of speaking see D. Hymes, *Foundations in Sociolinguistics. An Ethnographic Approach* (University of Pennsylvania Press, 1974), and for ethnoscience see W. Sturtevant, 'Studies in Ethnoscience', *American Anthropologist*, special issue on *Transcultural Studies in Cognition*, 66/3, part 2 (1964), pp. 99–131.
2 A. Schutz, of course, has also been referred to frequently by ethnomethodologists. See particularly his *Collected Papers*, vol. 1, *The Problem of Social Reality*, M. Natanson (ed.) (The Hague: Martinus Nijhoff, 1962).
3 Marxism, structural-functionalism and systems theory are examples of theoretical and methodological approaches which count as macro-sociological. For a summary presentation of macro-sociology see A. Etzioni and J. Porter (eds), *Macrosociology: Research and Theory* (Boston: Allen & Bacon, 1970).
4 R. Dahrendorf, *Class and Class Conflict in Industrial Society* (Stanford University Press, 1959), p. 159.
5 See A. Giddens, *Studies in Social and Political Theory* (London: Hutchinson, 1979), for an exposition of some historical origins and some theoretical aspects of the normative conception (chs 6 and 8).
6 E. Durkheim's discussion of social facts and his critique of methodological individualism is found in his *The Rules of Sociological Method* (New York: Free Press, 1962). His exposition of organic solidarity and of the moral integration of the conscience collective is found in his *The Division of Labour in Society* (New York: Free Press, 1956).
7 For T. Parsons's conception of the problem of social order see his *The Structure of Social Action* (Glencoe: Free Press, 1949).
8 Parsons talks about reciprocal sets of expectations in terms of the 'double

contingency' of social interaction: the reactions of each party in an interaction depend upon the contingent responses of others (1) which thereby potentially sanction the acts of the former (2) and vice versa. See T. Parsons, 'An Outline of the Social System', in T. Parsons *et al.* (eds), *Theories of Society* (New York: Free Press, 1965).

9 For example see A. Giddens, *Central Problems in Social Theory* (University of California Press, 1979), ch. 2.

10 The controversy over whether social action is to be explained in terms of (agents') reasons or in terms of (social and other) causes lies behind many of the differences between micro- and macro-approaches to social life. For two key volumes on the controversy see G. H. von Wright, *Explanation and Understanding* (Cornell University Press, 1971), and K.-O. Apel, *Die Erklären: Verstehen Kontroverse in transzendental-pragmatischer Sicht*, (Frankfurt/Main: Suhrkamp, 1979).

11 W. H. Goodenough, 'Cultural Anthropology and Linguistics', in P. Garvin (ed.), *Report of the 7th Annual Round Table Meeting on Linguistics and Language Study*, Monograph Series on Language and Linguistics, no. 9 (Georgetown University, Institute of Language and Linguistics), pp. 167–8.

12 Cf. C. Frake, 'The Ethnographic Study of Cognitive Systems', in T. Gladwin and W. C. Sturtevant (eds), *Anthropology and Human Behaviour* (Washington: Anthropological Society of Washington, 1962), p. 74.

13 Cf. O. Werner and J. Fenton, 'Method and Theory in Ethnoscience and Ethnoepistemology', in R. Naroll and R. Cohen (eds), *A Handbook of Methods in Cultural Anthropology* (Garden City: Doubleday, 1970), ch. 29.

14 See N. K. Denzin, 'Symbolic Interactionism and Ethnomethodology: A Proposed Synthesis', *American Sociological Review*, 34 (1969), pp. 922–34.

15 Paradigm examples of these kinds of results are found in the works of E. Goffman. See for example his *The Presentation of Self in Everyday Life* (Garden City: Doubleday, 1959), or his *Relations in Public* (New York: Harper & Row, 1971).

16 I am particularly referring here to the recent work of G. Lakoff and P. Fillmore which strongly questions the assumption that linguistic structures can be dealt with on an autonomous level detached from the pragmatics of linguistic performance. See for example G. Lakoff, 'The Arbitrary Basis of Transformational Grammar', *Language*, 48 (1972), pp. 76–87; or the papers collected in C. Fillmore, G. Lakoff and R. Lakoff (eds), *Berkeley Studies in Syntax and Semantics*, vol. 1 (University of California, Dept of Linguistics and Institute of Human Learning, 1974).

17 A. Cicourel, 'Interviewing and Memory', in C. Cherry (ed.), *Pragmatic Aspects of Human Communication* (Dordrecht: D. Reidel, 1974).

18 E. Goffman, *Frame Analysis, An Essay on the Organization of Experience* (New York: Harper & Row, 1974).

19 See D. Zimmerman and L. Wieder, 'Ethnomethodology and the Problem of Order: Comment on Denzin', in J. Douglas (ed.), *Understanding Everyday Life* (Chicago: Aldine, 1970), particularly p. 289.

20 For an example of conversation analysis see H. Sacks, E. Schegloff and

G. Jefferson, 'A Simplest Systematics for the Organization of Turn-Taking in Conversation', *Language* 50 (1974), pp. 696–735.

21 Cf. A. Cicourel, *Cognitive Sociology: Language and Meaning in Social Interaction*, especially chs 3 and 4.

22 An indication of this turn is the rise of the 'cognitive sciences' which enrol several disciplines (artificial intelligence, psychology, linguistics, computer science, education, philosophy, etc.) in the study of human cognition. For a summary presentation of some of the issues and advances in cognitive science see D. Bobrow and A. Collins (eds), *Representation and Understanding: Studies in Cognitive Science* (New York: Academic Press, 1975).

23 Cf. J. Douglas, 'Understanding Everyday Life', in J. Douglas (ed.), *Understanding Everyday Life*, p. 12.

24 W. J. N. Watkins, 'Methodological Individualism: A Reply', *Philosophy of Science*, 22 (1955), pp. 58–62, pp. 58f. For a presentation of the whole debate between methodological individualists and collectivists see J. O'Neill (ed.), *Modes of Individualism and Collectivism* (London: Heinemann, 1973).

25 E. Goffman, 'The Neglected Situation', in P. P. Giglioli (ed.), *Language and Social Context* (Harmondsworth: Penguin, 1972), p. 63.

26 G. Simmel, *On Individuality and Social Forms: Selected Writings* (University of Chicago Press, 1971), p. 23.

27 Ibid., p. 11.

28 G. H. Mead, *Mind, Self and Society* (University of Chicago Press, 1967), pp. 78f.

29 Cf. A. Brittan, *Meanings and Situations* (London: Routledge & Kegan Paul, 1973), particularly pp. 96ff.

30 See for example Weick's insistence that interacts rather than acts are the units of organizational analysis. K. Weick, *The Social Psychology of Organizing* (Reading, MA: Addison-Wesley, 1969), e.g. pp. 33f., 98.

31 E. Goffman, 'The Neglected Situation', p. 63

32 For an illustration of these results, see K. Knorr-Cetina, *The Manufacture of Knowledge: An Essay on the Constructivist and Contextual Nature of Science* (Oxford: Pergamon Press, 1981), particularly ch. 2.

33 A. Schutz, *The Phenomenology of the Social World* (Northwestern University Press, 1967), particularly the ch. on 'Meaningful Lived Experience'.

34 M. Mandelbaum, 'Societal Facts', in J. O'Neill (ed.), *Modes of Individualism and Collectivism*, pp. 223ff.

35 A. Cicourel, *Method and Measurement in Sociology* (New York: Free Press, 1964).

36 As an example see A. Cicourel, *The Social Organization of Juvenile Justice* (New York: Wiley, 1968).

37 N. Denzin, 'Symbolic Interactionism and Ethnomethodology: A Proposed Synthesis', pp. 272f. For those interested in these studies, Denzin provides further references.

38 Both psychoanalysis and Piaget's psychology locate the self within the cognitive processes of the central nervous system, while behaviourism identifies it with actual physical behaviour. See S. Freud, *The Interpretation*

of Dreams (New York: Avon Books, 1965), pp. 637f.; J. Piaget, *The Child's Conception of the World*, Totowa: Littlefield, Adams, 1975), p. 33; and B. F. Skinner, *Science and Human Behaviour* (New York: Free Press, 1965), pp. 29f. The 'cognitive' conception of the self can perhaps be traced back to Descartes and his separation of the *cogito*, i.e. the self-conscious mind, from the body.

39 For a brief summary of James's, Mead's and today's perspective on the self see A. Brittan, *Meanings and Situations*, pp. 183ff.

40 Cf. P. de Waele and R. Harré, 'The Personality of Individuals', in R. Harré (ed.), *Personality* (Oxford: Blackwell, 1976), pp. 190f.

41 Cf. for example Searle's outline of speech act theory which starts from Austin's conceptions. J. Searle, *Speech Acts* (Cambridge University Press, 1969).

42 See M. Kreckel, *Communicative Acts and Shared Knowledge in Natural Discourse* (London: Academic Press, 1981), for an example of the usage of the notion of tone-units.

43 Cf. D. Rumelhart and A. Ortony, 'The Representation of Knowledge in Memory', in R. C. Anderson *et al.* (eds), *Schooling and the Acquisition of Knowledge* (Hillsdale: Lawrence Erlbaum, 1976).

44 Max Weber, *The Theory of Social and Economic Organization* (Glencoe: Free Press, 1957), p. 88

45 For a brief and enlightened discussion of actor's meaning see H. Menzel, 'Meaning – Who Needs it?', in M. Brenner *et al.* (eds), *The Social Context of Method* (London: Croom Helm, 1978).

46 E. Gellner, 'Scale and Nation', in F. Barth (ed.), *Scale and Social Organization* (Oslo: Universitetsforlaget, 1978), p. 133.

47 Cf. for example H. Atlan, *Entre Le Cristal et la fumée: essai sur l'organisation du vivant* (Paris: Éditions du Seuil, 1979), pp. 74–6, for a discussion of these definitions.

48 Cf. R. Redfield, 'The Folk Society', *American Journal of Sociology*, 52 (1947), pp. 293–308, particularly p. 293.

49 See for example T. Schwartz, 'The Size and Shape of a Culture', in F. Barth (ed.), *Scale and Social Organization*, p. 217.

50 Cf. E. Gellner, 'Scale and Nation', pp. 134ff.

51 Cf. T. Schwartz, 'The Size and Shape of a Culture', p. 237.

52 Cf. H. Atlan, *Entre Le Cristal et la fumée: essai sur l'organisation du vivant*, p. 74.

53 Cf. S. Lukes, *Essays in Social Theory* (London: Macmillan Press, 1977), p. 4, where the idea that power is an 'essentially contested' notion is attributed to W. B. Gallie.

54 Lukes presents a summary discussion of some important definitions of power. Ibid., pp. 4ff.

55 Ibid., pp. 15ff.

56 Cf. M. Foucault, *Histoire de la sexualité.1.La volonté de savoir* (Paris: Gallimard, 1976), particularly ch. 2 'Méthode'; also *Surveiller et punir* (Paris: Gallimard, 1975), particularly pp. 29–33.

57 A. Cicourel, *The Social Organization of Juvenile Justice*.

58 R. Laing, *The Divided Self* (London: Tavistock, 1956); and R. Laing and A. Esterson, *Sanity, Madness and the Family* (London: Tavistock, 1964).
59 A. Brittan, *The Privatized World* (London: Routledge & Kegan Paul, 1977), p. 69.
60 I. Prigogine and I. Stengers, *La Nouvelle Alliance: métamorphose de la science* (Paris: Gallimard, 1979), p. 219. Prigogine has won the Nobel Prize for his work on chemical dissipative structures which entail models of self-organization.
61 See also R. Collins, 'On the Micro-Foundations of Macro-Sociology', *American Journal of Sociology* 86 (1981), pp. 984–1014.
62 A. Brittan, *Meanings and Situations*, p. 84.
63 For the notion of social class as a habitus of the individual acquired in socialization see P. Bourdieu, *Outline of a Theory of Practice* (Cambridge University Press, 1977), ch. 2.
64 In regard to these competitive endeavours, see particularly Bourdieu's notion of symbolic capital, ibid., pp. 171ff. See also his application of the concept to scientific fields in P. Bourdieu, 'The Specificity of the Scientific Field and the Social Conditions of the Progress of Reason', *Social Science Information*, 14/6 (1975), pp. 19–47.
65 See for example J. Habermas, 'Towards a Theory of Communicative Competence', *Inquiry*, 13 (1970), pp. 360–75, and 'What is Universal Pragmatics?', in J. Habermas, *Communication and the Evolution of Society* (Boston: Beacon Press, 1979).
66 I. Wallerstein, *The Modern World-System I* (New York: Academic Press, 1974), particularly the Introduction.
67 C. V. Wedgwood, *The Thirty Years War* (London: Jonathan Cape, 1967).
68 Ibid., p. 526.
69 Ibid., p. 12.
70 Cf. A. Cicourel, *Method and Measurement in Sociology*, and *The Social Organization of Juvenile Justice*, and *Theory and Method in a Study of Argentine Fertility* (New York: Wiley, 1974).
71 These possibilities are described in detail by an economist who had himself been engaged in econometric modelling in a leading position for many years. Cf. P. Fleissner, 'Wirtschaftsprognosen zwischen Orakel, Politik und Wissenschaft', *Wirtschaftspolitische Blätter* (1981), forthcoming.
72 For a more detailed exposition of the 'constructive', decision-impregnated character of scientific procedures in general see K. Knorr-Cetina, *The Manufacture of Knowledge: An Essay on the Constructive and Contextual Nature of Science*. The study is based on one year of direct observation of scientists at work in Berkeley, California. For a similar study which also supports the constructive nature of the scientific procedure see B. Latour and S. Woolgar, *Laboratory Life: The Social Construction of Scientific Facts* (Beverly Hills: Sage, 1979).
73 Cf. H. Grundmann, *Ausgewählte Aufsätze, Teil 1, Religiöse Bewegungen* (Stuttgart: Anton Hiersemann, 1976), pp. 364–416. I owe this and the following two references to Eric van Hove who has alerted me to the story

of the heresy of the Free Spirit but who has, unfortunately, not written up this story in a language spoken outside of Belgium.

74 See for example N. Cohn, *The Pursuit of the Millennium: Revolutionary Messianism in Medieval and Reformation Europe and its Bearing on Modern Totalitarian Movements* (New York: Harper & Row, 1961); R. Lerner, *The Heresy of the Free Spirit in the Later Middle Ages* (University of California Press, 1972).

75 Grundmann's article on the self-verifying character of the Inquisitors' interview procedure (see Note 73) was first published in 1965.

76 P. Fleissner, 'Wirtschaftsprognosen zwischen Orakel, Politik und Wissenschaft'.

77 F. G. Bailey, 'Tertius Gaudens aut Tertium Numen', in F. Barth (ed.), *Scale and Social Organization*, pp. 206ff.

78 Ibid., p. 201f.

79 Obviously, the assumption of such greater complexity is connected to the assumption of, or focus on, the interrelationship of events.

80 F. Braudel, *Civilisation matérielle, économie et capitalisme, XVe-XVIIIe siècle*, vol. 1 (Paris: Armand Colin, 1979), Introduction, particularly p. 8.

81 C. V. Wedgwood, *The Thirty Years War*, p. 13.

Part 1

The micro-foundations of social knowledge

1 Notes on the integration of micro- and macro-levels of analysis

Aaron V. Cicourel

[*Traditional sociological approaches have defined societal macro-structures as a particular level of social reality to be distinguished from the micro-episodes of social action. This has allowed them to conceive of and search for these macro-structures more or less independent of the observable practices of everyday life.*

Cicourel argues that (macro) social facts are not simply given, but emerge from the routine practices of everyday life. The macro in the sense of typified, normalized, context-free summary descriptions is a typical product *of organizational and interactive procedures which transform micro-events into macro-social structures. Thus a precondition for the integration of micro- and macro-social phenomena in our theory and methodology is that we identify the processes which contribute to the creation of macro-structures by routine inferences, interpretations and summary procedures.*

The paper also points out that differences between micro-sociologies parallel differences between micro- and macro-approaches. By focusing only on small fragments of conversational interaction, some versions of micro-sociology tend to ignore the context which informs the conversational interaction for participants themselves. The decontextualized accounts produced by such methods are not unlike the decontextualization which results from macro-sociological aggregate measurement procedure. Against this Cicourel (like Collins in chapter 2) argues for the generation of a comparative data base which includes not only the context of single interactions, but which also studies social phenomena systematically over different contexts.]

The title of this introductory essay seeks to call attention to methodological and theoretical junctures where interactions between macro- and micro-theories and research are routine aspects of the social organization of the group or larger entity being studied by the sociologist. The routine activities of an organization or group normally include the integration of micro- and macro-data and theory because all daily-life settings reflect several levels of cultural complexity.

Differences between micro- and macro-sociologies depend on the arbitrary ways in which researchers choose to theorize about the phenomena under study and the way they use research methods to generate particular kinds of data. The researcher's goals seem all too reasonable: utilize 'accepted' research strategies that guarantee a certain type of data base, and 'accepted' theoretical concepts. I will first summarize aspects of the strategies pursued by micro- and macro-researchers that enable them to ignore each other's activities, and then suggest a way we might begin to integrate the two levels.

The notion of integrating micro- and macro-sociological activities is a construction of the researcher and, therefore, is not a concept we can attribute to those members of a group whose normal activities create micro-macro integration. Yet the members of a group or organization who contribute to micro-macro integration in daily life often have their own ideas of the researcher's notions about levels of analysis and the methods required. The methods used by the members of a group invariably involve the creation of specific reports where a particular vocabulary enables insiders to interpret documents that are otherwise opaque or ambiguous.

1   The study of speech acts and connected discourse as social structure

The analysis of micro-processes is almost always conceived as a self-contained enterprise that is locally productive. This emphasis on the local production of social structures makes reference to such topics as the reflexive thoughts of participants of social interaction, conversational turn-taking rules, code-switching, and the constraints of external and local norms. In addition, some researchers address the role of locally emergent conditions that are perceived and attributed by participants to each other over the course of the interaction. The researcher tends to ignore the way the data used for analysis is part of the larger ethnographic or social organizational context from which fragments of conversations or large segments of discourse are taken.

Whereas some researchers examine intonation, stress and other phonological aspects of speech, others focus on gaze and body movements. For some students of conversation the primary focus is on turn-taking rules and the careful preparation of a transcript for analysis, while others are more concerned with code-switching as an index of the familiarity or social distance that marks speech between different groups. Still others are more concerned with the analysis of interaction as expressed by general speech-act categories like requests, promises, claims, orders, commands, and so on. A major focus of research on discourse or social interaction has been on the way persons orient their talk and actions to assumed typical meanings associated with utterances and actions and their paralinguistic and non-verbal elements.

Another point often mentioned by some researchers within the micro-view is that participants of social interaction must work at generating and sustaining normal appearances, and this work often includes talk about the setting itself, as well as various tacit assumptions about what is happening that are not vocalized but assumed to be operative throughout the interaction. The participants must work at sustaining the idea of a normal environment even if they believe it is unusual or deficient or deteriorating. The participants' talk and actions are assumed to express their competency as members of the local scene and/or some larger group.

A number of criticisms have been levelled at micro-studies and they are conveniently summarized by Collins[1] in the present volume. I want to call attention instead to issues that can be raised within the micro-tradition itself because they seem to parallel problems we encounter in the analysis of macro-data and in macro-theorizing. Two key issues can be identified. The first is the tension between the analysis of fragments of discourse and single utterances, and the analysis of a larger social setting in which considerable participant observation has occurred, and where audio or video tapes exist of the activities of the groups and individuals studied. This tension reflects both methodological and theoretical differences in the approaches to micro-phenomena. The second issue is really part of or an extension of the first and suggests that there cannot be a micro-sociology that claims to study social interaction as local, self-contained productions, any more than macro-theorists can claim that macro-social structures can ignore micro-processes. Acknowledging and incorporating micro-process into a study of macro-structures has often been called reductionistic. Neither micro- nor macro-structures are self-contained levels of analysis, they *interact* with each other at all times despite the convenience and sometimes the dubious luxury of only examining one or the other level of analysis.

The analysis of single utterances can be described from two perspectives. The first is frequently found in philosophical and linguistic studies of language[2] where syntactic and semantic studies focus on the notion of a bounded utterance and the use of a predicate calculus to deal with propositions whose truth or falsity has been established. The philosopher is concerned with the derivation of propositional meaning from a knowledge of predicates and referents in the utterance. The linguist uses single utterances to derive syntactic rules governing the word order of a sentence, the way syntactic, phonological, and semantic information are marked in the sentence, and a number of other issues associated with the speaker-hearer's competence to generate an infinite number of utterances from a finite set of elements that make up the grammar of a language. But these issues are not likely to be of immediate interest to macro-sociologists, and micro-sociologists are probably already familiar with these matters.

The issue that bothers macro-sociologists about research on micro-processes is the way a few fragments of a conversation or even several pages of discourse can presume to stand for the complex social structures identified in macro-theory, such as large-scale political, economic, demographic, and stratificational patterns. The fragments of discourse are seen as *ahistorical* and exceedingly *limited* from the perspective of the macro-theorist. The macro-theorist would object to any claim by the micro-theorist that these fragments represent recurrent aspects of interaction that could be viewed as systematic patterns for expressing a wide range of social phenomena that are ignored in macro-studies.

The transcriptions that are generated from audio tapes require considerable investment of time and energy, and, depending on the individual researcher, the final version of a transcript requires a personal attention to detail that cannot be delegated easily to a research assistant. The focus on conversational fragments trades on the fact that the sequential nature of discourse, and the requirements of some kind of allocation of time to speakers, if there is not to be a monologue, is necessary and is expected in most everyday settings. The analysis of conversation[3] has, for the most part, focused on exchanges in public and private settings that tend to be rather limited *vis-à-vis* their being linked to a more complex level of social organization. The fragments do not tend to be part of informal and bureaucratically organized settings in industry, education, the health field, and local, state, and national governmental agencies. But a few researchers have incorporated elements of conversational analysis in ethnographically oriented research, yet the conversational concepts are for the most part a minor part of the study.

Conversational studies tend to remain focused on fragments from spontaneous encounters between friends, members of a therapy group, and strangers calling at a public or private agency on a single occasion. The ethnographic or organizational context is seldom an explicit source of information for analysis of the fragments. The researcher, however, becomes especially clever at identifying subtle nuances and constraints in the way people try and succeed in obtaining speaking rights, the way greetings are initiated or terminated, the way topics are introduced or changed or terminated, the way interruptions are managed, and the way that utterance pairs are used as basic to conversational structure. Labov and Fanshel,[4] however, note that the key concept of adjacency-pairs in conversational analysis is not useful for understanding therapeutic discourse and the turn-taking issues do not become relevant for analysis of the discourse in question. An unresolved problem is that the content of the exchanges remains of residual interest, being primarily a tacit resource for information rather than a topic for analysis.

The micro-researcher interested in larger segments of discourse, and the extent to which they reflect more complex group or organizational structures, would not deny the relevance of many of the patterns found by the conversational analysts. But there are questions about the limits of such findings when larger socio-cultural contexts are included. The macro-theorist and researcher would, of course, want to make a similar charge against the micro-researcher doing participant observation and who also focuses on larger segments of complex encounters in a classroom or nursery school or prison or hospital or doctor's office.

2   The tacit interrelationship of micro- and macro-research

The micro-macro integration problem revolves around the following challenge: the micro-researcher doing a study of a complex organization but focusing on segments of discourse makes *indirect* reference to macro-concepts or at least must sustain their tacit relevance. The macro-researcher studying complex organizations or movements or historical trends will make reference to micro-activities, but only *indirectly*. In each case the challenge is to sustain one level while demonstrating that the other is an integral part of the discussion of the findings and the theoretical propositions advanced. *Within* the micro-group there are differences that parallel differences *between* micro- and macro-approaches to the study of social structure.

The micro-researcher interested in larger organizational or ethnographic settings finds the focus of conversational analysts too confining. Two points should be stressed here: (1) to what extent does the researcher's goal render different strategies of micro- and macro-analysis salient or significant?; and (2) to what extent are interactions between levels of analysis always presupposed and necessary regardless of the researcher's goals? These points are also pursued by Duster in this volume.

One way to illustrate a partial response to the previous questions is to note that restricting conversational analysis to notions of turn-taking and sequencing rules in conversation, means ignoring macro-levels of analysis and ethnographic research. A tacit reliance on more complex levels of analysis is unavoidable despite the claim that the primary goal is to identify the formal structures of conversational usage. But even researchers who focus on broader aspects of social interaction using a more ethnographically oriented approach will also create boundaries that enable them to avoid having to integrate their interview materials and field notes with survey and demographic data on the same topics. The researcher seeks to define his or her goals in accordance with the perceived practicalities of a group with similar methodological interests irrespective of a tacit reliance on other levels of analysis. These restrictive practices are commonplace in all normal science.

Macro-researchers who seek to generalize their findings from a sample survey to a larger population seldom address the possibility of serious discrepancies between the way members of a group respond to formal questions about diverse topics, and the extent and manner in which these topics are discussed by respondents when interacting with friends or family members or when actual courses of action are carried out. Being identified with particular methods limits the substantive goals of the macro-researcher. The overwhelming tendency is to employ survey questions about hypothetical cases (e.g. medical illness, legal issues), and to elicit opinions or attitudes about specific topics using individual respondents. The decisions that produce actual cases and the collective discussions in which opinions and attitudes are expressed do not become the focus of attention. The decisions that occur in actual cases within medical, legal, educational, corporate, governmental, military, and financial bureaucracies are obviously influenced by organizational practices and constraints that are also situated interactions between persons with patterned social and emotional relationships. Unless we engage in research that enables us to compare different micro- and macro-ways of examining the same or similar topics and issues, we will not understand the extent to which levels of analysis enjoy some kind of self-contained existence or are dependent on continual interaction across levels.

A theoretical example might be useful here. For micro-researchers interested in communication issues, the respondent's social and communicative competence refers to an ability to use language and interact appropriately with others in ways that are assumed to be typical and normal for a given social setting. The assessment of this competence is assumed to be accomplished by the way data are collected during participant observation, interviews, and tape recordings that take place in the social settings studied. For the macro-researcher, social competence refers to knowledge about values, norms, and institutional practices. This competence is assessed by examining the responses to questions asked of respondents or by examining documents that are presumed to reflect what others report based on testing procedures or some kind of official contacts. The respondent's ability to use language and to answer questions is seldom a topic of macro-research.

Micro- and macro-researchers manage to ignore each other's concerns with social or communicative competence. Neither is likely to study independently these forms of social competence as a prerequisite to the substantive goals each has projected despite the fact that social and communicative competence are necessary conditions for gathering and understanding the substantive data of interest to the sociologist.

If we restrict ourselves to rules that govern the way two or more participants to a conversation take turns in having the floor, the way that topics are introduced, altered, and dropped, and the like, and would like to focus initially on those aspects of these rules or conditions that seem to be invariant to the setting, participants, and larger social organization, then we would ignore the interests of most sociologists. But we can also examine the extent to which differences in the way persons carry out conversations are associated with gender, age, status differences, social settings, ethnicity, and so on. These differences would then reflect macro-concerns or complex organizational or ethnographic settings. Similarly, the way children are socialized into a culture, the way they acquire language, the way they acquire the use of conversational and interactional strategies, and the way they begin to understand notions like rules, require that we stress micro-processes within different family and school settings. Observing the same children and parents at different times becomes necessary in order to generate a comparative data base. The extent to which more narrow concerns with turn-taking, greetings, closings of conversations, topic shift, and so on, remain focal points of interest, is likely to change. More complex levels of data and analysis must be examined as we become interested in the content and form of the mother's (or father's) interaction with the child, and the child's interaction with playmates and siblings.

3   Micro-analysis and the study of social context

The discussion thus far implies that as we pursue goals at more abstract or complex levels of analysis the focus of our theoretical interests and data bases changes such that more micro-phenomena become less salient and more peripheral to our substantive and theoretical interests. There is a very difficult issue that needs to be addressed here. Interactions between levels of complexity must be specified if we are not to find arbitrarily a safe haven in a more extreme micro- or macro-analysis. We seek the safe domains of micro- and macro-analyses because we can then presume that each level is

more or less self-contained. One serious consequence is the theoretical and methodological convenience of only dealing with very global
or very narrow concepts and types of data.

Macro-theorists find it difficult to follow Collins's suggestion that
complex notions like a stratificational system should be studied and
conceived as an *aggregate of micro-situations* (see this volume). The
macro-theorist will find it difficult to accept the idea of aggregating
across countless exchanges that occur over the course of one day in the
offices of one large governmental agency much less several or many
large corporations.[5] Collins suggests that we conceive of an encounter
as similar to a marketplace. The individual brings cultural (or conversational) and emotional resources to the encounter. Specific styles
and topics of conversation are said to reflect membership in different
groups and thus constitute variable degrees of ritual compliance
vis-à-vis the maintenance of the structure of the immediate interaction
and more complex social patterns. The emotional energies that affect
ritual membership in encounters include a common emotional tone
and rhythm that lend success and solidarity to the interaction and the
topics or business conducted in this marketplace.

Collins suggests that a new form of social research is needed for the
study of micro- and macro-levels where the notion of encounters as
marketplaces is a central theoretical concept. The general idea would
be to sample conversations across a large number of different social
groups, repeating these conversational samples over time in order to
embed the encounters in some larger context. The suggestion by
Collins is quite innovative but may not be practical because it presupposes a number of research activities that he could not discuss in
the context and space of his paper. I shall address this methodological
issue below.

The macro-theorist may find (as I do) Collins's suggestions to be
quite provocative and an important way to reconceptualize sociological theory. He makes a convincing argument for the integration of
macro- and micro-concepts by showing that each presupposes the
other. I have suggested a parallel view in two recent papers.[6] Everyday encounters are an integral part of any discussion of macro-
structures even when their individual and aggregated forms are difficult to study and to integrate with some complex system of stratification. When we compare the conversational analysis of fragments of
discourse with more extensive segments of discourse as studied in a

larger organizational context, the turn-taking notions, topical introductions, closings, hesitations, and the like may be noticed but not be relevant to a discussion of the content. These conversational devices are not central to Collins's notion of cultural and emotional energies.

The analysis of conversations is similar to linguistic and philosophical studies of language. More complex levels of analysis are avoided or invoked indirectly as if the information being used was obvious and available to anyone. The logic of analysis is oriented to the study of single and local utterances as if they were self-contained meaningful units. The researcher thus restricts the context of analysis rather severely.

Everyday encounters are of importance because they reveal the social competence necessary for membership in a group or culture. Sustaining the appearances of a normal environment also contributes a sense of stability to the group or culture or organization. These encounters are necessary for intimate and formal social relationships between participants. The routine assessment of social competence, therefore, sustains and re-creates normal cultural environments and personal identities.

Tape recordings and transcripts of these encounters are selective sources of information for revealing the structure of daily encounters within an organizational context. The ethnographic or organizational setting, therefore, must become an *integral part* of the data base used for analysis.

We can illustrate the way that micro-sociological research is contingent on the researcher's use of several sources of knowledge, and ethnographic or organizational information, by a brief discussion of a recent sociolinguistic study of therapeutic discourse. If rules and structural elements identified as being integral to the structure of conversations can only achieve their self-contained objective status by ignoring a larger ethnographic or organizational context, then efforts by the researcher to abandon this posture because of lack of explanatory adequacy found in this perspective would provide us with a way to challenge more narrow views of micro-sociology.

In a recent study by Labov and Fanshel[7] on therapeutic discourse, the authors acknowledged their indebtedness to earlier, more narrow analyses of conversation, but found it necessary to challenge important aspects of this sub-field. The authors found that a part of the text they examined yielded alternative interpretations that required them to extend their analysis to elements of social life external to the therapy session itself. They refer to a theory of status and role relationships, including the use of notions like role strain and role conflict. But the role theory they cite remains abstract and lacks empirical content. The discussion of role obligations by Labov and Fanshel leads them to acknowledge the need for the therapist and researcher to be familiar with 'normal conventions of our society' as well as special knowledge about family social organization. The researcher, therefore, must employ considerable tacit reasoning and taken-for-granted special knowledge in order to link the discourse materials generated by the patient and therapist to idealized conceptions of status, role, role strain, and role conflict in Jewish families in the city of New York. More complex concepts and levels of analysis were found to be essential for dealing with a small portion of an extensive corpus of materials.

4 Aspects of micro-analysis

The study of micro-sociological events as part of a larger organizational context includes a data base of audio tape or video or film recordings and transcripts that are presumed to be a normal part of a group's daily round of activities. Gaining access to the settings that provide the basis for eventual tape or video recordings may require minimal (2 months) or extensive (perhaps 2 years) of field work. Different researchers seem to have reached an implicit agreement about what constitutes adequate transcripts in order for a reader to grasp some insight into a larger corpus of materials that will not be reported. Researchers dedicated to the careful analysis of isolated segments of conversation would dispute the question of what is an adequately prepared transcript and some would insist that most students of ethnographically oriented micro-sociological events are not generating adequate transcripts.

Students of micro-sociological events agree that the surface features of language use are inadequate if we wish to establish the meaning of utterances as recorded in context. These researchers stress the cultural basis of communication and underscore the importance of specifying the local context and the social relationships among the participants.

A basic assumption of the analysis of the transcripts and field notes is that participants assume they share enough of a common knowledge base with those they study to permit them to leave unreported many details about what is intended and believed to be true or false or irrelevant. Hence the actual talk that is studied always requires some kind of expansion. The expansion invariably leads to the invocation of often tacit external information based on a knowledge of prior events, the larger ethnographic or organizational context, and biographical relationships among the participants.

Another assumption is that utterances often perform several speech acts in a context in which actions and words can reflect present, past, and future circumstances. The extent to which a particular researcher makes reference to intonational cues and stress, non-verbal behaviour as revealed by eye gaze, facial expressions, and body movements, will depend on the objectives of the study and interests and expertise. The researcher's participant observation and field notes, and knowledge and analysis of segments of transcripts, presume interactions among several levels of analysis. A major goal of current work is to specify the nature of these interactions while recognizing that each level of analysis does not reduce to a lower level.

Micro-sociological research seeks data that can be examined by contextual inference rules in order to clarify how we go about transforming our observations and transcripts or interviews of interaction settings into summary statements about a much larger but unreported corpus of materials. Unless we can begin to specify some of the levels of complexity that enter into our selection, organization, and summarization of a data base, there is no clear way of integrating micro- and macro-theoretical perspectives.

An element that is often missing from most micro-sociological studies is the recognition that when doing participant observation and writing up field notes, and when observing interaction scenes that are being audio or video taped, the researcher ignores his or her limited capacities for processing information. The limited capacity processing problem is evident when we examine transcripts and/or interview protocols, but it is seldom addressed when talking about field research except to note that it is a difficulty everyone must face.

Neglecting the limited capacity processing problem often leads to a reification of our data base, such as attributing more information or

significance to limited amounts of data. This practice is often confounded by the tacit use of information from other sources of knowledge not identified for the reader. This reification is extreme in the
case of the analysis of single utterances, brief fragments of conversation, and in our use of interviews and questionnaires. Reification is
always present when we severely restrict the criteria that are used for
analysis, and when we can only present or study segments of a much
larger corpus. The study of the way we produce interpretative summaries of our participant observation and transcripts can clarify the
integration of micro- and macro-theories. These activities parallel the
way we must elaborate our interpretation of aggregated questionnaire responses, census and demographic materials, and historical
texts in order to endow them with some sense of their consequences
for understanding everyday living.

When a researcher becomes immersed in the reading of different
transcripts and listening to tapes over and over again either as part of
the transcription process or as part of the analysis itself, considerably
more information is generated than is ever seen by the reader. The
analysis involves an expansion of one's knowledge base about the
immediate transcript being examined, as well as altering the interpretation of the larger corpus of materials that has been gathered.
This expansion of knowledge about what is on the tape and in the
transcript is based on information from personal and systematic
participant observation and the ethnographic or organizational
structure of the group being studied. Only a small part of the information can be revealed to the reader. The results being reported seem
rather obvious and clear to the researcher because of the many
unstated details and general experiences that contribute to the
analysis. It is like trying to describe one's nativeness about language
and culture: these lived experiences appear obvious until we try to
describe them to others unfamiliar with their tacit aspects.

Micro-sociological research that is embedded in an ethnographic
or organizational context provides the researcher with a labour-
intensive understanding of tapes and transcripts. Listening to tapes
over and over again while fixated on the transcript and correcting it
many times exposes the researcher to subtleties and nuances that can
only be partially coded or marked for the reader who examines the
same transcript. Sources of information and inferences become un-
available to the reader. The analysis presumes a reader who is

familiar with the type of materials used and the kind of analysis presented.

Similar experiences occur to survey researchers if they have participated in pre-tests that have taken them into the field. These experiences provide unreported inferences and undocumented background knowledge with which to interpret aggregated findings. But a larger ethnographic or organizational context is likely to be missing or sharply truncated in the case of surveys although aspects of these settings can be discerned by visits to households or work sites.

Whenever a scholar immerses himself or herself in enormous quantities of materials in order to sift out and identify a selective corpus that will be used for a book or series of articles, subtleties and nuances are learned from examining countless sources of information. These sources are difficult to communicate especially when many of them are not directly relevant to the author's thesis about some topic. Yet these sources of indirect information provide the researcher with background knowledge that facilitates and enhances the analysis produced. The researcher seeks a level of sophistication which other experts in the field or in related fields can acknowledge as 'authentic'. Anthropologists and sociologists who routinely do field research will recognize this last point as a central way in which ethnographic work is assessed. We must always rely on some indulgence on the part of the reader, and this sympathetic indulgence often hinges on the reader's own experiences with the kind of research being reported.

The interaction between different levels of analysis is often obscured in survey and demographic research. When we aggregate across individual responses to items of a questionnaire we are forced to restrict severely if not eliminate the local and larger contextual conditions that could clarify the respondent's perspective. The aggregation is a summarization process that obscures our thinking of the way local context and individual responses contributed to the larger picture. The summary becomes a constructed account of a collective or group or class response. I return to this point below.

The integration of micro- and macro-theories is not at heart a methodological issue, but it should be clear from the preceding discussion that methodological issues influence the way concepts are created and explored when substantive findings are obtained, organized and analysed. The dependence of any one level of analysis on other levels remains the heart of the argument.

The micro-sociological researcher often eliminates macro-issues by focusing on the local conditions of social interaction captured by the tapes and transcripts while indirectly making use of the larger ethnographic or organizational context. The student of fragments of conversations chooses to pretend that even local ethnographic conditions are irrelevant, yet cannot avoid using these conditions implicitly in the analysis of turn-taking, openings, closing, and the like. The macro-survey researcher employs methodological devices to eliminate the direct relevance of analysis termed micro. Individual differences and their reflection of lived or daily-life group perspectives are never studied and reported independently of the survey itself. The aggregated responses provide their own collective reality by the choice of variables for creating classes or 'groups'. The decisions that lead to distributions by income, education, social classes, occupational groups, and the like, create collective entities in the larger society regardless of whether these 'groups' have any coherent organized existence that can be studied by other means.

5   Micro–macro integration as reflected in everyday settings

A central thesis of this chapter is that micro- and macro-levels of analysis are integrated in everyday settings as a routine feature of all cultural or social organization. The members of a group or society have created their own theories and methodologies for achieving this integration. The chapter by Callon and Latour in this volume discusses the related topic of the constructed nature of the macro-level of analysis in their remarks on power.

Western societies have created complex bureaucratic organizations that have been studied extensively by sociologists and other social scientists. The notion of bureaucracy as a macro-structure can refer to physical and socio-cultural properties that imply some kind of co-ordination of interpersonal and documented interaction in the sense of meetings, telephone calls, letters, memos, reports, and the like. Offices may contain different kinds of equipment and spatial arrangements that often follow some notion of hierarchical status and task demands, and the kinds of physical and personal objects that will be permitted or voluntarily placed therein. A key function of organizations is said to be the way they limit the range of decisions that their members can make in order to achieve some sense of rationality in choosing among alternatives.[8] The practical problem of making choices has been studied in field and laboratory settings. My concern with rationality and organizational goals is limited to the way internal bureaucratic practices are developed and used to reach decisions on the adequacy of routine work that lead to promotions or complex tenure assessments. In school settings teachers must evaluate classroom performance and produce a summary statement or assign a grade at the end of specified periods of time. Bureaucratic organizations typically produce reports of routine and special board-meetings, or meetings in which a group decides whether to give someone a loan, a grant, or a fellowship. In medicine and law patients and clients are interviewed and a medical history or legal statement or brief is prepared that summarizes an interview and the assessment of tests and documents. In all of these cases, and many more that can be easily identified as routine practices within bureaucratic organizations, there are fairly explicit procedures that have been adopted or that have emerged. These practices and procedures are culturally organized knowledge structures that can be said to be in the environment and not simply in the head of members of the culture. The interaction of members of a group is needed for the practices and procedures to achieve 'structural' status. This 'rationalization' process has increased over the past 100 years and shows no signs of diminishing. Everyday settings, therefore, abound with highly organized ways of dealing with and producing macro-evaluations, reports, and summarizations of relentless micro-events. There are many ways in which everyday micro-events are evaluated and/or reported and/or summarized. In each case the activities are routine aspects of some organization and are independent of the way social scientists design and carry out their research.

The everyday settings alluded to above are of interest because they make it possible for organizations to achieve their own macro-inferences about their own day-to-day activities. Organizations have developed methods for resolving complex problems of evaluation, reporting, and summarization that constitute natural experimental settings for the social scientist interested in micro–macro integration. These everyday settings demand assessment as a routine part of achieving and evaluating organizational goals. Summary statements that are said to reflect the evaluation and description of everyday micro-events require problem-solving[9] under conditions of limited capacity processing of information. But students of organizational behaviour seldom study the contextual inferences that take place routinely day-by-day. The accomplishment of these inferences enables us to assess the way supervisors, managers, teachers, physicians, credit managers, fellowship committees, tenure committees, board-meetings, and the like, carry out their work and transform their activities into a condensed summary of what happened during a meeting, a work day, a work week, a day in class, an interview with a patient, and so on. Oral and written summaries reflect macro-inferences made about the attainment of organizational goals or the extent to which an individual, a group, and an organization can be said to be functioning in a normal manner.

There is nothing new in recognizing this routine and relentless processing of information necessary in order to create macro-structures or summaries out of micro-events. What I propose is new is identifying those processes and inferences that transform micro-events into macro-structures. If we can begin this task then progress on the integration of micro- and macro-theory will be within our reach. We must study the way human decision-making in complex micro-settings contributes to the creation of macro-structures by routine problem-solving activities necessary for the simulation or realization of basic organizational goals. These accomplishments presuppose a sense of micro–macro integration by the members of an organization and strategies for pursuing this integration.

In the preceding remarks I have outlined a few elements of a macro-level of analysis in order to show its dependence on interactional activities to sustain its structure. Interactional activities contribute to the production of outputs that are viewed as structural indicators of complex organizational or institutional trends and objectives. The idea of environmental knowledge is again relevant here because it refers to a basic aspect of micro–macro articulation; the interaction between particular physical sites, forms of organization, and emergent social exchanges.

The reader may gain a more realistic picture of the natural settings that routinely accomplish micro–macro integration if we present a brief discussion of doctor–patient interviews.

6   Doctor–patient interaction and medical histories

In a series of publications[10] I have described the way that physician–patient interaction and the creation of medical histories can provide us with information about the routine integration of micro- and macro-theory and substantive findings. The basic format followed by most medical facilities in Western countries is fairly straightforward. The physician may see a patient for approximately 10 to 60 minutes, and this time period may also include a physical examination and/or a related activity such as an X-ray or laboratory specimen. The physician may write down a few notes, or take an extensive history, again depending on the kind of health care delivery setting involved, how long the doctor has known the patient, and how serious the physician feels the case may be. Some physicians do nothing more than write down a few cryptic notes on a 'progress sheet' or something comparable, while others proceed to dictate their impressions while using their notes as a resource for recalling what happened during the interview. The written version of the interview becomes a part of an official record that takes on legal significance as well. The transformation of the micro-event we call the interview, in which there is a combination of unstructured questions and answers and considerable inductive and deductive hypothesis-testing on the part of the physician and often the patient, requires that macro-conceptions of disease held by the doctor and patient be explored by reference to specific types of micro-events and utterances.

Macro-conceptions of disease refer to entities like cardio-vascular disorders, or those labelled rheumatic, pulmonary, or urologic. Specific forms of a disease can be identified by reference to presenting symptoms of the patient, radiological evidence, biochemical analysis, and information based on a physical examination. Macro-conceptions of disease are also developed by public health and health care delivery bureaucracies because the categories provide convenient ways of aggregating related instances of a disease within a larger system of classification. The mental models and language used by patients, nurses, and physicians to represent diseases and symptoms are not always in correspondence with public health conceptions of disease categories and their empirical study. A study of the aggregation process, therefore, should include the way the physician interprets the patient's presenting symptoms and conceptions of disease with the physical examination and radiological and laboratory tests. We want to know the way these activities contribute to the creation and use of macro-categories of disease by public health officials.

A wide variety of medical interviews occur rather relentlessly in Western medical settings. I can only describe a small fragment of a complex activity. Many encounters between the patient and physician are fairly routine and the resulting history is rather brief and not always informative. But a patient with suspected or confirmed cardio-vascular disease can become involved in a rather complex way with his or her physician. The physician's medical history taking can touch on the patient's life history, the everyday lives of his or her family, the kind of work done, recreation, and the backgrounds of many other family members who are part of an extended kinship system. The physician is deliberate in wanting the patient to provide accounts, often orchestrated by the physician, about routine and intimate aspects of marital life, relationships with others outside of the home and at work, as well as details about personal eating, work, and recreational habits. The physician transforms information gathered in a context of privacy and highly individualized social interaction, into a medical history that can be used by several other health professionals. Those interested in a medical history could also include researchers who want to focus on specific aspects of the history that may be summarized in hospital records and then aggregated for state and national epidemiological studies or reports.

The physician is authorized and obligated to transform micro-events into statements that have macro-significance. The context in which the physician interprets the micro-events or accounts by the patient is not available from reading the history. The discourse produced by the interview is reduced to a highly selective account, an account that enables the physician to create a goal-oriented, factual interpretation of often rambling, incoherent, and highly fragmented remarks.

For example, a patient that comes to see a physician for hypertension may be interviewed at great length by one internal medicine specialist and for only a short time by another doctor. The first physician may probe for unusual events in the patient's life, including changes in blood pressure associated with events at home, at work or with pregnancies. There may be probes about possible stress or mental illness associated with these events, but the medical history version of what happened is likely to be highly condensed with few if any details.

The physician who places minimal emphasis on sources of stress will give more attention to family members with similar complications. The patient will not be encouraged to describe signs of stress, anxiety or mental illness. The history may not reveal sources of stress even if the patient volunteers such information directly. The physician simply does not ask about emotional problems and minimizes any reference to them by the patient. There are patients, of course, who will want to minimize the role of emotional problems with the first type of physician mentioned above and others who are concerned about the role of emotional problems will be bothered by the physician who minimizes such issues.

The physician does not bring an explicit framework to the interview with which to process the kinds of micro-details and intimacy conveyed by the patient about day-to-day stresses and social relationships at home, at work, with friends, or problems associated with career aspirations, identity problems, and the possible reciprocal impact of illness on all of the above conditions. Many physicians are not interested in or incapable of dealing with the patient's day-to-day problems and they will seldom be concerned with establishing and sustaining a good 'bedside manner'.

The physician must search for medical coherency from among often fragmented narrative statements in which the patient seldom completes an account about some event or symptom. The physician often asks leading questions, and the language used can seriously complicate the comprehension and attribution of intentions and knowledge conveyed. The patient's rambling, often fragmented narratives, are not coherent in and of themselves unless considerable contextual information is attributed to what is said or information is gleaned from other sources within and outside of the interview. The physician does not work from a transcribed text when writing up his or her medical history, but must often compile information while conducting the interview. Hence he or she often cannot trace later inferences to contextual elements influencing interpretations that occurred at the time of recording cryptic notes or the actual history or progress notes. A micro-analysis, however, seeks to create from the discourse, as tape recorded and transcribed, a coherent account of what the patient intended by different utterances and paralinguistic and non-verbal movements. The micro-researcher must go beyond the information given by trying to be explicit about the significance of missing elements of dialogue, the use of conventional and unconventional terms or phrases, metaphors or similes, changes in voice intonation and stress, and facial movements or hand gestures. The goal is to create a coherent perspectival view from the patient's and physician's vantage-point, while seeking to embed this view in the larger organizational and institutional context of their lives.

The physician is not trained to deal with micro-events as socio-cultural, cognitive, and emotional manifestations. But the physician will nevertheless employ his or her folk theories in trying to create a medical history where socio-cultural, cognitive, and emotional elements may be present. But such folk theories are seldom if ever evident in the medical history except when expressed in terms that seem to match medical terminology about the patient. So the patient can be described as having had a 'depression' or 'nervous break-down', or 'stress' associated with her place of employment or because of a divorce or death of a child. But we could not recover any of the richness of the actual interview from reading the medical history. Medical histories are often not representative of what is said during the interview; we do not obtain much insight into the patient's mood, socio-cultural life, emotional concerns, and the like, even when they are provided voluntarily by the patient or elicited by the physician. The physician is 'programmed' to look for certain patterns, symptoms, associations, that can provide a quick diagnosis and which also signify an underlying causal network he or she can specify by reference to categories that are explicitly linked to biological concepts. The physician wants to link his or her history to existent disease classes so that others who are trained in a similar way can interpret the history with relative ease.

To summarize, the physician–patient interview and medical history can be viewed as routine examples of continual micro–macro integration which combines several levels of complexity. The substantive content of the discourse becomes the vehicle for tracing the ways in which micro-events are transformed into macro-structures. The transformation permits certain symptoms and illnesses of a patient to be coded and then aggregated over large samples and correlated with different variables.

7   Social mobility as macro- and micro-social structures

The study of social mobility at the macro-level of analysis seeks answers to several questions that have integral aspects of traditional theories of social stratification. Sociologists have long been interested in the extent to which a society is governed by an elite and the relative access of outsiders to the inner circles of power. The extent to which social mobility is possible from one social class to another, the possibility of downward mobility, and how a society is organized to facilitate or inhibit such movements, have been important sociological questions that many theorists and researchers have addressed. Contemporary studies of social mobility have been concerned with the extent to which low-income and minority groups' generational social mobility has changed over some period of time, whether movement up or down has increased, and what structural conditions seem to promote movement up or down. Some researchers have been concerned with the policy implications of such questions and seek to make recommendations *vis-à-vis* education curricula that might alter existing conditions of social stratification.

Two sets of goals at the macro-level can be noted for purposes of the present crude and limited discussion of social mobility; identifying general trends in social mobility relative to different social classes and ethnic or racial groups, and the consequences of these trends for increasing or decreasing class conflict, social upheavals or revolutions. Social theorists are also interested in the clarification of policy issues and possible changes that can be made to alter existing conditions and trends. The next question we must ask is if a micro-level of analysis would ask different questions. Are these questions at variance with those posed by the macro-theorist and researcher?

In this short essay I cannot pursue a variety of micro-questions. I will therefore confine myself to a few issues that seem to have clear empirical consequences *vis-à-vis* the way social mobility is addressed by macro-theorists. Many traditional studies of social mobility examine the school and occupational records of, say, a cohort of adults, or adolescents and young adults, interview a cross-sectional sample of high school students and young adults, survey the respondents about their fathers' social mobility, and their own educational and occupational careers. We can pose somewhat different questions.

We might examine the processes that make up the different ways in which careers are pursued, including the way decisions made at different points in a person's educational and occupational career have influenced the outcomes measured by a survey of adolescents, young adults, and adults. Space does not permit us to describe a prior type of study which would focus on interaction and the extent to which this interaction contributes to the child's success in school. For example, we might find that middle-income parents are consistent in exposing their children to cycles of questions and answers. We would want to know if this exposure to particular forms of discourse is associated with success in school when question–answer sequences are used for classroom assessments and intelligence testing. Socialization prior to school is of obvious importance. For present purposes, however, I want to focus on the fact that judgments by school personnel can influence a child's achievement in school. The strategy is not to pose the macro-issues associated with social mobility and social stratification systems, and then to survey a representative sample to ask questions that operationalize the concepts and hypotheses. Instead, we would study day-to-day activities in classrooms, the use of standardized testing, and decisions made by teachers, counsellors, and administrators to promote, advise, or discourage students *vis-à-vis* taking particular types of programmes or courses. These processes create certain educational career patterns that generate interactional and structural conditions that close off or discourage, or open up or encourage, occupational opportunities.

The social organization of educational institutions creates its own accounting systems and decision-making activities whereby the micro-events of the classroom and testing situations are transformed into macro or aggregated information. We can then speak of the way a society, as represented by educational institutions, can use information from its own bureaucracies to monitor the way it exerts an influence on the social mobility of its members. But the schools do not monitor the way its own record keeping about the success and failures of its students articulates what takes place in the classroom, during standardized testing, and the grading and promotional decisions by teachers, counsellors, and administrators.

The tacit bureaucratic integration of micro- and macro-events pertaining to the area sociologists call social mobility can be observed to take place with relentless consistency in the schools by the way that summary measures of achievement are routinely constructed for any given cohort of students. The limitations of field research become immediately obvious when we seek an articulation between classroom activities, teacher–counsellor–administrator decisions, standardized testing, and the aggregated distributions of the success and failure of students by cohorts designated by the schools. Such a project can be achieved only by studying one or two classrooms at a time for a number of months or a few years. The research requires a rather tedious dedication to detail and the patience to deal with large amounts of uncertainty in the form of a changing sample of students and school personnel, daily problems in obtaining tapes and transcripts whose comprehension is not readily available by using a standardized set of coding procedures. The kinds of data generated would be a nightmare for the macro-researcher because they do not fit into the categories normally found in the use of surveys or in the study of organizational records.

An organizational study of school records relies on several forms of aggregated information. The processes that generate the records tend to be ignored. In the case of a micro-study these records become a resource for identifying the way the institution creates macro-information about the frequency of certain careers and their distribution by age, gender, socio-economic status, and so forth. But the records are also a topic for independent investigation by asking what micro-processes were involved in their construction as objective indicators of educational failure, stability, and mobility. The study of micro-processes reveals differences in language facility, family influence on academic success, the way teachers can influence students, and the way that peer group pressures and activities can influence the way children learn to use native, family, and environmental (the classroom itself) resources in achieving certain levels of success or failure on tests and in the classroom. An understanding of these processes becomes severely restricted if we seek the way they are reflected in school records versus the oral history that teachers, counsellors, and administrators create.

The micro-researcher views the administrative records on school performance as a macro-indication of processes that must be given independent study. These records are not merely obvious social facts to be correlated with other social facts. But at a macro-level of analysis the administrative records *are* social facts when school administrators, counsellors, and teachers use them in order to make decisions about a student's educational placement, advancement, denial of promotion, or whatever. But such decisions do not simply make use of whatever information is available from an official record; the school personnel's knowledge about the student based on first-hand experiences or encounters with other personnel (the oral history or collective memory) will interact with the documented summary.

The micro-researcher's task is to show how the official record is constructed – the way micro-information is transformed into macro-representations – and the way micro-events or day-to-day encounters draw on a wider knowledge base from memory and the social interaction itself in order to interpret official records about a student's career, placement, advancement, disciplinary problems, and the like. The laborious process whereby a student's educational career is constructed, based on evaluative summaries by the teacher in writing or during face-to-face encounters with other teachers, counsellors, or administrators, is the concern of the micro-researcher. The study of this process, when combined with aggregated evaluative summaries that become part of an official record for each student, constitutes a data base for the integration of micro- and macro-concepts. The day-to-day processes that lead to unofficial and official evaluative summaries on each student, and the use of these summaries as social facts, are routine, normal organizational activities, and they typify the ways in which the everyday world integrates micro- and macro-aspects of socio-cultural life.

The concept of social mobility can be used to explain the way evaluative written and oral summaries mark student educational careers to reveal the micro-processes that facilitate or inhibit the possibility of later occupational careers. The same study design can be used to study the way employees achieve occupational careers within and between different organizations.

What remains unclear from the above discussion of social mobility is whether or not a micro-analysis of social mobility would draw different conclusions from a study using official records and survey interviews with adolescents, young adults and older adults. Current research[11] suggests that many children will be tracked so early in the educational process, or treated so differentially, that their educational mobility will be restricted severely long before crucial decisions are made in junior high (or middle school) and in high school. These decisions seriously influence the pursuit of vocational or college-preparatory courses.

Macro-analysis of educational careers is not very helpful for an understanding of these tracking and classroom processes and the decisions about taking courses in junior and senior high school. But macro-data can suggest that certain educational goals of a society are not being met. But these data do not identify the processes that produce the macro-outcomes. The issue is not simply one of dismissing one level of analysis or another, but showing how they must be integrated if we are not to be convinced about one level to the exclusion of the other by conveniently ignoring competing frameworks for research and theorizing.

8   Conclusion: the aggregation of micro-events in accounting practices

The discussion of the integration of macro- and micro-concepts began by noting differences within micro-researchers as to what might constitute an adequate data base for the analysis of micro-events. These differences revolve around a focus on an elaborate transcription and detailed ahistorical analysis of fragments of conversation, versus the use of more extensive discourse that is recognized as being embedded in a larger organizational or ethnographic context. Macro-researchers find it difficult to accept either of these micro-sociological positions. The study of more abstract levels of analysis leads to little interest in micro-events despite indirect references to everyday processes. Each view sees its own perspective as more or less self-contained.

The tacit bureaucratic integration of micro- and macro-levels of analysis can be found in everyday life as a routine part of Western social organization. I believe the same argument can be made on a cross-cultural basis, but the study of such integration in non-Western societies would require that more attention be given to oral histories, folktales, the organization of ritual ceremonies, firmly established routines in the culture, and the particular cultural use of Western forms of bureaucracy.

At one point in this paper I referred to the importance of cognitive constraints on social organization and its study. I want to close with a brief discussion of the role of limited capacity processing for an understanding of micro- and macro-levels of analysis. I will make use of the notion of an *interactive model* as used in cognitive psychology[12] to illustrate the discussion.

The physician's creation of a medical history from an interview requires an integration of many complex micro-events in order to produce summary statements that can be used for macro-inferences about classes of patients and a range of disease categories. These activities reflect the more general study of comprehension in discourse and stories or textual materials. The comprehension process is analogous to the integration of micro- and macro-levels of analysis. When a teacher must evaluate a student there is an *undocumented integration* of countless reading sessions, reading tests, arithmetic lessons and tests, and standardized tests that can be district-wide and state-wide. The evaluation process is also like the comprehension of discourse and stories or textual materials in a laboratory setting, but the time factor is more extensive.

When we examine educational records as a way of obtaining indicators of educational careers we aggregate the information contained in the records without worrying too much about the ways in which these records were created. When we use survey questions to access a respondent's memory of educational and occupational experiences for himself or herself and that of the parents, we provide questions that are already abstract summary statements about prior experiences. We cannot say very much about how the respondent has created his or her own summary of these prior experiences by accessing information stored in memory and now reorganized in order to deal with specific questions and a few response categories. The constructions of a response will not be as comprehensive as that used by the teacher but it will be similar.

The notion of an interactive model addresses micro-events such as those aspects of comprehension that deal with the recognition that word meanings change when they are embedded in sentences, and that the meaning of sentences can change when they are part of a larger unit like a paragraph, section, and a report or story. The general idea here is that when we study discourse, there are phonological, prosodic, non-verbal, and social setting features that constitute different sources of information that are *activated in parallel*, as would be the case (adding orthographic features) when readers seek to comprehend sentences by integrating lexical, syntactic, and contextual information. There is an interaction between different sources of information and with stored information about these sources.

The physician, like the teacher and respondent, in their respective contexts, would like to create what is assumed to be the most plausible interpretation of the information available to him or her. The production of a plausible account is central to the idea of comprehension. As researchers, we are interested in the way the physician, teacher and respondent create interpretations that are deemed plausible. For Rumelhart[13] comprehension is a process whereby elements or units of knowledge (schemata) are selected to produce a plausible account of some story. The notion of a schema is viewed as a data structure by which generic concepts stored in memory can be represented, and where these schemata also contain information about how the knowledge contained therein can be used. The idea is to develop a notational system that could model what *might* be in a person's head. As in any theory a central concern is whether or not the notational system is sufficiently powerful to account for observable actions, experiences, and our understanding and telling of the experiences.

I do not have the space to spend more time on the notion of an interactive model. I introduced it here as a way of discussing the integration of micro- and macro-research and theory in a context in which we can acknowledge that the physician, teacher and respondent all face the task of *aggregating* across many micro-events in order to satisfy the organizational requirements of a clinic, hospital, or quality assurance board in medicine. The teacher must satisfy school bureaucratic requirements, and the respondent is expected to satisfy the survey format. In each case, the physician, teacher, and respondent, must create accounts that *integrate* micro-events in such a way so as to produce macro-interpretations of experiences that cannot be explicitly documented. The limited capacity processing and language categories available to the physician, teacher, and respondent are integral parts of the micro–macro transformation as is also the case for the researcher. There is always the problem of information overload and the necessity of selecting a metalanguage and concepts that will convey enough information so that the reader can employ his or her knowledge resources (schemata) in order to interpret the summary statements or accounts presented as findings.

The study of micro-events is an essential part of all macro-statements. We must be able to indicate differences between what takes place in a medical interview and physical examination, and what is written in the medical history. We must examine classroom and testing activities, how grades are assigned, and how placement into different classes or reading groups is made. Similarly, we must study the way respondents process survey questions in order to choose one of the categories provided by the researcher, and the extent to which inferences the researcher makes from the aggregated responses reflect the respondents' knowledge and decision processes.

If surveys are viewed as one more form of organized activity that is natural and routine to a society's daily functioning as with the sample surveys of, say, the Census Bureau, then the above organizational conditions provide us with a laboratory for studying the integration of micro- and macro-research and theory. The study of this integration recognizes the relative autonomy of each level of analysis, but also insists on viewing sociological theory as reflecting the interaction of different levels if we are to generate plausible substantive findings with theories and methods that reflect the structure of everyday life.

Notes

1 Randall Collins, this volume.
2 A. V. Cicourel, 'Language and Social Interaction: Philosophical and Empirical Issues', *Sociological Inquiry*, 50 (1980), pp. 1–30.
3 H. Sacks, E. A. Schegloff, and G. Jefferson, 'A Simplest Systematics for the Organization of Turn-taking for Conversations', *Language*, 50 (1974), pp. 696–735.
4 W. Labov and D. Fanshel, *Therapeutic Discourse: Psychotherapy as Conversation* (New York: Academic Press, 1977).
5 Randall Collins, 'On the Micro-Foundations of Macro-Sociology', *American Journal of Sociology*, 86 (1981), pp. 984–1014.
6 A. V. Cicourel, 'Three Models of Discourse Analysis: The Role of Social Structure', *Discourse Analysis*, 1980, pp. 101–31. Cicourel, 'Language and Social Interaction'.
7 Labov and Fanshel, *Therapeutic Discourse*.
8 P. M. Blau and W. R. Scott, *Formal Organizations* (San Francisco: Chandler, 1962).
9 J. G. March and H. Simon, *Organizations* (New York: Wiley, 1958).
10 A. V. Cicourel, 'Interviewing and Memory', in C. Cherry (ed.), *Pragmatic Aspects of Human Communication* (Dordrecht: D. Reidel, 1974), pp. 51–82;

'Discourse and Text: Cognitive and Linguistic Processes in Studies of Social Structure', *Versus: Quaderni de Studi Semiotici*, Sept–Dec (1975), pp. 33–84; 'Language and Society: Cognitive, Cultural, and Linguistic Aspects of Language Use', *Sozialwissenschaftliche Annalen*, 2 (1978), pp. 25–58; 'Language and Medicine', in C. A. Ferguson and S. B. Heath (eds), *Language in the USA* (Cambridge University Press, 1981).

11 A. V. Cicourel, K. Jennings, S. B. Jennings, K. Leiter, R. Mackay, H. Mehan, and D. Roth, *Language Use and School Performance* (New York: Academic Press, 1974); F. Erickson, 'Some Approaches to Inquiry in School-Community Ethnography', *Anthropology and Education Quarterly*, 8 (1977), pp. 58–69; S. Phillips, 'The Invisible Culture: Communication in Classroom and Community of the Warm Springs Reservation', Unpublished PhD dissertation (University of Pennsylvania, 1975); R. McDermott, 'Relating and Learning: An Analysis of Two Classroom Reading Groups', in R. Shuy (ed.), *Linguistics and Reading* (Rawley: Newbury House, 1978); H. Mehan, *Learning Lessons* (Harvard University Press, 1979).

12 D. E. Rumelhart, 'Notes on a Schema for Stories', in D. G. Bobrow and A. M. Collins (eds), *Representation and Understanding: Studies in Cognitive Science* (New York: Academic Press, 1975), pp. 211–36; D. E. Rumelhart, 'Toward an Interactive Model of Reading, paper presented at the Sixth International symposium 'Attention and Performance', Stockholm 1976, in S. Dormic (ed.), *Attention and Performance VI* (Hillsdale: Laurence Erlbaum, 1978).

13 Ibid.

2 Micro-translation as a theory-building strategy

Randall Collins

[*Chapter 2 can be seen as proceeding in three distinctive steps. First, it surveys and analyses the criticism micro-sociological perspectives have advanced against macro-sociological theory and methodology as well as the critique of micro-sociology by which more macroscopically inclined authors have countered the attack. Second, it promotes a model of macro-social reality as composed of the aggregate of micro-social episodes (see the 'aggregation hypothesis' discussed in pp. 25–30). And, third, it argues for the systematic micro-reduction of socio-logical conceptions and explanations to that which happens in the micro-episodes of social life, as a general theory-building strategy for sociology.*

The paper admits only to time, space and number as pure macro-variables. All other sociological variables and concepts can be translated into people's experience in micro-situations. Collins conceives of a radical micro-sociology as engaged in the radical empirical reconstruction of social theory and methodology along these lines. The macro consists of aggregates of micro-stituations in time and space, but these play a part in social reality only in so far as they bear upon people's motivations in everyday micro-interactions. Somewhat analogous to Harré (chapter 4), Collins sees any other view of macro-structures as rhetorical.]

A debate has been emerging in recent years between micro- and macro-sociology. Earlier versions of this debate went on between symbolic interactionism and various forms of macro-sociology; for a time a compromise seemed available by such linking devices as role theory, exchange theory, and Parsonian action theory. But the debate has revived in much stronger terms, with the development of radical forms of micro-sociology, above all ethnomethodology. And this newer micro-sociology faces a strong critique from the macro-side, especially from contemporary structuralism and Marxism.

In the following, I will argue pragmatically that we cannot do without either micro- or macro-sociology. But the most recent round of the debate does not leave us at the earlier point of compromise. For the newer, radical micro-sociology is epistemologically and empirically much more thorough than any previous sociological method; and it claims a number of important discoveries about the ways in which social realities are constructed. The task of micro-research has hardly been finished, and many of the key micro-discoveries are doubtless yet to be made. But I would suggest that the effort coherently to reconstitute macro-sociology upon radically empirical micro-foundations is the crucial step toward a more successful sociological science.

I shall review the micro- and macro-critiques of each other, and attempt to resolve the debate by locating in time and space the types of sociological concepts usable in causal explanations, and by undertaking micro-translations of these concepts. This effort at translation enables us to see what elements of macro-concepts are irreducible and which are not; and it prompts a search for the mechanisms by which long-term and large-scale social processes are reproduced in micro-situations.

Recent micro-sociology has become increasingly 'radical' in several senses. Through the use of audio and now video recordings, it has been able to concentrate on much finer detail empirically than previous micro-sociologies. Instead of loose participant observation of a chain of situations, we get carefully scrutinized analyses of interaction in segments as small as 'the first five seconds'.[1] This shift, moreover, has been away from the more idiosyncratic or dramatic events that occasionally occur in behind-the-scenes manoevring, to the mundane routine that is apparent throughout everyday life. All previous sociological theories and research methods are called into question from this radically *empirical* stance.

Micro-sociology has also become *philosophically* radical. Where the symbolic interactionists have generally accepted the pragmatist version of an ongoing construction of a conventional world, the ethnomethodologists have imported the stance of Husserlian phenomenology. Thus radical micro-sociology brackets the ordinary pragmatic assumptions in order to examine their foundations. Unlike in the practice of philosophers, however, this is done empirically. Instead of examining only the observer's own philosophical subjectivity, the micro-sociologist now examines cognitive and epistemological issues via the close analysis of conversation,[2] and of the construction and use of written texts in social organizations.[3]

The unique thrust of recent, 'radical' micro-sociology is in its combination of an extreme micro-empiricism with a stance which attempts to question all sociological as well as philosophical presuppositions. This questioning is not necessarily relativistic, although it can be that. It is at its most useful, I would claim, where it aims at discovering the fundamental grounds for the topics with which other social analysts concern themselves. Its concerns cut in two directions: towards the grounds of all social structures, and towards the grounds of cognition, especially as displayed in commonsense social reasoning. The two concerns are sometimes brought together, as when radical empiricism is turned upon the sociological research process itself, to show the ways in which the world as portrayed by sociologists has been constructed by observers relying implicitly upon their own use of ordinary practical reasoning. The problems of reality-construction begin at home, and the observer's own cognitive strategies are a first order of materials to be examined in any truly radical empiricism: they are topic as well as resource.

For the present, however, I would like to consider only one of these issues: the implication for conventional macro-sociology of having a vigorous new research tradition which concentrates on ordinary social activity in second-by-second detail.

1 The micro-critique of macro-sociology

Micro-sociology has a strong claim to be considered the only directly empirical form of sociology, with materials that are the only empirical reality there is. Empirical reality is that which is given in experience; as such, it is always experience in a particular time and place and by a particular observer. Human experience is always a *selection* from the totality of sensory experience, since the total amount in all modalities can easily overload the perceptual and information-processing capacities of the human organism. One task of micro-sociology is to discover the structure of the 'filters' and of the semantic memory by which actors in particular situations experience what is empirical for them. But even before we have fully uncovered this inner organization of the individual, it is possible to criticize the conventional notion of empirical reality as held in macro-sociology. For empirical evidence is necessarily bounded by the time-span of the observer's presence; any 'evidence' that is more than a report on the observer's flow of attention becomes indirect and introduces elements which are cognitive constructions of a different sort from the primary empirical materials.

The term 'empirical' has often been used misleadingly in social science to mean numerical evidence or 'hard data', although the latter is actually several removes from empirical in the experiential sense.[4] What is the empirical reality underlying a numerical measure of social mobility, for example? First, there is the actual empirical situation in which an interviewer confronts a subject with a question. Micro-sociologists concerned to be strictly empirical examine this situation to see just in what senses the procedures of formally asking and answering such questions create the kind of data produced. Beyond this, there is the process by which the subjects transform an enormous amount of their previous social experience into a few words: their 'father's occupation' and their 'own occupation' can be rendered in two words, but they summarize materials that empirically, minute by minute in their previous lives, consisted of a variety of social interactions, negotiations, efforts, cognitions. The processual detail by which their career was actually made is compressed into a few nouns, given a hard and object-like form, and thence enters into the sociologist's fund of 'data'.

There are further transformations that a micro-sociologist can observe in applying micro-analysis to the research process: the practical and cognitive contingencies of the coder's actions, the juxtaposing and rearranging of many subjects' answers, reflections upon these arrangements in the form of counting, and then various operations upon these numbers according to theories of statistics, mathematical exposition, and substantive sociology. The final product depicting 'social mobility' in tabular form on the printed page has the appearance of thing-like reality. However, it is, in fact, the product of numerous transformations of the basic empirical materials – the long sequences of social behaviour which alone have sensory, time-and-space reality. Many radical micro-sociologists have thus tended to despair of the problems of arriving at any general explanation of large-scale social processes. Under these circumstances, all sociology can do is examine its own processes; at most, it might be able to uncover the universal micro-mechanisms by which people deal with the daily epistemological problem of producing or at least negotiating ordinary reality.

From this perspective, macro-sociology fails in several regards. It misses the actual here-and-now, enacted nature of social life behind it ignores its own reality-constructing activities, especially the artificial bias given by the practical contingencies of research and by the bias given by the practical contingencies of research and by the forcing of social reality into the alien mould of numerical categories. It ignores the limited cognitive mechanism that sociologists share with all other social actors. The most important of these are *indexicality* (the embeddedness of any communicative reference in some unexplicated, taken-for-granted aspect of the situation), and *reflexivity* (the potentially infinite regress of self-regarding viewpoints that an observer may enter upon when attempting completely to account for the possibility of understanding any situation). In both cases, the empirical inference is that everyday thinkers do *not* act because they have a full and self-conscious view of the grounds for their inferences, but precisely because they avoid questioning what is taken for granted. It is from this point of view that the cognitive presuppositions of symbolic interactionism and other traditional micro-sociologies have been questioned. For none of them assumes there is any fundamental problem in taking the role of the other, recognizing an exchange, or applying a norm (whatever the case may be with particular theories), whereas ethnomethodology claims that ordinary social action could not be carried out if people continuously and explicitly had to recognize these cognitive objects. In fact, social action can be carried out at all only because people do not usually have to think about such things.[6]

Radical micro-sociology applies this type of criticism not only to the standard forms of empirical macro-sociology, into which category it fits not only large-scale research but virtually all quantitative research of any scale, but also to historical sociology and macro-level theorizing in general, and especially to structural-functionalism. Moreover, it claims that macro-theoretical concepts are not only empirically ungrounded and inaccurate, hence at best *glosses* on the underlying reality, but that there is a crucial element of ideology or *reification* in macro-sociology. A *gloss* may be potentially unfolded to reveal a fuller description, albeit an infinitely expandable one; a *reification*, however, is not a failed effort to expound reality but a successful effort to construct a particular mental reality that can constrain people who accept it as true. Hence ethnomethodologists[7] may claim that social researchers and theorists have no superiority to the people they study, since they all use the same fundamental cognitive procedures, such as avoiding explication of glosses because this is an endless and hence impractical task, and one which is usually ignored lest cognitive chaos result from realizing this predicament. And if ultimate reality can never be reached, sociologists had better turn to another task, puncturing dangerous illusions in everyday life such as stratifying practices which create the sense of 'social classes'.

In so far, then, as people take the 'state' to be not an intermittent collection of actions by certain people, some of whom have weapons, but as an expression of the collective will of the people, or a manifestation of God, or simply as a self-subsistent entity, they bolster the power of those who enact the 'state'. The same can be said of concepts of 'property', or 'position', or 'organization', or 'culture', or 'society' itself. Actors in everyday life and sociologists in their analytical constructions are alike, from this viewpoint, in using reifications and thereby contributing to the privilege of those individuals who benefit from the deference they thereby receive in real-life micro-situations. In this critical stance, radical micro-sociology can be very radical indeed.

2 The macro-critique of micro-sociology

A number of criticisms have been made in the other direction, some of them expounded against earlier versions of micro-sociology, some directed at contemporary phenomenological versions. Schematically, these are the criticisms of subjectivism, triviality, historical and structural situatedness, and reductionism.[8]

It can be claimed that micro-sociology is simply another form of subjective idealism, an incursion of long-standing philosophical positions into sociology, a clever argument by which hard material realities and the constraints of social organization are reduced to phantoms in the mind. Such an argument focuses on the human being only as thinker, rather than actor, and leaves out the surrounding physical world and its constraints. The fact that such arguments, taken to the extreme, end in solipsism or mysticism is in itself a refutation of them by reduction to absurdity.

It has also been charged that micro-sociology is trivial. It is a method without substance, or at best a focus upon the minor details and surface appearances of encounters. In either case, it is trivial because it misses the important sociological issues – stratification, politics, social conflicts and movements, social change – all located on the macro-level.

Further, the patterns of behaviour studied in micro-sociology are themselves the results of macro-patterns. For micro-sociologists study styles of interaction and cognition which are specific to a particular social class or ethnic group, or at least to a particular society at a particular time in history. Micro-sociologists are oblivious to the situatedness of their own observations, and hence they not only overgeneralize their findings to the entire social universe, but fail to see how their patterns are themselves the results of larger historical and structural patterns. Gouldner[9], for example, sees the ethnomethodologists as symptoms of the youth world of the 1960s, in which all was uncertain: drugs, sex, school, family, religion. He argues that Garfinkel's breaching experiments were a kind of hippie happening, expressing not only the underlying normlessness of the youth culture, but a sadistic pleasure in disrupting people's ordinary lives. This particular interpretation may be rather speculative, to be sure, as well as rather anachronistic about the timing of Garfinkel's work; but the more general point does have force, that micro-behaviour is not necessarily an historical constant, but itself varies in a larger historical context.

Finally, there is a long-standing argument against micro-reductionism. Durkheim[10] pointed out, in opposition to individual, psychological explanations of social behaviour, that the individual is constrained by the entire structure of interaction; one's location in a particular type of division of labour, for instance, is an externally constraining force upon the individual. Just as physiology is an independently organized level of analysis above chemistry, sociology is a level of organization above psychology – and by extension, macro-sociology is independent of micro-sociology. The reductionist error is to miss the structure of relationships among the parts, and its determining influence upon the parts, by focusing only upon the parts. This critique has subsequently been applied to Homans's attempt explicitly to reduce sociology to the principles of behavioural psychology,[11] and it may be applied equally to radical micro-sociology. Contemporary structuralist Marxism in particular[12] has been adamant in proclaiming that the economic and other formal structures of a society are independent of any subjective, individual level of experience.

3   A confrontation

Micro-sociology produces five main criticisms of macro-sociology. Macro-sociological research (and to some degree, theory) is criticized: (1) as unexplicated gloss; (2) as false construction because it forces social reality into an inappropriate mould through bureaucratic research procedures and/or numerical concepts; (3) as impossible in principle because it shares a mode of everyday cognition that can never fully account for its tacit grounds; (4) macro-concepts are criticized as reifications; (5) Micro-events *are* the empirical reality of human actors, and hence situational reductionism *is* appropriate – in a sex-neutral version of Homans's dictum, 'bringing people back in'.

Macro-sociology makes four main criticisms. It claims that micro-sociology is: (1) idealistic; (2) trivial; (3) causally contingent; (4) reductionist.

Only the last point in each series confronts the other directly. Let us examine the others seriatim.

The first four micro-criticisms do not seem to me impediments to doing valid macro-sociology, at least in some sophisticated fashion.

(1) Macro-evidence as presented may be a set of unexplicated glosses, but this fact can be taken not as a condemnation but as an invitation to unpack those concepts into their constituent parts. Micro-sociology, though, points to several different directions in which explication could proceed: *externally*, into the details of subjects' real-life situations that are usually referred to cryptically as a 'career', or even more abstractly (i.e., after several more cognitive operations) as a 'mobility rate', etc.; and *internally*, into the processes by which researchers construct their data as finally presented. Of these two types of explication, the former (external explication) is more directly important for rebuilding macro-concepts on a firm foundation. The latter, internal explication of the research process itself, may have

some corrective value (see the following point), but as a substantive issue it cuts in a different, and far more general, direction than the effort at external explication of glosses. Internal explications, as a substantive (rather than methodological) concern, can contribute to the discovery of universally present micro-mechanisms of cognition, which must be one component of any total explanation of a macro-pattern. But they are one component only, and they may be discovered from other types of analysis than an explication of macro-research procedures. Hence to lead all efforts to explicate the glosses in micro-research in this internal direction would be to miss the more useful type of explication that can be supplied here.

(2) Micro-sociology also contributes a methodological critique of macro-research. Such a critique does not destroy macro-research. It shows instead how crude an approximation is being tendered, in some instances; in other instances, it proposes that particular types of methods or concepts may be entirely inappropriate to certain phenomena. In either case, it clears the road to improved macro-research.[13]

(3) The most extreme micro-criticism is that absolute truth is never possible on the macro-level (or any level) because research and theory can never escape from such properties of everyday cognition as un-explicated glosses and other tacit grounds of communication. No matter how much explicating one does, there is always more to do. Yet to dismiss macro-sociology on these grounds would be to make a choice for an absolute ideal of truth, while it is quite possible to live with a pragmatic ideal of truth which recognizes successive approximations rather than some final resting point as its aim. The importance of pragmatic approximations can be seen by the following example. What would be required to give a relatively full explication of every gloss involved in a macro-concept such as a mobility rate? It would require, to begin with, an explication of every cognitive moment in the lives of every individual referred to in the mobility rate. To do this, even without adding much analysis, and leaving the analyst's reflexivity at each point out of the question entirely, would take at least as long as the sum of the times of all the lives involved. To say anything in this fashion about world history would take many times longer than the length of world history itself. Given these stringent requirements, it is no wonder radical micro-sociologists often confine themselves to very small slices of data. More practically,

one must conclude that typifications (glosses) by means of strategic samplings and summaries are inescapable. The task of micro-sociological critique should not be to prevent us from doing it, but to enable us to do it better; indeed, to point us to the crucial junctures at which macro-institutions are reproduced or changed.

(4) Micro-sociology charges that macro-concepts are reifications. This is a suggestion worth following, above all as a direction for research. For it is not only the practice of sociological *theorists* that may contribute to reifying the social world, but the practice of people in everyday conversations, and the effects of the latter are by far the more important. It is a research question, though, rather than a theoretical given, because everyday usage may vary a good deal in how much reification it involves, and locating these variations among particular people and particular situations may go a long way towards demonstrating the ways in which a stratified world is produced.

Macro-sociology, then, seems possible, and in a fashion that is consistent with the enhanced sophistication and empirical precision of radical micro-sociology.

In the opposite direction, several of the macro-critiques of micro-sociology can also be disposed of.

(1) Although some micro-sociology resembles idealist philosophy, and much of it owes historical debts to this philosophical tradition, many versions are not susceptible to this critique. Indeed, radical micro-sociology is highly empirical – on its own terms, arguably more so than macro-sociology. Micro-sociology certainly need not slight the external side of experience, for all its frequent emphasis upon the problems of the internal processes of cognition. It is true that some versions of ethnomethodological hyper-empiricism stay entirely within the cognitive constructs by which actors experience concrete situations. In the history of philosophy, such analysis has been the gateway to idealist systems, which concentrate upon supposedly universal and transcendent mental categories, and end by denying the reality of concrete moments in time and space. Phenomenologic-ally inspired sociologies are in danger of travelling the same route.

As a corrective, I am suggesting that radical micro-sociology should hold fast to the concrete experience of individuals in time and space, and not jump immediately to the categories or alleged 'rules' by which they cognitively structure their situations. There is no doubt that the bare physical encounter of human bodies in some particular place is an abstraction – a construct by a theorist such as myself. My argument, however, is that this is the most fruitful starting-point for sociological explanation. It is the touchstone by which we may test the reality of various kinds of cognitive constructions, both those of theorists and those of everyday actors. Only in this way can we avoid the path of trying to explain what people do by accepting common-sense ideologies. This error has vitiated much of previous sociological theory of a more conventional sort, such as functionalism, and it threatens to reappear in a new form in so far as phenomenological micro-sociology takes an exclusively cognitive stance. This is not to say that cognitions play no part in social life. But we need to show realistically just what part they do play: they are parts of chains of the experiences and of the speech actions of particular people at particular times and places, and are to be understood as part of people's efforts to deal with *that situation*, not as the rules of the social structure itself. In short, radical micro-sociology can avoid idealism by locating people's cognitions in their concrete, lived experience, instead of cognitivizing the entire social world.

(2) Micro-sociology, like any other form of specialized research, may appear trivial to outside observers who do not see the theoretical issues with which it deals. I would suggest that not all micro-sociologists themselves are aware of the theoretical issues for which their materials are relevant, but these issues are certainly there. Micro-materials touch on every important issue in sociology, in so far as every macro-theoretical concept is a gloss upon a series of micro-events. And even without this effort at translation, the leading work in micro-sociology aims explicitly at a crucial theoretical issue for the entire field, whether one couches it as 'the basis of social order' or 'the construction of social realities'.

(3) It is unfortunately true that virtually all micro-sociology is oblivious to the historical and often the class context of its materials. Nevertheless, this critique of micro-sociology is not as devastating as it might seem. For if one claims that micro-interactions are caused by historical and structural patterns, the question arises: what are those historical and structural patterns themselves? *Empirically*, they are made up of long sequences and aggregates of other micro-situations. At most, then, this critique states that micro-behaviour in certain situations is due to micro-behaviour in other situations. For example, the social class variable invoked to explain micro-conversational

styles may be translated into previous micro-situations involving interaction in the realm of work, handling money and other property, etc.[14] One may still ask: why do these working and property-handling situations exist, and why do particular individuals get into those situations? In so far as one is unwilling to admit that these questions may be answered by citing still further chains of micro-events, one is claiming structural irreducibility of the larger pattern. Hence the whole of the macro-critique of micro-sociology devolves upon the crucial question of (4) reductionism.

4   Micro-reduction as a theory-building strategy

The issue of reductionism has generally evoked extreme positions. On one side, reduction is declared to be impossible, seeking for explanations of structural phenomena on a level where the phenomena cannot even be found. Thus the term reductionism itself is taken as epithet, and pinning it on an opponent is taken as sufficient disproof. On the other side, rather strong stands have been taken in favour of reduction by several types of micro-sociologists. Ethnomethodology and Homansian behaviourism alike have usually stressed that the micro-situation alone is empirically real, and that explanations which are not grounded in real people in real places are false conceptualizations. If one seeks for causal explanations, then Homan's dictum applies: the analyst must bring people back in every instance, for only real physical people can actually make social events happen. The radical side of symbolic interactionism expresses the point even more strongly: in Blumer's[15] terms, there is only a series of ongoing situations, and there are no larger sociological laws or patterns because situations can always be created anew.

Yet the case for or against reductionism is not logically either all or nothing. One can make (at least) three different claims against reduction: that it cannot be done at all; that it cannot be done in an important number of cases; that it is not necessary or desirable for the progress of sociology.

The third claim is the mildest and the most defensible. It holds that work on the macro-level of analysis does not depend on work on the micro-level; one does not need to have a successful explanation of individuals' situational behaviour in order to make progress in analysing, for example, stratification patterns or long-term social changes. In the same way, Durkheim[16] pointed out that research in physiology is not dependent upon research in chemistry, even though the empirical components of a living body are chemical; physiology could move ahead at its own pace and by generating its own explanatory concepts. But this argument, although acceptable, is not a decisive reason not to attempt micro-reduction. For although physiology did indeed progress without reduction to chemistry, the more recent developments of biochemistry and molecular biology show that a more advanced theory can usefully proceed by seeking for the micro-mechanisms that produce the larger pattern.

The question, then, remains: is micro-reduction generally impossible, sometimes impossible, or always possible? I would suggest the question has never been conclusively settled, but only argued programmatically for one extreme or the other. Yet it is not a hypothetical question but an operational one. The only way we will know the answer is to attempt micro-reduction systematically across the range of sociological conceptualizations and explanations. The answer, as we can see, may not be conclusively yes or no: some aspects of sociology may prove irreducible, while others are not.

There are several advantages of attempting micro-reduction, and these advantages hold whether reduction proves to be fully possible or not. Reduction produces an empirically stronger theory, on any level of analysis, by displaying the real-life situations and behaviours that make up its phenomena. In particular, it introduces empirically real causal forces in the shape of human beings expending energy. It enables us to discover which macro-concepts and explanations are empirically groundable, and which are not, thus enabling us by a strict criterion to separate out hypostatizations. And to the extent that hypostatizations are part of people's social realities, we can clearly situate them in people's cognitive usages in particular times and places.

These advantages appear to be entirely formal, the micro-sociologist forcing an increased degree of empirical and conceptual accountability from the macro-sociologist. But we may see advantages from the opposite direction. Micro-reduction increases the plausibility of macro-theories. For although I do not wish to discourage anyone from producing macro-analyses of any degree of historical and theoretical scope, I would suggest that such analyses are almost always merely plausible in a general way. They are pictures of the world that make sense but are rarely demonstrated rigorously. This is especially true of analyses of entire societies or of large historical events such as the Industrial Revolution or the rise of world capitalism, for here one cannot sample randomly from a large universe of cases or make a full range of controlled comparisons for all important variables. History simply does not provide enough cases.[17] In my view, this is not a reason for abandoning large macro-analyses; surely one learns more from an analysis of world history, even if it comprises only one case, than from ignoring that wealth of material. Sampling procedures of a given kind (like any other methodological device) are not a *sine qua non* of valid sociological research; they are merely a device for increasing the plausibility of an empirical argument. There are other means of increasing plausibility. In the case of a large-scale macro-theory (such as Weber's or Wallerstein's theories of the rise of captalism),[18] one may improve its plausibility by showing that it involves a network of explanatory principles, which we have reason to believe are true because there is evidence for them in other contexts. In other words, a macro-analysis, like any analysis, is strengthened when its implicit structure can be made coherent with the rest of social theory. In so far as macro-theoretical principles can be tightly knit together with micro-principles in a single explanatory web, the macro-analysis has a stronger claim to being correct. In arguing among rival macro- or macro-historical explanations, then, the theory that can be better micro-grounded is much more plausible than one that cannot.

My argument, then, is not that macro-sociologists should cease their work and become micro-sociologists, but only that they should realize that their work is theoretically incomplete. No macro-analysis is a strong argument until it can show not only that a particular historical pattern exists, but why that particular pattern exists rather than another. The requisite cases to compare may not be available on that macro-level, but systematic theory linking micro and macro can provide empirical substitutes as a repository of principles whose plausibility has been more strongly demonstrated in other, smaller contexts.

There is a final advantage in attempting micro-reduction across the entire range of sociological theory, precisely in the event that there are genuinely irreducible macro-components of explanation. In this case, micro-reduction should give us a clearer idea of just what irreducible macro-concepts may consist of. We will be able to distinguish among different types of macro-usages in sociology, and macro-variables, if they genuinely exist, may be economically reduced to a finite and possibly quite small number. Let us call this process 'micro-translation', to avoid the negative connotations of the term 'reduction'; it should be thought of as a revisualization of social theory in micro-terms, a sort of X-ray vision of the micro-components and linkages that make up macro-structure.

Previous efforts at micro-translation may appear implausible, primarily because of the weakness of the particular micro-theory applied. The weakness of Homans's[19] efforts at reduction may be attributable to the specific formulations of social behaviourism, rather than to micro-approaches generally. Thus the effort at micro-translation should also have benefits for improving micro-theory by showing which models of the actor and the situation are most adequate for explaining macro-patterns. The effort at micro-translation, however, should be applied to genuine macro-principles, not to makeshift ones such as 'Golden's Law'.[20]

5   Four types of macro-reference

Elsewhere[21] I have presented approximately 300 propositions and sub-propositions, designed as an interconnected series of causal explanations across the range of sociological materials. Although varying in degrees of empirical support and in tentativeness of formulation, the propositional structure claims to codify major principles on both micro- and macro-levels, ranging from face-to-face interaction at work and in conversation, through organizational structures, up to such long-term and aggregate phenomena as the organization of the state, patterns of social mobility, and the distribution of wealth. In general, the claim is to ground all propositions, as much as possible, in micro-interactions. However, when one analyses each proposition in terms of its empirical referents in the world of time and space, one discovers that there are a variety of ways in which even quite micro-situational propositions generally imply certain types of macro-reference. Explicit macro-propositions, on the other hand, can be analysed more closely into more fundamental micro- and macro-concepts. Thus the argument against reductionism turns out to be valid to a degree, but the effort at reduction does open up a more complex view of the types of interplay between micro- and macro-levels.

There are four main types of macro-reference.

(1) *Individual micro-histories* Avowedly micro-principles are of the form: the greater the value of a situational independent variable (IV), the greater the value of a situational dependent variable (DV). Yet even such principles tend to involve some implicit macro-reference, i.e. they refer to more than a small segment of time and space which comprise a particular situation. Thus:

1.1   The more one gives orders, the more one is proud, self-assured, formal, and identifies with the organizational ideals in whose name one justifies the orders.[22]

This proposition is designed to give a micro-situational basis to the main pattern of class cultures. Nevertheless, it refers not only to a particular situation but to a number of situations. 'The more one gives orders' implies that the IV is stronger as one experiences more situations of this sort (though 'more' may also mean that a particular experience is more emphatic, and also that it may last longer within the situation). The same is true of the DVs. One is more 'proud, self-assured, formal', in the sense of acting and feeling thus in a larger number of subsequent situations (as well as possibly in the other senses indicated for the IV). Thus micro-propositions usually refer to repeated situations, for both IVs and DVs; further, these may be different situations for the IVs and the DVs – e.g. giving orders in one set of situations, acting proud and formal in other situations.[23]

Such propositions may refer not only to repeated situations but to a variety of situations. For example:

2.2   *Cosmopolitanism* The greater the diversity of communications one is involved in, the more one develops abstract, relativistic ideas and the habit of thinking in terms of long-range consequences.[24]

The IV 'diversity of communications' refers to experiencing a variety of different situations over time, as compared to experiencing situations of the same sort. The same implicit comparison of types of situations may be found in the DV as well (e.g. 5.3, below).

In short, even principles which refer explicitly to action in micro-situations for both IV and DV involve an implicit aggregate of situations. Micro-principles of this sort, then, refer not only to particular points in time and space, but to a micro-history of situations which may possibly extend considerably in time.

(2) *Situational macro-views* Micro-principles often refer to people in situations who take account of the macro-structure itself, whether they do this by referring to other micro-situations or to more reified macro-concepts.

In 2.2 (cited above), the DV is a continuum between 'one develops abstract, relativistic ideas and the habit of thinking in long-range consequences,' and '[one] thinks in terms of particular persons and things, short-term contingencies, and an alien and uncontrollable world surrounding familiar local circles.' These are situational views of the macro-structure, of varying types of abstractedness and reification. (Their *accuracy* is not given within this proposition; both types of macro-views may well be highly inaccurate.)

Some propositions make the reification explicit:

5.5 *Publicly announced relationships.* The more ritually an ideal symbolizing an interpersonal contract to carry on certain types of exchanges is announced to third parties, the more reified and constraining the ideal relationship becomes for the participants.[25]

Reified macro-views may also appear as the IV:

10.3 The more one gives orders in the name of an organization, the more one identifies with the organization. [Cf. 1.1, cited above.][26]

'The organization' here is a complex of situations in time and space, but is referred to cryptically (and often only implicitly) when one gives orders or otherwise represents the organization to another.

On the other hand, macro-references may not be reifications or glosses, but explicit situational understandings of the variety of other possible situations:

5.3 The more unique and irreplaceable a conversational

exchange, the closer the personal tie among individuals who can carry it out.[27]

Here 'the more unique and irreplaceable a conversational exchange' may mean a person's explicit recognition that s/he can have certain conversations with only a few people (or conversely, with many).

Finally, the macro-views of the individuals in situations may vary precisely along the dimension of how clearly one can see other micro-situations that may occur in the future:

15.1   The more unique the product or unpredictable the problems of the task, the less reliance on rules and the greater the decentralization of authority.[28]

Here 'uniqueness' and 'unpredictability' imply types of situated macro-views in which future situations are explicitly vague.

Situational macro-views, then, can take a variety of forms. They may be reifications, glosses, or explicit understandings of other micro-situations. Moreover, they can be conscious or unconscious, in varying degrees. Just how macro-views are produced, especially unconscious ones, is not well understood and constitutes a key problem for micro-sociological research. It also provides two important bases for the actual linking together of micro-situations into macro-structures: *rituals* (the IV in 5.5, above) are the central micro-procedures for producing reified macro-views; and *markets* (the IV in 5.3, above) involve an array of different interaction situations, the choice among which becomes part of the actor's cognitions in any one particular situation.[29]

(3) *Pure macro-variables: time, space and number* I have argued that the empirical reality of sociological concepts is people's experience in micro-situations. Nevertheless, the sheer numbers of situations and their dispersion in space may enter as IVs (e.g. 14.4) or as DVs (19.11).[30]

Terms such as 'centralization of authority' can be translated into micro-situations. But the pure macro-variable here enters neverthe-less in the form of the number of 'links in the chain of command' – unpacking the metaphor, one should say the number of situations involving different combinations of people, either passing along orders or giving orders on their own initiative. Hence structural variables often turn out to be sheer numbers of people in various kinds of micro-situations.

> 6.81 The more efficient the technology of transportation and communication, the greater the potential diversity of communications, and the lower the potential level of surveillance.[31]

Here the IV 'efficiency of technology' is a gloss that can be translated into the amount of time it takes for people to communicate over a given amount of space. Hence the degree to which a variable is macro or micro is itself a variable.

There are more complex macro-concepts than those given in these examples. Some of them, such as the concept of 'social mobility' or the 'distribution of wealth' are very complex glosses, which can be unpacked into a number of levels of analysis.[32] A few of these will be further considered below. The principal point here is more abstract: that pure macro-concepts do exist in causal propositions and do survive micro-translation. But the macro-concepts as ordinarily stated ('centralization of authority', 'organization structure', etc.) are not the irreducible variables themselves; those variables are always some combination of number, time, and space applied to the micro-contents of situations.

This conclusion is consistent with an overview of the possible forms of empirical evidence. If the sum of all possible empirical evidence in sociology consists ultimately in a set of 'filmstrips' giving the sensory and subjective experience, moment by moment, of every person who has ever lived, then macro-references can arise only in these ways: (1) each strip consists of micro-situations, but it runs on in time (for a lifetime), and hence gives the aggregates of situational experiences that make up micro-histories; (2) often people at particular points in time refer to the future or past of their own 'filmstrip', or to some aggregate of other people's filmstrips, whether individually or in the form of a reification; and (3) there is the sheer number of micro-strips of various sorts, their configurations in space, and their lengths in time.

All social reality, then, is micro-experience; but there are temporal, numerical, and spatial aggregations of these experiences which constitute a macro-level of analysis.

(4) *Analysts' macro-comparisons* There is a further way in which sociology involves references to larger segments of the time–space continuum than momentary situations. In formulating any proposition, the analyst must refer to situations which are not included in the proposition. The analyst not only states the linkage within or among situations referred to in the proposition, but also compares this linkage with other possible linkages (i.e. with other situations or relations among situations) in order to ascertain that that relationship holds and not some other. Thus the analyst always engages in macro-references and must have at his or her disposal some knowledge of a larger macro-world than is contained in the propositions. Put differently, the analyst must always be able to range about more widely in time and space than the contents of any proposition. In terms of the 'filmstrips' metaphor, the analyst always takes a number of filmstrips (or of aggregates of strips) and compares them with other strips or aggregates.

This procedure holds even if one is dealing with pure micro-propositions. For, it should be noted, there are such propositions in which both IV and DV are confined within a single micro-situation and do not depend on repetitive situations for the strength of the variables. Ultimately, in fact, all sociological principles should be built up from such pure micro-principles. There is no exhaustive or even well-established list of such pure micro-propositions, but the following illustrate that they do exist:

4.3   The greater the common focus of attention among physically copresent human beings, the more likely they are to experience a common emotional arousal or mood.[33]

4.6   The stronger the emotional arousal, the more real and unquestioned the meanings of the symbols people think about during that experience.[34]

10.1   Coercion leads to strong efforts to avoid being coerced.[35]

11.1   *Surveillance.* The more closely a supervisor watches the behavior of subordinates, the more closely they comply with the observable forms of behavior demanded.[36]

The DVs in 4.6, 10.1 and 11.1 may last through a number of situations, but they are directly manifested in the immediate situation. All of these propositions, though, do involve the *analyst's* transcendence of the paticular situation. The terms 'the greater the common focus', 'the stronger the emotional arousal', etc., refer to the analyst's comparison of several situations.

Analysts' micro-comparisons, however, are on a different level of analysis than the previous three types of macro-references. The first three are within the frame, whereas the fourth refers to the frame itself. In the first three, we examine the contents of the picture; in the fourth, we examine how the picture itself was constructed. (If we wish to treat them all on the same level, one would then say that type #4 is merely an instance of type #2 – the analyst, situated in a micro-situation such as sitting at a desk or reading a piece of paper, is constructing macro-references – hopefully, in this case, accurate ones.) It is useful to keep the contents of the frame distinguished from the framing itself, however. If we do this, we can see that pure micro-propositions are possible *in* sociology, and explore how these become entwined with other propositions that contain macro-references of various sorts.

6   Conclusion

The reductionist or micro-translation strategy, then, suggests the following results. There are pure micro-principles, and these should be at the core of all empirically causal explanations in sociology. There are also pure macro-variables, but these take only three forms: space, time, and number of combinations of micro-situations. All other variables are characteristics of micro-situations, whether these extend into micro-histories, become referred to in situations as macro-views, or make up more complex combinations, as in the conventional glosses expressed as macro-variables.

What substantive value is there in doing this kind of micro-translation? One value is to make macro-theories truly empirically grounded. Here micro-translation is a defence of macro-sociology against the most radical micro-attacks. There is also a critical side. For not all macro-concepts survive translation. Entities like 'system', or the 'society' with its autonomous needs, or the 'state' with its purposes, turn out to be abstractions without causal reality; at best they are social actors' concepts, living forms of rhetoric which have misled sociological theorists into taking them as literally true.

Micro-translation is also a method for building explanatory theories. It helps to move us from empirical generalizations to a more basic level of causality. For example, organizational research shows a number of relations among types of technology and the 'shape' of the occupational distribution, the authority channels, and other conventional concepts of organization 'structure'. Micro-translation shows that the connections can be explained on the basis of quite general principles of personal interaction; the 'structures' are the results of differing outcomes of micro-control struggles in various physical arrangements of work.[37] The same translations may be made of historical models of political change. Barrington Moore, for example, proposes on the basis of half a dozen historical cases, that modern fascism, communism, or democracy are the results of alternative property arrangements between landowners and agricultural workers during the transition to commercial agriculture.[38] Micro-translation of this model has not yet been carried very far, but even some early steps in this direction show that this large-scale process hinges upon the typical interests of members of various social classes as they engage in political and economic situations in their daily lives.[39]

Micro-translation thus makes us aware of the empty spaces within existing sociological models, and provides us with a technique for putting a real skeleton inside the superficial skin. Micro-translation may also provide new substantive hypotheses. In the area of social mobility, for example, there has been a yawning gap between the conventional independent variables – family background, ethnic origins, education – and the subject's current occupational status. Leave aside the problem that these independent variables, which are really a long string of interactional experiences at home and in school, are treated as if they were entities; even without going into the real empirical meaning of these IVs, it is clear that the conventional model ignores what happens in all the years after people leave school. It is small wonder, then, that these models are able to explain only a relatively small part of the variance in occupational achievement. But what happens after the completion of school is hardly a matter of 'chance', as some writers[40] have argued. It is just that all the daily interactions that make up a career have not been formulated into some conventional variables that researchers might take as thing-like entities, and thus enter into their path models. If we micro-translated a person's career, it is possible to see that the motivations, resources, and contacts that lead from one job to another appear in a succession of personal encounters.[41] I have proposed, therefore, that each link in the occupational chain is mediated by a friendship network, which generates and reinforces both conversational styles and social motivations. Individuals' careers remain on the same occupational level if their friendship networks are stabilized in that milieu, and shift upwards or downwards if their friendship networks are skewed in those directions. These friendship networks, of course, can be taken apart into yet more micro-processes encompassing both the details of conversational negotiation which results in people becoming (or failing to become) friends, as well as aggregate features of 'conversational markets'.

A micro-translation strategy need not stop at extending existing theories. It is also possible to strive for a comprehensive theory of macro-structures built up entirely on the basis of micro-research.[42] One of the main findings of ethnomethodological research, for example, is that humans operate within limited cognitive capacities, and hence tend to make social life as much as possible into a taken-for-granted routine. It is not 'rules' or 'norms' that uphold social structure, then, but precisely people's incapacity to operate with such rules in the real-life world. The inference from this, I would argue, is that the repetitive behaviours that make up social structures are primarily based upon the *physical* plane. People base their routines upon particular physical localities, particular human bodies, and particular things; it is the sheer physical structure of the world that makes for what social orderliness there is, rather than the impossible requirement that each individual should have a cognitive map of the whole social world or of some abstract rules allegedly applying to all of it.

It follows that the most basic element of social structure is *property*, in the real-life sense of individuals' relations to the physical objects that make up their life-worlds. But the degree to which individuals respect one another's property, as well as defer to authority, depends upon their tacit monitoring of the social coalitions that can threaten or support them. Again, this cannot be done by conscious calculation, but requires some tacit mechanism. I suggest that it is done by a very common social activity, namely conversation. But it is not the referential content of talk that is important for checking out social alliances, but the ritual aspect of conversation. People tacitly recognize particular kinds of conversational practices as symbols of common memberships; and their social motivations come from the feelings of confidence or lack thereof which they get from these implicit tests of group belonging in various interactions.

The aggregate of all conversational encounters across the physical landscape makes up what might be considered a conversational market. Individuals acquire conversational and emotional resources from their chains of encounters over time, and the match-up of such resources among individuals who come together at any point determines their current degree of solidarity or antagonism, domination or subordination. It is through such chains of encounters that property and authority are stabilized or changed. A conversational 'market' is more complex than the conventional economic model of a market, because there are both generalized cultural 'currencies' as well as quite particularized conversational media, and there is a flow of emotions as well as of verbal symbols. The conversational 'market' links together micro-encounters in a non-reified way; macro-variables enter this model only in the form of the numbers of conversational encounters among people and their dispersion in physical space and time.

From this model it is possible to show the conditions for the stable micro-reproduction of the aggregate social structure, as well as for social changes of various types. There are several basic sources of structural change, corresponding to the several major components of conversational rituals. A great deal of structural change flows from shifts in *particularized* cultural media, especially the *reputations of specific individuals* which tacitly define their place in social coalitions. Power, as well as a fall from power, is a self-fulfilling prophecy, which operates along mutually reinforcing chains of conversation. Hence the macro-organization of politics hinges upon the micro-transmission of particularly dramatic events which are used as barometers of social confidence in the ability of public figures to muster support. On the other hand, the entire structure of personal relations across a society changes into a different form when the sheer amount of *generalized culture* is increased or decreased, via such culture-producing activities as religion, education, or entertainment media. A third source of change might be referred to new 'technologies of emotional production' – new devices for self-dramatization which change the aggregate amount of impressiveness or solidarity of individuals in their daily encounters. Major historical changes, such as the shift from patrimonial to bureaucratic forms of organization, or to the peculiar conditions of present-day 'Goffmanian' society, are the results of such changes in the resources available for putting on everyday interaction rituals.

This cryptic summary is intended to do no more than suggest the possibilities of building general macro-theory upon a micro-basis. Perhaps there are other ways of carrying out such a project. One obvious difference among approaches is between those (such as Giddens's paper in this volume) which try to build macro-structures upon actors' knowledge of social 'rules', and those (like my own) which build macro-structure upon micro-actions and emotions. For the reasons given above,[43] I would contend that grounding macro-structure in the contents of cognitions is impossible, and that the 'rules' are only constructs of the theorist rather than matters to which actors really attend. There may be yet other alternatives to these models. The important thing is that micro-translation be tried, and especially upon substantive theoretical issues. Only in this way can a truly coherent sociology be established.

The challenge of radical micro-sociology is among other things a call for a radically empirical reconstruction. The dynamics as well as the statics of the larger social world ultimately depend upon its only living elements, people in micro-situations. Structural aggregates of micro-situations in time and space are on another level of analysis, and play a part in social causation only as they bear upon people's situational motivations. It is within micro-situations that we find both the glue and the transforming energies of these structures. Any other view of them remains metaphorical.

Notes

1 Emmanuel Schegloff, 'The First Five Seconds', unpublished PhD dissertation (University of California, 1967).
2 Harvey Sacks, Emmanuel Schegloff, and Gail Jefferson, 'A Simplest Systematics for the Organization of Turn-taking in Conversation', *Language*, 50 (1974), pp. 696–735; Jo Ann Goldberg, 'A System for the

Transfer of Instructions in Natural Settings and the Amplitude Shift Mechanism: a Procedure for Utterance Affiliation in Sequence Construction', unpublished PhD dissertation (University of California, 1977).

3 Aaron V. Cicourel, *The Social Organization of Juvenile Justice* (New York: Wiley, 1968); Stewart Clegg, *Power, Rule, and Domination: A Critical and Empirical Understanding of Power in Sociological Theory and Everyday Life* (London: Routledge & Kegan Paul, 1975).

4 Aaron V. Cicourel, *Method and Measurement in Sociology* (New York: Free Press, 1964).

5 This point has also been made by George Homans, 'Bringing Men Back in', *American Sociological Review*, 29 (1964), pp. 809–18; and by Herbert Blumer, *Symbolic Interactionism* (Englewood Cliffs: Prentice-Hall, 1969), although without as great an emphasis upon micro-detail as by the ethnomethodologists.

6 Harold Garfinkel, *Studies in Ethnomethodology* (Englewood Cliffs: Prentice-Hall, 1967).

7 Hugh Mehan and Houston Wood, *The Reality of Ethnomethodology* (New York: Wiley, 1975).

8 A sampling of the many expressions of these criticisms may be found in Guy E. Swanson, Anthony F. C. Wallace, and James S. Coleman, 'Review Symposium on Harold Garfinkel's *Studies in Ethnomethodology*', *American Sociological Review*, 33 (1968), pp. 122–30; and Lewis A. Coser, 'Two Methods in Search of a Substance', *American Sociological Review*, 40 (1975), pp. 691–700.

9 Alvin W. Gouldner, *The Coming Crisis of Western Sociology* (New York: Basic Books, 1970), pp. 390–5.

10 Émile Durkheim, *Sociology and Philosophy* (New York: Free Press, 1974; originally published 1924). Pierre Bourdieu, *Outline of a Theory of Practice* (Cambridge University Press, 1977), p. 3, explicitly turns this criticism against the ethnomethodologists, as a one-sided subjectivism opposed to an equally one-sided objectivism. Bourdieu goes on (p. 81):

We are insisting, against all forms of the occasionalist illusion which consists in directly relating practices to properties inscribed in the situation, that 'interpersonal' relations are never, except in appearance, *individual-to-individual* relationships and that the truth of the interaction is never entirely contained in the interaction.

11 Robert R. Blain, 'On Homans' Psychological Reductionism', *Sociological Inquiry*, 41 (1971), pp. 3–25; Jonathan H. Turner, *The Structure of Sociological Theory* (Homewood: Dorsey Press, 1974), pp. 242–57; George C. Homans, 'Reply to Blain', *Sociological Inquiry*, 41 (1971), pp. 21–3.

12 Nicos Poulantzas, *Classes in Contemporary Capitalism* (London: New Left Books, 1975); Louis Althusser, *For Marx* (New York: Pantheon, 1970).

13 Aaron V. Cicourel, *Theory and Method in a Study of Argentine Fertility* (New

York, Wiley, 1974); Randall Collins, *Conflict Sociology: Towards an Explanatory Science* (New York: Academic Press, 1975), pp. 450–6.
14 Randall Collins, *Conflict Sociology*, pp. 49–160.
15 H. Blumer, *Symbolic Interactionism*.
16 E. Durkheim, *Sociology and Philosophy*.
17 The world-system argument (Immanuel Wallerstein, *The Modern World System*, vol. 1 (New York: Academic Press, 1974) makes this methodological criterion all the more difficult to meet, because it points out empirically that different societies are by and large not independent of each other, and that these intersocietal linkages are exactly the key to many problems of social change.
18 Max Weber, *General Economic History* (New York: Collier, 1961; originally published 1924); I. Wallerstein, *The Modern World System*, vol. 1.
19 George C. Homans, *Social Behavior: its Elementary Forms* (New York: Harcourt Brace, 1961). It should be apparent that *psychological reductionism* – the reduction of all social processes to the principles of individual psychology – is not the same as *situational reductionism* – the reduction of social processes to concrete situations of interaction among individuals. Homans advocates psychological reductionism, whereas I am proposing situational reductionism.
20 R. R. Blain, 'On Homans' Psychological Reductionism'.
21 R. Collins, *Conflict Sociology*.
22 Ibid., p. 73. I have changed the pronouns in these quotations to a sex-neutral form.
23 Notice the same sort of reference to micro-histories rather than to micro-situations in Blau's principles, e.g. 'Principle 2. The more a person has exchanged rewards with another, the more likely are reciprocal obligations to emerge and guide subsequent exchanges among those persons.' (Peter M. Blau, *Exchange and Power in Social Life*, New York; Wiley, 1964, p. 90.)
24 R. Collins, *Conflict Sociology*, p. 75.
25 Ibid., p. 159.
26 Ibid., p. 301.
27 Ibid., p. 157.
28 Ibid., p. 324.
29 Randall Collins, 'On the Micro-Foundations of Macro-Sociology', *American Journal of Sociology*, 86 (1981), pp. 984–1014.
30 R. Collins, *Conflict Sociology*, pp. 320, 355.
31 Ibid., p. 218.
32 Ibid., pp. 434–6.
33 Ibid., p. 153.
34 Ibid.
35 Ibid., p. 298.
36 Ibid., p. 307.
37 Ibid., pp. 315–29.
38 Barrington Moore, Jr, *Social Origins of Dictatorship and Democracy: Lord and Peasant in the Making of the Modern World* (Boston: Beacon Press, 1966).

39 R. Collins, *Conflict Sociology*, pp. 396–9.
40 Christopher Jencks *et al.*, *Inequality; A Reassessment of the Effects of Family and Schooling in America* (New York; Basic Books, 1972).
41 R. Collins, *Conflict Sociology*, pp. 451–4.
42 A fuller exposition of this model is given in R. Collins, 'On the Micro-Foundations of Macro-Sociology'.
43 These arguments are amplified and documented in ibid.

3 Intermediate steps between micro- and macro-integration: the case of screening for inherited disorders

Troy Duster

[*The thrust of chapter 3 is that it presents a methodological model for the social sciences consistent with Cicourel's call for generating a systematic data base across different contexts of social action (see chapter 1). Duster conceives of these contexts as hierarchically ordered on a ladder of abstraction. This implies that the context of law or of an income tax regulation will have to be studied as another level of empirical inquiry in addition to that of, say, community-based programmes dedicated to the enactment of the law or the regulation.*

The model calls our attention to the transformations *of social reality which occur between levels, and proposes to account for them by drawing upon cross-level data. One underlying assumption here is that the general characteristics of different social groups play a crucial role in their observably different handling of issues which appear to be 'the same for all' on a more abstract level (like a government regulation).*

By admitting to different levels of abstraction of social reality and inquiry, Duster challenges the assumption of the essentially microscopic *nature of* all *events for which the preceding chapters have made a point (see also sections 4 and 5 of the Introduction, pp. 25–40). Note that a case can be made for these different levels if we start from the perspective of participants for whom the (micro)activities of a political administration take on the form of an (abstract) regulation, and if we admit to differences in the reach and consequences of different levels of (micro)action.*]

1 Rungs in the ladder of methodological abstraction

Every generation of social scientists has its own set of injunctions about the importance of connecting theories to observations. Sometimes, the swing of the pendulum to one end is so dramatic as to produce powerful reaction. At the turn of the century, an early generation, led by Franz Boas, reacted against the grand theoretical systems of evolutionism with an emphatic swing to lengthy, comprehensive field observations and detailed taxonomy. At mid-century, Merton led a balanced attack against both grand theory and low-level empiricism with a plea for 'middle-range' coverage of the empirical world.

But it is late in the twentieth century and the age of specialization is well upon us. We are presently confronted with a situation of thousands of workers in apparently unrelated vineyards, the proliferation of theoretical and methodological camps, and a wide split between those who work on what have come to be called 'micro' studies of specific scenes and those who attempt 'macro' studies of gross national, international, and comparatively informed historical trends in the polity and the economy. Accordingly, the sages of this period calling for the integration of theory and observation enjoin us to draw relationships between macro-analysis of social structures and micro-studies of local scenes. The obstacles to accomplishing this, however, are paradoxically 'spacy' and intangible. A close-up study of farm workers in the Central Valley of California may produce an elegant leap to world systems theory, but, no matter how graceful, unless the warrant is established with intermediate connectors, the critic has an easy mark. Likewise, when grand functionalists and grand Marxists alike see evidence of 'the system' in every setting, both are open to effective broadsides that range from reification to tautologizing.

It may well be a matter of taste or style with regard to the direction one moves from microscopic to macroscopic work. But, for either, it is a precipitous fall or a wondrous catapult if no rungs are available on the notches in between the base and the top. If we follow the metaphor of the ladder a bit further, we see some of the problems to be encountered when trying to place intermediate rungs. A major obstacle is that each of the rungs is often associated with a different kind of methodology. The bottom rung, direct empirical observation, requires ability to engage in either participant observation, the use of sympathetic informants, or experimental manipulation in a laboratory setting.

Depending upon the problem studied, the next rung might be

'formed' by utilizing local and regional demographic analysis of patterns of migration, employment, age and sex pyramids, review of the racial and ethnic composition of the workforce, and a review of the educational and welfare systems. The context can be forged by the ferreting and interpretation of historical materials that draw the prospective reader, where relevant, to a comparative treatment of the relative credibility of documents and the accounts of old timers. Excellent histories themselves contain many tiers of analysis, observation, and interpretation, and a model for this kind of work is Fernand Braudel's monumental *Civilisation matérielle, économie et capitalisme*.[1] Braudel is a historian whose earlier work on Spain achieved a notable integration of both detailed portraits of daily peasant and village life and heavy attention to patterns of gross mercantile trade. While his students and followers frequently went off in the direction of local and limited descriptions of daily life, Braudel himself reasserts in this most recent work the primary importance of framing these local scenes with the larger economic and political landscape.

For a study of the *contemporary* world, however, another rung can be crafted from analysis of the structure or organization, both with regard to the nature of accountability to the relevant overarching organization in a highly bureaucratized world, and also with respect to the nature of the network of linkages between relevant organizations.[2]

When we finally reach the highest levels, however, we are left more with 'indicators', less with the direct observation of behaviour. Economies and polities cannot be seen, as units, in motion. Rather, what we observe are national rates of employment, gross rates of growth, surveys of attitudinal change along the political spectrum, summaries of voting trends, or, in wartime, bodycounts of the enemy killed. From these indicators, we try to weave a picture of national and international complexity and scope. A measure of success is the degree to which the audience determines the weave between levels, observations, theorizing, and indicators to be compelling. It is the kind of enterprise attempted by William Shawcross in his account of the destruction of Cambodia.[3] Shawcross's analysis takes him from the organization level at the State and Defense Departments, through the analysis of documents of committee meetings and memos from key figures, through direct interviews with embassy personnel in

Saigon and Phnom Penh. Shawcross is not an academic trying to
generalize about the use of theory and methods. He is a journalist
giving an account of a particular historical development in two countries. However, the methods that he employs and the case that he
presents are both excellent models for the integration of levels in
inquiry.

As a journalist, Shawcross was not limited by the 'trained incapacity' of the academic specialist who uses only a limited arsenal of
methods. Academics in the social sciences go through a training in
which there is a subtle process of differentiation and stratification that
accompanies the learned use of a specific method. We may be told by
the writers of methods textbooks, and by graduate instructors that a
method is only as good as its applicability to the specific question it is
designed to help answer. However, the structure of the disciplines, the
weighting of graduate curricula in methods at the 'better' departments and the path to publication in the 'better' journals quickly give
graduate students the message. Methods are stratified!

There are exceptions, but the pattern is irrefutable, and few object
to graduate methods courses being taught overwhelmingly by
specialists in surveys, factor and network analysis, and model
building. Status positions in the professional hierarchy produce an
entrenchment to the use of preferred methods. Method 'A' gets
professionally treated as superior to Method 'B' quite independent of
the problem addressed. While methods are stratified, it does not end
there. No less than with theories, methods carry with them ideologies.
The qualitative camps fight back with their own journals, increasing
the specialization. Feeling embattled, the survey researchers counter
with ideological formulations about 'field methods' as being prior to
the *real* testing of hypotheses. Direct observation is characterized as
hypothesis generating, little more.

This career preference for certain methods is one reason why, on
any given research problem, it is difficult to connect the micro-studies
to macroscopic analysis. The intermediate steps (links, rungs, or
connectors) often call for the use of different methods.

Before I turn to an illustration of this, it will be useful to specify
what is meant here by this notion of intermediate steps, and why this
may be theoretically as well as empirically useful. A 'ladder of
abstraction' carries the implicit notion that direct observation of a
local setting (especially in contemporary urban, bureaucratized,

technologically advanced countries) is insufficient to understand the social forces that help explain the social behaviour observed.

While one kind of explanation can be taken from the people in the scene (their stated motives and interests), actors themselves are often unaware of historical, demographic, and other factors that can better account for what occurs than the stated motives.

Interposed between the individual in the local scene and the gross explanations of social, economic, and political patterns we have strong theoretical grounds for assuming that an intermediary inter-polation exists, an institution, organization, or bureaucratic structure. Grounds for this assumption can be located in every forum, from classical theory (Weber) to a wide spectrum of empirical studies of formal organizations to contemporary prognostications and obser-vations about the 'bureaucratization of the world'.

If much of the world is broken down into intermediate organiz-ations that mediate much of social life between grand cultural ethos or federal law, or international cartel, then a strategy for apprehending that world must include a concern for this level.

The choice of levels of analysis is generated from our broadest understandings of the relevant points of reference and sources of decisions, policy, action, and behaviour in Western cultures. As we have just noted, almost all behaviour in these cultures can be located in an institutional or bureaucratic context. Whether it is the practice of medicine, the marketing of a product, a small local business enter-prise, the education of the young, or whatever, most of human social life that we would like to study can be situated in an organizational context that approximates the old sociological notion of 'formal organizations'.

In a study of a particular empirical or theoretical problem, the choice of the specific organizational level should be dictated by the theoretical question posed. For example, in studying local policy in an elementary school, one could choose variably between the local school board, the regional superintendence, or state department of public education. While ideally one might wish to deal with all three levels of organizational context, practical limitations might necessi-tate a theoretically dictated selection. In any event, the organiz-ational frame is one of the 'rungs' that we can reasonably con-ceptually interpose between the micro-level of individual situated, local action, and grand federal, or national, policy in education.

Technically, the demographic, epidemiological, or historical analyses of a particular local scene are, of course, not so much different levels (with respect to abstraction) as they are ways of placing context around the scene and providing grounding. Before we move to different levels of abstraction, we need to take an early step of mapping the larger terrain. Again, choice of *how* one enlarges the scope is determined by the theoretical bent of the researcher and the empirical problem under investigation. If we return to the example of a study of a school, if it is a new experimental school, we won't have as much history as a study of a school steeped in tradition. However, the former might better choose to place a greater emphasis on the changing migration and birth patterns that generated the constituency for a new school.

All social action can be conceived as local in the sense that it must occur in settings bounded by local time and local space and the local constitutive expectancies of social exchange. It may ramify and serve as a future point of reference for many other local scenes, both temporally and spatially. Great moments in history and great centres of power share this characteristic, and in this sense there could be resistance to the characterization of these situations as 'local'. But the question of whether the local scene has some future historic import is a problematic matter for empirical assessment. That it is local is the empirical given, and provides justification for taking the natural setting as a central point or origin of social research.

The choice of a local scene is determined by some practical or theoretical concern. In this chapter, I want to turn to a specific empirical problem to illustrate possible ways to achieve the integration between the micro-observations of the local scene and the gross general patterns and understandings of larger social and political forces.

However, before moving to the substantive empirical problem, I would like briefly to address the focus for the methodological stance that I have taken, and give the reasons behind it.

2   The 'natural setting' as the starting-point

Ethology emerged from the naturalistic critique of the zoological method.[4] The latter took highly controlled surroundings, the zoo, as an adequate setting for the close and systematic observation of animal life. The ethological critique stressed the inviolate character of the natural habitat as the starting-point of observation, despite the obstacles to direct observation in natural settings.

If one were searching for an analogue to zoology in human life, it would be penology. Clearly, certain important things can be learned about humans from studying them in prisons.[5] It is equally clear that the prison has features that prohibit one from learning about other important aspects of human social life. Two basic considerations are the variable transmutations of sexual energy by locking out the opposite sex, and the powerful constraints on exchange/market relations. Would we not be grossly misled about key elements of Italian, French, or American life if we were restricted to the study of Italian, French, and American prisons?

For humans, the 'natural setting' means something quite different from what it means for animals. The corporation, the law office, the factory are not in the same way naturalistic as the forest, riverbanks, and wild habitats. For humans, 'natural settings' in this usage means simply the places where people would ordinarily or routinely be doing what they are doing as they live out their lives. If one is to study or measure 'intelligence' among humans, then, even if one assumes capacity for abstract reasoning to be central, the best place to do it would be in the natural setting in which intelligence is called forth as a feature of living. With both parties using abstract reasoning powers, a factory worker might be measured as far more intelligent on the shop floor than the corporation lawyer. If we take them both out of their 'natural setting' and put them in the 'neutral' setting of an IQ test, it may be more like studying animals in zoos and people in prisons, in that it so removes the participants from the natural setting that it distorts the meaning of intelligence. With such 'neutral' IQ testing, the lawyer might do better precisely because this test setting more closely approximates his or her natural setting (routine way of living) than that of the factory worker. Such tests are zoological. Likewise, a two-hour interview, a mailed questionnaire, a laboratory experiment, while useful techniques for certain purposes, are all analogous to the zoological study of animals. To repeat, important things can be learned from prison studies or zoological studies. However, such research needs to be complemented by other kinds and other levels of research if we are to have confidence that the findings apply to human social behaviour in the setting in which it ordinarily occurs.

If we combine observation in the natural setting with these other methods, we may be able to supplement our knowledge in the same way that zoologists and ethologists can complement each other's work.

To return to the notion of the ladder, I noted earlier that an attempt to move from local empirical detail and grounded observation (micro-studies) to a highly generalized understanding and explanation of gross economic, social, or political trends means that, if we are to avoid a gigantic 'leap' to the highest rung, we have to place more rungs on the ladder.

In this chapter, I would like to suggest a way of doing that, not in the abstract, but with a particular empirical problem. I have chosen to illustrate the integration of methodological levels and issues by discussing some ongoing research on the new technology in micro-biology that has permitted genetic screening of part of the population. Before I turn to the issue of adding the 'rungs' to the ladder of abstraction, it is necessary to give some background to the empirical issues that are the subject of the research effort. Any of a number of subject-matters could also be approached by a multi-tiered strategy; this is simply a convenient one to use at this time.

3   Screening for inherited disorders: a brief overview

Screening a population for genetic disease is a very new form of health screening. It is distinguished from all previous forms because of the unique relationship between the ethnic and racial boundaries of many genetic diseases and the social stratification of ethnic groups. Genetic screening, although less that 20 years old in the USA, has already raised many important questions for public policy. Legal mandates to screen populations for inherited disorders have existed only since Massachusetts passed the first such law in 1963 for Phenyl-ketonuria.[6] Within the short space of 4 years, forty-three states passed PKU screening laws, and, by 1972, these laws and associated regula-tions governing screening programmes generated considerable con-troversy. Because most genetic diseases are ethnically and racially linked, genetic screening has come inescapably to involve the attitudes, information, and experiences of the nation's different ethnic groups, and of those who seek to represent these groups politically.

At the very outset, giant insurance companies are involved in the health screening from a highly interested perspective. For a private insurance company, it is simply good business, and bad for profits, to insure people who are chronically ill. Federal and state laws that mandate screening are in a very delicate area whenever they specify 'target' populations, for these populations-at-risk to be designated ethnically or racially is to raise the ugly spectre of Nuremberg. Finally, on the more local levels, as we gain more knowledge in this area, public concern with 'defects' tap deeply into the experiences of individuals, families, and communities, and their most strongly held beliefs about life. These issues take us into the heart of the medical profession, and thus engage matters of social and political organization that are local, regional, and national. They reverberate into such diverse loosely knit associations as religious organizations and consumer protection groups. All of this means that it will make it possible to use this empirical instance as one in which the various rungs to the ladder can be specified and in ways that may bring some clarity to the methodological strategies suggested.

Unlike contagions, genetic diseases are ethnically and racially linked. That is, while smallpox crosses over all ethnic and racial boundaries, most genetic diseases are found primarily in populations that have intermarried for generations and centuries. To mention but a few of the better-known examples, Tay-Sachs disease is empirically associated very strongly with Ashkenazic Jews, Sickle Cell disease with blacks, and Thalassemia with Mediterranean peoples. Cystic Fibrosis is rare among Asians, and twice as likely to affect whites as it is to affect blacks. White children get Spina Bifida twelve times more frequently than Japanese children, but the Japanese have the highest incidence of cleft lip and cleft palate of any ethnic or racial group.

This linkage of genetic diseases and race and ethnicity means that laws which mandate screening for such diseases already provide examples of the practice condemned so sharply by the Nuremberg trials of German war criminals after the Second World War: the specification of ethnic and racial groups in legislation by the state. Coming in the wake of the genocidal annihilation of Jews and gypsies, the Nuremberg trials served to dramatize the moral consensus of the war's victors against the scapegoating of a single ethnic or racial group by state power. Before and during the days of Nuremberg, moreover, enlightened anthropologists in Western nations had declared with authority that 'race' was merely and only the social construction of the unenlightened, the prejudiced, and the malevolent. Today, we are forced to be more humble and cautious in our formulations about biological, social and cultural linkages of race and ethnicity, as laboratory scientists learn more about the genetic code and gene pools. The dilemmas posed to societies which espouse equality before the law for their citizens will be sharpened by the designation of ethnic and racial groups to be screened genetically as a matter of law.

Genetic screening acquires another social-political dimension through the social stratification of ethnic/racial groups. Some societies are relatively homogeneous, ethnically and racially, as with nineteenth-century Sweden. Such societies tend to experience clear estate and class stratification. But, in those societies where there is considerable ethnic/racial heterogeneity, social stratification typically parallels and overlaps the ethnic and racial groupings.[7] In Malaysia, for example, Gardner found that select occupations were dominated by the Chinese, while others were dominated by the Indians, the Malays, or the English.[8] Such facts will serve to distinguish genetic screenings from all previous health screening, since – quite in contrast to mass screening for contagious diseases – it cannot be made appealing to all groups for the common or collective good. Being linked to ethnic/racial groups which are socially stratified, genetic diseases also are socially stratified, not merely biological, socially 'neutral', characteristics. The same is true, inescapably, for medical and legal measures to deal with them, which raise not only humanistic ('ethical') or politically neutral ('policy') questions, but socially and politically controversial ones as well.

Because genetic diseases affect different groups in the population differently, different screening/prevention procedures are necessary to equalize citizens' treatment before the law. This is true, not only because the diseases themselves differ, but because the groups primarily affected by them are different, also – historically, culturally, and in their positions on the hierarchies of political and economic power. Such facts sharpen the difficulties which decision-makers face in answering the hard questions about how scarce national resources are to be spent. Which diseases are most important? Which groups are most deserving, or most needful, of government-supported action?

Decisions about such issues are very much subject to the forces of political manipulation. For example, the Nixon administration's espousal of Sickle Cell screening in 1972 was portrayed as an indication of official concern about the disease's effects on black citizens. In retrospect, however, the programme then created has been widely viewed as a prime example of how genetic screening should *not* be done.[9] It has been interpreted by many black leaders as a cynical attempt to 'buy' black votes with a public relations campaign, behind which the actual screening programme was a great disservice to the persons it purported to help. Objections have also been raised, as we shall see presently, against state regulations in California, mandating Sickle Cell screening of all blacks admitted to hospitals for whatever reason. Thus, in very concrete and specific ways, genetic screening is inevitably joined to the matter of power and control over that screening, and to the issue of which groups exercise it.

Most genetic diseases are chronic. For many, such as Tay-Sachs and Sickle Cell diseases, there is no treatment which can alleviate the basic symptoms, much less their underlying cause. In other instances, such as Haemophilia and Thalassemia, victims must be given repeated transfusions and cared for in ways which make them continually dependent on others. It is one thing to screen for a disease which can be cured by known means, but quite another to screen for a disorder that will not go away even when discovered. This element of chronicity provides a reservoir of latent, recurring fears about the motives of those who would *prevent* genetic disease rather than *treat* it.

An historically unique combination of scientific genetics, medical technology, and legally mandated mass screening is producing a new and complex interplay of biological and social/cultural processes. There is nothing new about genetic disease, or about its specific location in an ethnically or racially definable population. Populations 'at risk' are defined by the socio-historical fact of gene-pool homogeneity, occasioned by long periods of intra-group marriage. What is new is the scientific knowledge of genetic diseases, the technology which allows detection of carriers and prenatal diagnosis of disease, and the increasing lay knowledge that screening for these diseases is possible. Biological and social processes are joined here, but not in the neo-evolutionary sense of a 'socio-biology' which sees social relations as largely determined by biological factors.[10] Instead, there is a powerful new fusion of the two sets of forces, in which the objective diagnosability of disease and the subjective, cultural definitions of the group (nation, race) are both inescapably present – and deeply consequential.

4   Levels and methods of inquiry

In order to carry out research in this area and to integrate the 'micro' empirical scenes, ultimately, with a 'macro' analysis, a research plan is imperative. In this section, I will suggest a plan to incorporate four distinct, complementary levels of inquiry into the problem of genetic screening. The goal is to draw the interrelationships between these levels, partly by tracing problems through them to illuminate the nature of the connections, or lack of connection. The four levels are:

1   *The step to macro-analysis*
Law and lobbying: vertical integration of federal and state, with intersection of lobbying interests that are potentially international.
2   *Intermediate steps to vertical integration*
Administration and organization: vertical integration of federal (Public Health Service), state (State Department of Public Health), and the local clinic or hospital level.
3   *Two micro-observational levels*
(a) Physician and client: vertical integration of physician as professional (thus, connection to organizational base, with ideology and interests) with client or patient (lodged in particular community or cultural base).
(b) Family and community: loop back integration to lobbying federal and state; tie-in to clinics with communal sanctions, positive and negative, for participation in screening programme.
4   *History and context as grounding step*
Discussion of the history of mass health screening, and the technological changes that have permitted new forms of screening for inherited disorders. The context has already been provided in the earlier section of the paper, namely, the discovery of an association between ethnicity, race, and populations at greater risk

for inheritable disorders. Since this discussion has already framed this section, we will turn now to the first three levels to illustrate the vertical integration and interaction between levels.

4.1   Law and lobbying (the step to macro-analysis)

Sometimes, federal law sets the tone and frames what occurs in state law. But health is one of those residual matters left up to the state. (It is certainly true that the federal government enters into the health picture with great effect with the power to tax.) In this area, action by the states preceded that of the federal government. Not only did the various states have earlier laws mandating screening, but the mistakes that they made were for the most part avoided by those that developed into national legislation. For example, many states had made genetic screening compulsory.[11] The National Sickle Cell Anemia, Cooley's Anemia, Tay-Sachs, and Genetic Disease Act of 1976 expressly forbade compulsory screening and demanded that any federally funded screening programme be 'voluntary'. But it is necessary to go back to the first national legislation on Sickle Cell to understand how and why the latter bill developed into such a conglomerate.

In 1972, the National Sickle Cell Anemia Control Act was signed into law, with an authorization of over 100 million dollars for the establishment of screening and counselling programmes, and for research. While state laws mandated screening, and sometimes provided limited funding for these programmes, this degree of support at the federal level engendered interethnic group competition, envy, rivalry, and an increasing demand for 'our fair share' of concern and money from other ethnic and racial minorities.[12] People from the Mediterranean, especially southern Italy, are at greater risk for Beta-Thalassemia (Cooley's Anaemia). As it became clear that blacks were going to get 'their' disease control funded, the Mediterranean constituents of Congressman Giaimo persuaded him to introduce a bill, also in 1972, for a National Cooley's Anemia Control Act. That bill passed. Ashkenazi Jews are at greater risk for Tay-Sachs. Within a few months, a Jewish constituency put pressure on Senator Javits to secure passage of a National Tay-Sachs Control Act.

At this point, a very interesting controversy surfaced. Should there be a proliferation of specific laws and programmes tailored to specific inherited disorders, or should there be a centralized programme, with one omnibus law? Initially, Javits and others moved to introduce and support a separate bill for Tay-Sachs. Later, they became persuaded that a single comprehensive bill covering all diseases should be developed. In Congressional hearings on the bills, Blacks almost universally testified in favour of keeping the national legislation for Sickle Cell separate.[13] They argued that a composite bill would dilute the interest, concern, and funding for Sickle Cell. They feared that control of the Sickle Cell programme would shift more and more away from blacks. But the medical establishment brought out all of its artillery to these hearings, and argued the language of efficiency quite strongly. They won, and Congress passed the comprehensive law in 1976.

There is considerable regional, state, and local variation in the USA among constituencies for genetic diseases. Moreover, the terms 'voluntary' and 'informed consent' mean quite different things at Congressional hearings and in the routines of state hospitals or local clinics. The translations of these concepts into practice must necessarily vary with locale and consumer constituency.

Massachusetts has been a front-runner in the creation of screening programmes for inherited disorders.[14] In 1963, the state of Massachusetts enacted the first law mandating screening for Phenylketonuria (PKU). In 1971, the state legislature passed a law requiring blood tests for both Sickle Cell trait and Sickle Cell disease as a prerequisite to school attendance. These programmes generated considerable controversy, and helped fuel the recombinant DNA controversy, which also flared early in Cambridge.[15]

California was also an early state to pass laws requiring screening of the new-born. In 1965, the state legislature passed legislation requiring screening at birth for PKU. Very shortly thereafter, the Bureau of Maternal and Child Health received a federal grant to establish a special unit dealing with hereditary defects. In 5 short years, the California legislature enacted a requirement of blood-typing of all pregnant women. As has been noted earlier, one of the most salient issues in screening for inherited disorders is the capacity for medical intervention. With some problems there is a solution, as in the birth of an RH+ mother (the administration of immunoglobulin can prevent this disorder). But, in 1971, the California legislature directed its Department of Public Health to develop a policy for control of Sickle Cell Anaemia. Since there is no cure for Sickle Cell, the idea of 'control' became ominous and odious to many black medical practitioners in California, who reacted vigorously when the legislature passed a law permitting the Public Health Department to require testing of blacks 'wherever appropriate', as illustrated by the following articles which appeared in the *San Francisco Chronicle*:

Big Furor Over Sickle Cell Tests

Amid widespread confusion and without public announcement, the State Health Department has just ordered California hospitals to obey long-delayed regulations aimed at testing all hospitalized black patients for sickle cell anemia.

Although the test is not supposed to be mandatory, black physicians throughout the state are up in arms at the abrupt decision to enforce the two-year-old rules.

Lobbyists for the California Hospital Association are also working to change them; the California Medical Association opposes them, and one CMA official terms the rules 'offensive.'

The regulations require physicians to administer sickle cell anemia tests to every black patient admitted to a hospital, and to enter the test-results in the patients' medical records. But they allow patients to refuse to take the screening test.

The renewed political furor over the mass screening program is only beginning, for it involves many serious problems:

The Golden State Medical Association, which represents California's black physicians, charges that state health officials – no matter how benign their motives – are actually practicing 'Big Brother' medicine by singling out a specific racial group for genetic testing.

Medical care for minorities is in fact so often hurried and sketchy that many blacks who are to be screened cannot possibly give their 'informed consent' to the procedure, even though the regulations do permit them to refuse to take the test.

Because test results must be noted in each patient's medical records – and thus become part of health insurance computer records as well – the ultimate result could be job discrimination and discriminatory insurance premiums aimed at blacks who do not even have sickle cell disease many doctors fear.

Finally, the regulations require that patients receive

'appropriate information and education' about the nature of sickle cell disease, but even health department officials agree that large numbers of doctors have themselves received little or no training in the problems of the illness or the nature of the test.

When the storm broke in medical circles yesterday over the abrupt decision to implement the sickle cell testing rules Dr. Jerome Lackner, California's Director of Public Health, conceded that he had never read the regulations.

'The first I heard about it all,' Lackner told The Chronicle in a telephone interview, 'was when people called in and wanted to know what the hell was going on.'

In view of the furor he told The Chronicle, he will ask medical leaders to meet with him on the problem, to study possible changes in the regulations, and perhaps to delay their implementation for a few months while changes are being studied.

Sickle cell anemia is a hereditary blood disease that is confined mostly to black people, although a small but significant percentage of persons from Mediterranean stock also are subject to it. The disease is estimated to affect 50,000 blacks each year in America.

People who inherit the 'sickling' gene from only one parent carry the trait but do not suffer from the disease. However, a child of parents who are both carriers has a one-in-four chance of developing the lethal illness itself.

The disease causes severe anemia, crippled limbs and recurrent crises of excruciating abdominal pain. Few patients with sickle cell disease live beyond the age of 40.

Because no cure is known, voluntary efforts at mass screening programs and genetic counseling have been going on for some time in the black community. Doctors feel that pregnant black women should be required to undergo the test early in pregnancy.

In 1971 the California Legislature passed a law requiring the State Health Department to launch an early detection program for the disease, but not necessarily to screen everyone for the sickling trait.

Two years later the State Board of Public Health – an agency subsequently abolished by the Reagan Administration – shelved a mass screening requirement and agreed to a modified program aimed at finding children who were actually afflicted with sickle cell disease.

But a year later the Department of Health adopted more far reaching regulations even though they were opposed by virtually all major medical organizations in the state.

The regulations require physicians to test the 'sickle cell status' of all blacks admitted to hospitals and to record the test results. Hospitals were required to submit statistical reports quarterly on the numbers of patients with sickle cell trait, the numbers with disease, and the numbers who refused to take the test.

But the 1974 regulations caused a new storm and the Health Department agreed not to enforce them pending further study.

Last month, however, Dr. George Cunningham, chief of the department's maternal and child health services, began notifying hospitals they would have to comply with the rules. Some hospitals were not informed until this week.

Cunningham told The Chronicle he felt that enforcing the rules would prod physicians to learn more about the genetic disorder. He insisted that under the regulations hospitalized black patients would merely be 'offered the opportunity' to take the test.

But Dr. Lonnie R. Bristow, a black San Pablo physician who is president of the California Society of Internal Medicine, insisted the rules amount to mandatory testing, that the results cannot be kept confidential and thus will cause blacks economic hardship, and that current tests are both poorly standardized and expensive.

Dr. Vertis R. Thompson, an Oakland obstetrician and immediate past president of the Golden State Medical Association, was even more vehement:

'It's a damned shame, and that's putting it mildly,' Thompson said. 'It's outrageous, and we're going to do everything in our power to make the department revise the regulations.'

A California Medical Association spokesman noted that his organization's policy is to recommend sickle cell testing only when a physician feels it is necessary and only 'where there exist adequate counseling and resources to deal with the problems and anxieties that are created by a positive sickle cell test.'

Those resources, noted one CMA official, obviously don't exist in hospitals where so many of the state's 1.5 million blacks are often treated (David Perlman, *San Francisco Chronicle*, 3 July 1976).

Sickle Cell Test Rules Scrapped

Controversial State Health Department regulations aimed at screening all black hospital patients in California for sickle cell anemia were scrapped yesterday.

A six-month moratorium on enforcing the regulations was ordered by Dr. Jerome Lackner, the state's director of public health, and at the same time Lackner named a prominent black physician to head a committee that will rewrite the rules.

The committee will have all the time it needs to draft new regulations, Lackner said – even more than six months, if necessary – and will be given staff assistance by the Health Department.

Dr. Lonnie Bristow, a San Pablo physician who is president of the California Society of Internal Medicine, was named to head the committee. Bristow has long been an outspoken leader in the effort by black doctors to encourage widespread testing for sickle cell anemia without imposing mandatory tests that ethnic minorities feel are offensive invasions of privacy.

Bristow and several of his colleagues held a press conference here yesterday to discuss their concerns about sickle cell testing and to announce Lackner's message to them that he was holding up enforcement of the mass screening rules.

The regulations were first drafted in 1973, after a new California law declared it state policy to 'detect, as early as possible, sickle cell anemia, a heritable disorder which leads to physical defects.'

But the first regulations were rejected by the State Board of Health, an expert advisory agency abolished by the Reagan administration.

The Health Department itself published the regulations two years ago, but delayed enforcing them. Then a department official, without consulting Lackner, notified all the state's hospitals last month to begin obeying them now. This unexpected decision caught black physicians by surprise.

The rules require physicians in hospitals to 'determine the sickle cell status' of all black patients by giving them an approved blood test. Patients are permitted to refuse to take the test after the nature of both sickle cell anemia and the test have been explained to them. But the results of the test, or a patient's refusal to take it, are to be entered in the patient's chart. And sickle cell test statistics are to be forwarded regularly to the health department.

Sickle cell anemia is a hereditary disease most prevalent among blacks. Where both parents carry the genetic trait for sickle cell blood, each of their children has a one-in-four chance of developing the disease itself. Carrying the 'trait' alone rarely leads to any illness at all.

When the disease does strike, however, it is marked by severe painful and crippling recurrent crises; most victims die before they are 40, and many die long before that.

At yesterday's press conference Bristow noted many difficulties with mass sickle cell tests: It's not always possible to determine 'who is black or how black is black,' he said.

There is never a guarantee that hospital records will remain confidential, he added, and as a result insurance companies, which can easily learn the sickle cell status of patients are apt to increase premiums on racial grounds alone.

Nor do most hospital staffs include either doctors or other health workers skilled or sensitive enough to counsel black patients on sickle cell problems, Bristow said (David Perlman, *San Francisco Chronicle*, 8 July 1976).

We can see from the news stories from the *San Francisco Chronicle* that the attempt at organizational implementation of state genetic screening laws and regulations for Sickle Cell Anaemia ran into serious difficulties, complications, and ultimately, reversals. If we remain only at the organizational level, we cannot account for the behaviour of the State Department of Public Health. We learn from the article that virtually all major medical organizations opposed the Sickle Cell screening regulations. From having contextualized the 'local' problem of the State Department of Public Health, we have strong grounds for concluding that it was caught from above (a top rung) by a desire to spring for federal funding. Yet, from below, and with parallel organizational pressures from the state medical establishments, the state bureaucracy was buffeted about amidst the political winds. There is nothing particularly new about cross-pressures on a state agency, especially if one is studying the agency itself. The thing that is of particular theoretical and methodological interest for our purposes here, however, is the portrait of the varying levels of articulation that permit a connection between local, community, clinical activity in the specific social scene under investigation, and the grand level of decision making at the federal level. This is certainly not the only way to integrate micro- and macro-social theory and observation, but it is one way.

4.2   Administration and organization (intermediate steps for vertical integration)

The link between legislation and this level is direct, in that administrative regulations are created to help and carry out the intent of the genetic screening laws. Indeed, in many instances, new agencies had to be established, or new wings of old agencies created or supplemented, in order to carry out the legal mandate. But while the link is direct, it is hardly complete. The law is general and abstract, while administrative regulations to implement these laws are (a) quite specific in the nature and direction of that implementation, and (b) themselves bend and reshape in the hands of particular interests that surface at the organizational level. The local policies and professional relationships within organizations which conduct genetic screening programmes have a large effect on the ways in which these programmes are conducted.[16]

I have just mentioned in the preceding section an example of these points in what happened in California about the Sickle Cell regulations. Here was an instance in which the implementation of the law has had quite different effects on the experiences of various screening programmes. The law can hardly take into account the variability of the economic, social, and political positions of the ethnic and racial groups screened. Yet, as soon as the programmes are set up for administration, the relative economic and political position of the groups comes to the fore. In California, for example, Tay-Sachs screening has gone on without much in the way of vocal negative public reaction. It is interesting to note, however, that the bureaucratic structure for the administration of Tay-Sachs screening is quite different than that for Sickle Cell Anaemia, although the language of the laws that generate and underpin such programmes gives no indication of this. In southern California for example, Tay-Sachs screening is funded through a principal investigator, a private physician, who then in turn makes funding allocations to various agencies and organizations that wish to participate in Tay-Sachs screening. The situation is quite different for Sickle Cell Anaemia. Screening programmes for this disease must be approved by a central co-ordinated agency of state government. The agency sends out 'requests for proposals' and then assesses whether the various applicants meet the criteria to warrant funding.

This difference can be explained by a number of factors, but a social scientist looking at the problem cannot help but isolate as a central factor the relative structural location of Jews and blacks, their attendant relationships to the medical profession, their relative educational and economic positions, and the comparative level of trust and confidence one might therefore expect these programmes to generate.

Sickle Cell Anaemia screening programmes came on the heels of the black power movement in the late 1960s. The Black Panthers collected for Sickle Cell on the street corners of major cities, and, with others in the movement, used political rhetoric to reshape the consciousness of much of the population to the neglect of this disease. When community and neighbourhood groups emerged to direct and staff such programmes, they often did so with the rhetoric of 'control over our own lives'. This meant the black groups from the black community should be in charge of these programmes.

The reasons are not hidden. The hostility and suspicion with which blacks would have treated white medical professionals who suddenly showed up in the black community to conduct genetic screening in 1969–72 would, predictably, have been fierce and unbearable. But a very uneasy relationship was to develop out of these programmes precisely because blacks are at the base of the economic order. The very groups that surfaced to work on any well-funded black community-based programmes were those groups who had been poverty warriors, but who had been shunted aside when Lyndon Johnson's war on poverty gave way to the Nixon–Moynihan policy of benign neglect. Suddenly out in the cold, many of these emeriti of poverty warriors would discover a natural affinity with community-based Sickle Cell programmes.

It was the same with the methadone maintenance clinics across the country. They were frequently based in the black community, and federal and state funding was essential to the continued livelihood (at a certain level) of the staff. As the sociologists of organizations and bureaucracy have long noted, the interests of the staff in the perpetuation of the bureaucracy will almost perforce supersede the original intent of a programme. Methadone maintenance became an essential element in the continuation of funding, and so it became the interests of the staff to find more people to serve as warm bodies in the body count in the war on heroin. There was a parallel development with Sickle Cell programmes. Imagine, then, that with this economic reality at the base of such programmes, how an entrenched, establishment, physician-oriented and controlled State Department of Public Health would view such groups: 'fly-by-night', 'storefront', 'jive', 'on the make', 'hardly serious', and certainly in need of close scrutiny, monitoring, and overseeing.

We cannot escape the fact that the social-economic stratification of Jews and blacks will re-create itself in 'community-based' programmes that attend the medical problems of the two groups. For blacks, the staffing of these programmes may be much closer to a basic fundamental issue of economic livelihood. For Jews, the health issue can become paramount precisely because the economic interests at the base are a given, or at least substantial.

We would be at a loss to explain these differences if we looked only at the screening programmes themselves, for it is necessary to move to gross data on the income, educational, and occupational situations of the two groups to help explain these developments. They manifest themselves again at the administrative and organizational levels in the way in which genetic screening programmes for Jews and blacks are developed, funded, and responded to by the respective communities and potential clients of screening.

4.3 Two micro-observational levels

Physician/patient/counsellor

A set of issues that cuts across all levels is the combination of concern for voluntary participation in the screening process, informed consent and confidentiality. One way to ensure continuity between levels (making sure that the rungs are on the same ladder) is to follow issues that obviously surface at every level of empirical inquiry. For the purposes of illustration in this area of work, we can take the three related issues of voluntary participation in the screening process, informed consent, and confidentiality. Each taps a quite different political and conceptual problem. The matter of confidentiality takes us into the interests of giant international insurance conglomerates, but it is also a matter of an exchange and trust in the relationship between the individual and the physician. In sharp contrast, 'informed consent' is simply an ideal set up by a number of quite different interests at many levels, but it is quite difficult to monitor. By observing what occurs in the actual setting in which 'informed consent' is a requirement, we come to understand how it ties into the medical profession's image in the minds of consumers of medical services.

If viewed as an isolated problem, informed consent seems hardly an issue that could generate much concern or interest. However, it is tied up with a vital nerve of all genetics controversies between the state and the individual, the degree of voluntarism in participation. Federal law and government regulations insist on the non-coercive assurances built into any genetic screening programmes. The primary device for ensuring that voluntarism is the requirement that participants be fully informed (sometimes verbally, usually written) that they have the right to refuse a fully explained screening detection procedure.

But while federal and state laws are clear and unequivocal on this matter, the implementation of the ideal is fraught with almost insurmountable problems for the administering agency, the clinic, and the physician. Regulations call for standardization, yet the populations being screened are infinitely variable. In the state of California, how does one individual achieve the assurance that a recently arrived Asian from Hong Kong or Cambodia, a recently arrived 18-year-old black from rural Alabama, and an Armenian professor of engineering, get 'standardized' consent forms that ensure informed consent? Implicit in 'giving' consent is the background assumption that the individual feels or senses no hidden coercion and expects no negative sanction if he or she says 'No!' The forms may require that the person be 'read' that participation is totally voluntary, but individuals from certain groups come to the bureaucratic setting with widely varying expectations of what will ensue once one rejects or refuses what are described as routine procedures.

At the level of close observation, then, between physician or medical para-professional and screenee, informed consent may take on quite different shapes than anticipated in the panelled walls of a Congressional hearing on required assurances for voluntary participation. The Congressional action is important, and serves as a guideline for interpreting the spirit and intent of the law. However, only by climbing through various layers (or rungs) to get to the bottom of it, where informed consent and confidentiality are practised, can we make connections between theorizing about genetic screening and the many local scenes where it is practised.

Family and community
In the decision of whether or not to accept or participate in genetic screening, the implicit, subtle, and yet prevailing definition in the individual's family and community can be overwhelming. For example, we have noted how the Jewish community has accepted screening for Tay-Sachs disease to a much greater extent than any other racial or ethnic group has accepted or participated in screening for the relevant inherited disorder. In many areas throughout the country, donations from private sources and considerable volunteer work has made Tay-Sachs screening a model of private, voluntary participation. A number of factors converge to help account for this. First, and perhaps foremost, Tay-Sachs is one of the most devastating and fatal of genetic diseases, with far less variability than such diseases as Thalassemia, Cystic Fibrosis, or Sickle Cell Anaemia. A child with Tay-Sachs will not live beyond the age of four. A second set of reasons is the combination of social class and formal education. The median education of Jews screened for Tay-Sachs in one study was one year of post-graduate (*sic*) study, while the mean education of blacks screened for Sickle Cell was 3 years of high school.

Still a third factor is the relative trust the blacks and Jews have of the medical profession. In 1978, the test for detecting Thalassemia and Sickle Cell *in utero* was the same, with more than a 10 per cent chance of causing a miscarriage. Yet, while native Italian women are giving up a life's savings and flying to San Francisco for the test, black women in the San Francisco Bay area rarely agreed to the procedure, to the surprise and consternation of the clinical staff.

This kind of development could not have been anticipated at the 'macro' level, and unless or until such empirical patterns are uncovered locally, it is difficult to see how even a well-intentioned legislative body can create legislation that serves the interests of such diverse community responses to screening programmes. I think that the best way to achieve this is to co-ordinate a large number of specific empirical studies in different locations. The major problems with 'classics' of ethnography is that they often come to stand for the relationships that they portray, across time and space. Rather, what we need is not one Tally's Corner, but ten such studies on different corners throughout the cities of the nation. We need not only one *Street Corner Society*, but a dozen. Accordingly, in this area, what is needed is a co-ordinated series of ethnographies of clinics and community responses to such clinics, including case studies of families afflicted with a member with an inherited disease.

We should always keep in mind the question of how we get from the clinical setting where the client is being screened for genes that indicate an inherited disorder, or from a physician–patient exchange on treatment for such a disorder, all the way to national legislation on the topic, and an understanding of international insurance cartel activity. A deductive strategy won't do, otherwise there would be identical replicable little scenes at the local level. A singular inductive strategy fails for different but related reasons: which elements from the local scene are to provide grounds for induction?

5 Summary

In contemporary sociology, we can find a general advocacy of attempts to integrate studies of local scenes with analysis that comes from our broadest understandings of cultural, social, political and economic forces. This advocacy could possibly have greater persuasive powers if it were accompanied by an articulation of how such an integration might be achieved. In this essay, I have tried to provide an illustration. My strategy is to argue that, for a study to achieve this integration, there should be inclusion of separate levels of entry into the empirical world, buttressed by a fourth strategy of substantive contextualization. Then, by raising the empirical question of how the phenomenon under investigation manifests itself at each of these levels, there is an implicit injunction in this device to draw the relevance (or reaction) of levels one to the other.

Three levels of entry are: (1) direct observation of behaviour in the local setting in which it routinely occurs, the grounding for the 'micro' base of the study; (2) observation and analysis of the administrative, bureaucratic, or organizational unit(s) that are interposed between the local scene; and (3) the 'macro' trends, rates, or perhaps law, or federal policy developments. The precise content of what will be observed is of course dictated by practical considerations like access, the theoretical orientation of the researchers, and the substantive research problem.

The fourth strategy is not really a level of entry, but an attempt to provide some greater context to the problem under investigation. The attempt to provide the longitudinal context is the analysis of historical records and the use of oral histories. The horizontal context might be provided from demographic analysis of migration patterns, rates of employment or literacy in the area, and so forth. Again, as in the choice of organizational level, the empirical problem addressed and the conceptual orientation should determine what kind of demographic or historical data provides the relevant context. It is the method of procedure for achieving the integration of levels that has been the focus of interest here, not the substantive problem nor the theoretical camp.

Notes

1 Fernand Braudel, *Civilisation matérielle, économie et capitalisme* (Paris: Armand Colin, 1979).

2 One may certainly study organizations through direct observation, but the concern for formal as well as informal structural arrangements alters the research strategy, in that a key question for all parties becomes the tension or degree of fit between the formal and informal.

3 William Shawcross, *Sideshow: Kissinger, Nixon and the Destruction of Cambodia* (New York: Simon & Schuster, 1979).

4 This discussion is indebted to David Matza.

5 John Irwin, *The Felon* (Englewood Cliffs: Prentice Hall, 1970).

6 Philip Reilly, *Genetics, Law, and Social Policy* (Harvard University Press, 1977), pp. 39–61.

7 Tomatsu Shibutani and Kian M. Kwan, *Ethnic Stratification: The Comparative Approach* (New York: Macmillan, 1965).

8 Stuart W. Gardner, 'Ethnicity and Work: Occupational Distribution in an Urban Multi-Ethnic Setting, Georgetown, Penang, West Malaysia', unpublished PhD dissertation (University of California, 1975).

9 Tabitha M. Powledge, 'Genetic Screening as a Political and Social Development', in D. Bergsma (ed.), *Ethical, Social and Legal Dimensions of Screening for Human Genetic Disease* (New York: Stratton, 1974), pp. 25–55.

10 E. O. Wilson, *Sociobiology: The New Synthesis* (Harvard University Press, 1975).

11 National Academy of Sciences, *Genetic Screening: Programs, Principles, and Research* (Washington, DC, 1975).

12 P. Reilly, *Genetics, Law, and Social Policy*, pp. 79–83.

13 US Senate, 94th Congress, *Hearing, Subcommittee on Health, Committee on Labor and Public Welfare, First Session, on S1619, S1620, S1714, S1715,* July 15 1975.

14 Gerald James Stine, *Biosocial Genetics: Human Heredity and Social Issues* (New York: Macmillan, 1977), pp. 507–8. See also T. Powledge, 'Genetic Screening as a Political and Social Development'; and National Academy of Sciences, *Genetic Screening: Programs Principles and Research*; Marc Lappe, *Genetic Politics: The Limits of Biological Control* (New York: Simon & Schuster, 1979); P. Reilly, *Genetics, Law and Social Policy*; and Samuel P. Bessman and Judith P. Swazey, 'PKU: A Study of Biomedical Legislation', in E. Mendelsohn, J. Swazey, and I. Taviss (eds), *Human Aspects of Biomedical Innovation* (Harvard University Press, 1971), pp. 55–7.

15 David A. Jackson and Stephan P. Stich (eds), *The Recombinant DNA debate,* (Englewood Cliffs: Prentice Hall, 1979).

16 Irene Taviss, 'Problems in the Social Control of Biomedical Science and Technology', in E. Mendelsohn, J. Swazey, and I. Taviss (eds), *Human Aspects of Biomedical Innovation,* pp. 3–45.

Part 2

Action and structure: the cognitive organization of symbolic practice

4 Philosophical aspects of the macro-micro problem

Rom Harré

[*Chapter 4 may be called another attempt at a radically micro-sociological reconstruction of macro-phenomena based on differentiations such as between individual and structure. Harré argues that the talk about macro-collectives as a separate (and separately researchable) layer of social reality makes sense if these collectives can be proven to be structured. To have structure means to have emergent (macro) properties* by virtue of *the structure and* in addition to *those displayed by individual members. However, such structures can only be proven to exist for middle-range collectives like families or organizations. Consequently, true macro-concepts like that of a social class must be considered as rhetorical classifications which have no empirically identifiable referent other than that of the component individuals of which they form a sum.*

Harré also holds that there is another group of macro-phenomena which consist of the effects of the unintended consequences of micro- or middle-range action. These macro-effects can only be proven to exist indirectly, since by definition we have no way of knowing them in advance. It is the macro-order composed of such effects which acts as a selection environment for social action, for example by determining which of the micro-mutations of social life will take off and persist as a component of social change. As we shall see, there is some similarity between Harré's hypothesis of unintended consequences (see section 4 of the Introduction, pp. 25–30) and the conception proposed by Giddens in chapter 5.]

In order to understand the difficulties which beset the realization that the social order may extend beyond those relations which are under individual control, and even beyond those of which an individual can be aware, we need to get some metaphysical distinctions and foundations entirely clear and well-ordered. The study of these foundations is complicated by the fact that there seem to be two distinct metaphysical questions about the way the concepts of micro- and macro-social structures are to be properly formulated, which are yet closely interrelated.

1   Metaphysics

The first problem that emerges directly from contemplating the possibility of a structured and causally efficacious social order 'larger' than the institutions and other collectives we can comfortably comprehend, is that of the ontological status of collectives in general. The problem of the metaphysical status of collectives is already present in the relationship between human individuals and micro-social orders, for example families. However, if we can get a grip on the metaphysical questions as exemplified in concepts appropriate to smaller-scale collectives it might be possible to transfer, by analogy, some of those insights to the understanding of collective concepts as they might apply to some vast macro-order. I am not at present concerned with addressing the more radical question of whether, if the macro-order exists, any of its properties could be known, or the even more radical question of whether it is proper to talk of macro-orders existing or not existing at all. The issue at this level of analysis is addressed on the assumption that at least it is intelligible to entertain existential hypotheses.

Why should anyone have doubts about the status of social collectives? A little elementary analysis suggests that co-ordinate mass behaviour of groups of people might be the product of several different forms of collectivity, of deeply different metaphysical status. Mass behaviour can originate from groups of people, each of whom has similar beliefs, dispositions or aspirations to each of the others. I shall call groups of this kind 'taxonomic collectives'. There are no real relations between the members, by virtue of which they are members of this kind of collective. The similarities between their beliefs is something which is conceived in the mind of an observer, as a ground for grouping them together. Social psychologists are prone to speak of 'groups' and 'group behaviour' when they have identified merely taxonomic collectives, with 'shared' beliefs.[1] But 'shared' is ambiguous. It could refer to real sharing, where something unitary is divided or even replicated by some causal process from one individual to another. For instance one individual can teach or persuade another to accept a belief. Usually when one speaks of something shared this refers to no more than a similarity between the beliefs of one individual and another; and this does not entail the existence of any real relation between them.

But there are human groups whose collectivity comes about through real relations between the members, such as those engendered by legal or conventional demands, systems of respect and deference, or the social realization of biological links. A collectivity of this sort has a structure, and usually involves roles and role-holders, and opens up the possibility of representative or vicarious action, such as that undertaken by presidents, kings and ambassadors on behalf of their nations or corporations. Some structured collectives are so tightly ordered and so closely bounded that they may appear as supra-individuals.

The psychological processes involved in the maintenance of a collective and in modes of action within it will be very different, depending on whether the collective is structured or merely taxonomic.

(a) Are some structured collectives *supra-individuals*? I pose this question not as an issue of fact but of metaphysics. A metaphysical question is answered by setting out the criteria for judgment, in this case for anything to count as an individual, that is, to be a distinct being, and then asking oneself whether a being such as a structured collective could meet these criteria. The simplest criteria, applicable in the physical world, and to a qualified extent in the world of human beings, can be set out as follows. For an entity to be counted as an individual:

(i)   it must be *continuous in time*;
(ii) it must occupy a *distinctive* and *continuous* region of *space* or a distinctive and continuous path through space;
(iii) it must have *causal powers*.

The third requirement is necessary in order for us to be able to distinguish individuals from mere spatio-temporal regions. The claim that there is an individual present in some region of space-time is empty (though not necessarily meaningless) unless there is some way in which that individual can influence the world as we experience it, directly or indirectly. It must have causal powers. Clearly, in the physical world, there are many collectives, aggregates of parts, which are supra-individuals, according to these criteria. An animal is an individual, though it has parts that are individuals, its cells. Characteristically, in a scientific analysis of the physical world, hierarchies of types of individuals are set up, 'higher' types being aggregates of 'lower'. Here we have a model for the understanding of supra-individuals, and criteria for their ready identification.

(b) Do collectives have distinctive properties? The physical sciences recognize the distinction between molar properties, that is properties of collectives considered as individuals, and molecular properties, that is properties of components considered as lower-order individuals. There is no presumption in the physical sciences that the parts of a collective should exhibit the same range of properties as the collective itself (a hot collective need not be presumed to have hot components); nor that the only properties possible for a collective should be aggregates of the properties of its parts. For example, that which used to be called the 'valency' of a chemical atom is not an aggregate property of the characteristic properties of the protons, neutrons and electrons that make it up. Equally, the characteristic properties of cells do not include the capacity to think, though certain aggregates of cells do have that capacity. Thus we are accustomed to the idea of 'emergent properties'.

The criteria by which we would identify a property as *emergent* are implicit in the above brief discussion, namely that a determinable manifested by the whole is not manifested by any of its parts, for instance colour will be emergent if we have reason to think that the colours of material things are not to be found among atomic individuals, which are neither coloured nor not coloured. The claim that no part manifests an emergent property of a whole must be qualified by the restriction that it must not manifest that property when it is considered as an independent individual. For instance it is not clear that when *a* cell is part of a brain, there might not be occasions when, as a brain component, it might not properly be described as thinking.

In the physical and biological sciences the existence of an emergent property is explained by introducing hypotheses of *structure*. If an aggregate, considered as a collective, has properties which its components do not, there must be some extra property which is responsible for the collective supra-individual having causal powers which are manifested as emergent properties. In the physical and biological sciences the 'extra' property has turned out, almost without exception, to be structure. When isolated parts are brought together into a true collective particularly when the collective is sufficiently bounded to count as a supra-individual, they are likely to form a structure. When iron molecules are brought together to form a key, the emergent property or power that the key has to open a lock, is explained by the structure of the key, a structure which reflects a myriad relationships between individual iron molecules, but individuates the key.

There is little that is in any way problematic about any of this. Puzzles about emergence are routinely resolved in the physical and biological sciences by careful application of the distinctions and criteria I have briefly set out above. There is no particular difficulty about emergent properties if they are grounded in structure, since forming a structure is the most unproblematic way in which individuals can be brought together to form a collective which manifests a novel property. I suggested that one way of proceeding with the problem of supra-individuals in the social sciences is to try to transfer the arguments and insights that seem to work well in the theory of the natural sciences to the new arena.

Which, then, of the arguments, insights, conceptual distinctions and so on, comes over from the physical to the social context, and which do not? I want to suggest that while there is a natural application for the idea of structure and emergent property, there are difficulties with the concept of supra-individual, in social examples.

First of all, it is not at all clear that the spatio-temporal criteria, which are of such central importance in the physical sciences, have a *general* application in the techniques by which social collectives might be individuated. Many collectives, such as institutions, are obviously temporally discontinuous. For example what should we say about a university in the dead of night? The fact that this seems rather a silly question shows the relative unimportance of temporal continuity in individuating institutions. But some human collectives, such as an army in the field, are spatio-temporally bounded. When they cease to be spatially coherent they are a mere rabble.

Let us turn then to the third criterion, namely that a supra-individual should have distinctive causal powers. Here we are on firmer ground. It may be that one of the criteria which one might be inclined to employ would be that an individual, basic or supra, exists if 'it' can reasonably be said to have noticeable effects (though the absence of noticeable effects is no criterion for denying that it exists). If we could demonstrate distinctive causal powers, we might be able to justify the claim that committees are distinct beings from their members, that firms are supra-individuals distinct from the aggregate of their workers, and so on. But, even if such a case could be made, we are not entitled to ascribe to supra-individuals any properties other than powers to act in these ways. To demonstrate in what attribute these powers are grounded is another and much more difficult matter.

Take, for instance, the nuclear family. The individuals that make up such a collective, considered in relation to it, are constituted or created *as* father, mother and children by virtue of their relations to one another. The relational system creates both the social categories of membership and the individuals as satisfying the requirements for membership, and, *inter alia*, the family itself, since it is a set of individuals standing in those relations, that is a family. Perhaps structure, which was introduced in the physical case through the need to explain the manifestation of emergent properties by certain aggregates could serve as a fourth criterion defining an ultimate grounding for the idea of supra-individuals whether macro or micro, relative to the social order.

If collectives have causal powers distinctive from those of their component parts, the argument in (b) above suggests that the most economical hypothesis to explain such cases is that the collective is a structured aggregate of parts. In developing the arguments of this chapter I want to contrast extremes in a continuum of collectives of differing 'magnitude'. I shall presume that the ontological status of nuclear families and the like is indubitable. Sociologists and some historians blithely talk about such dubious entities as social classes, economic systems and historical forces. I shall focus my attention on this kind of talk. Universities, business firms, hospitals and the like present their own range of problems for conceptual analysis but I shall not deal with any of them in this paper. But the fact that macro-collectives do not satisfy any obvious spatio-temporal criteria for individuality need not bother us, since *structure* and *causal efficacy* have turned out to be the crucial attributes. I shall have occasion later in this paper to discuss the question of the causal powers of macro-collectives, macro-individuals and macro-structures. We shall see that these causal powers are, at least as far as they can be experienced, undifferentiated in their exercise and our concept of them is likely to be vague. So though even for large-scale collectives we are justified to some extent in accepting the idea of distinctive causal powers and of emergent properties, it is to claims about structure that we must look for the ultimate justification for taking macro-collective talk literally. It may be that, just as the family consists of internally related categories of beings, a macro-collective may consist in its members standing in certain internal, category-creating relations, the aggregate of such members being the collective and the internal relations its structure. This idea has considerable merit and has been made use of both by Adorno and by Bhaskar[2] in recent years. It will be discussed in more detail in connection with the epistemological problems of admitting collectives into our ontology with distinctive ranges of properties.

But we are not yet free of the tangles of metaphysics. There is a second class of metaphysical problems which stems directly from the assumptions that have been made above in connection with the possibility of using structure to identify supra-individuals. The question is more tractable if discussed in terms of micro-collectives. If some headway seems to have been made in that discussion its results can be cautiously generalized to include collectives of greater scale. The second range of metaphysical questions concerns the opposite analytical trend from that I discussed above. How are individuals influenced by having their being in collectives? There is an analogous problem in the physical sciences. Are there any mechanical properties which an individual could still properly be said to have if it were the only being in the universe? Mach's Principle, defining one form of contemporary cosmic mechanics, asserts that even that most apparently individualistic property, inertia, should be thought of as a relational property manifested by *a* body only by virtue of its location in the system of material bodies. In this and other cases physical scientists are familiar with radical relational analyses of attributes that are, at first sight, unique and stable attributes of individuals, *per se*. Could we say the same of the important properties ordinarily ascribed to individuals who are members of social collectives? Some properties that are attributed to individuals are clearly constituted by virtue of that individual standing in a certain relation to some other. For instance though we say that this or that woman is a wife, that state is constituted wholly by virtue of the woman standing in the marriage relation to a husband. There is no sense in which a single woman can be a wife, in the strict sense. In similar ways there is no sense in which a self-employed worker can be a manager or a faith healer a medical practitioner. There are very many such relational attributes constituting many commonsense categories.

The metaphysical question that this prompts is whether there must be a core human identity which is *absolutely independent* of the relational network, and which is, as it were, the essence of what it is to be a person. The question is somewhat more complicated than it looks, since like many questions that emerge from social analysis it can be posed in both a moral and a metaphysical sense. J. S. Mill conceived the question pretty much in a moral sense. One may recollect that he thought there were certain psychological features of human life that should be the province of individuals, and in which the possibility of their moral autonomy lay. The philosophical argument turned on how the boundaries of the sphere of privacy were to be defined, which in the end depended on arbitrary assignments of value to certain human goods.

The metaphysical form of the original question is not empirical either. It is partly an invitation to determine the concept of a person, defining what is to count as a human being properly so called. If a human mode of being is defined in terms of emergent properties generated by personal location in networks of social relations then there could be no core of identity by which a human being could be identified as a person independently of the social order, e.g. the relations constitutive of 'Soviet Man'. At most there could be biological criteria for identifying members of the species *homo sapiens*, criteria which could be used by Martians wholly unfamiliar with human social organization. But those who hold to a socially constructivist view of personhood could quite properly insist that membership of the species did not entail that the being was properly a person. There could be no empirical refutation of that view.

But the question of the kind of criteria properly to be adverted to is not entirely a matter of convention and political and moral conviction. Since human beings can be categorized by biological attributes such as sex or colour which are independent of the social network, and notoriously these attributes play a role in the handing out of respect and contempt, should they not be thought of as defining a core identity? But in order for an attribute, even a physical attribute, to be a socially relevant property it must be endowed with social meaning. But whether the meaning it gets is degrading or enhancing of social standing, for instance, must depend upon the actual society which defines it. That this philosophical point correctly identifies the logic of these attributes is confirmed by the facts of historical relativity of the social meaning of these and other physical attributes.

How does this dénouement relate to the micro-macro problem? A proof of the causal efficacy and hence the reality of the most macro of social orders would be forthcoming if it were demonstrable that there were person-defining categories which derived from the location of people in relational networks of the largest scale. However those person-categorizing relations that we do find actually effective in social life are constitutive of modest collectives of the order of firms, families and the like. Apart from the tendentious and highly problematic alleged attribute of 'social class' there seem to be no person-constitutive relations which are of greater scale than can be found in institutions of the middle range. To use observable 'class differences' to infer the existence and structure of an alleged class system is a *petitio principii*, since it pre-empts the prior question of whether observable 'class differences' can be explained by reference to more modest and local relational systems defining more domestic social orders. Further it may be possible to show that macro-class talk is a mystifying technique by which the real issues of social reform can be concealed in a cloud of rhetoric.

To summarize the argument of this part I set out three main distinctions within which discussion of the macro/micro 'problem' ought to be framed.

(i) The first distinction was between a set of individuals who form a group because each member has a property that is like that of each other member. Such a group may have no real interrelations, and the similarity may be only a matter of thought. I called groups like these '*taxonomic collectives*'. They exist, as it were, in the mind of the classifier. On the other hand, there are groups which are constituted by a structure of relations by which individuals come to have their identifying properties. A *relational or structured group* has at least the possibility of forming some stronger kind of aggregation than merely that of being classified as one group, and in particular its structure could be so articulate as to ground emergent properties.

(ii) Once structure has been admitted amongst the relations constitutive of the group and its members one can differentiate groups relative to the *kinds of relations* that obtain. For instance an institution is liable to reveal and to depend upon asymmetrical rather than symmetrical relations, for instance authority, respect and the like, rather than friendship. Though economic relations are certainly real it is very doubtful if they form a sufficiently articulated structure to admit of grounding emergent properties.

(iii) Finally it is possible to consider structured groups as to whether and to what degree they are bounded in space and continuous in time; or exhibit some other form of *boundedness*. Only groups which have this further level of integrity can be considered as possible *supra-individuals*.

I am now in a position to lay down some fairly stringent conditions for the possibility that a macro-grouping on whatever scale should exhibit interesting, for instance causal, properties. If a macro-grouping is merely taxonomic, as it might be with the group of British passport holders, then little of interest can be concluded from the demonstration that such a group exists, other than historical matters and questions raised by the presence of the group. But if it can be established that the grouping involves properties which are constitutive both of members of the group and of that group itself by virtue of the existence of internal relations, then all sorts of possibilities can now be considered, including the possibility that the group is a supra-individual. However, it should now be obvious that merely showing that a taxonomic group exists in a certain population is no ground for concluding that that group has any other, more elaborate, structure. And if it is the case that inductive sociological methods can establish no more than the fact of taxonomic groupings when the scale is greater than that of institutions and the like, there is a clear limitation to the empirical employment of macro-social concepts.

2   Macro-social concepts as rhetorical devices

Later in this paper I shall be arguing that epistemological considerations force one to be fairly sceptical about the knowledge claims that have been made by macro-sociologists concerning the properties and even the existence of the collectives to which they make reference. I have in mind such entities as Wallerstein's 'world-system'.[3] In consequence the status of alleged large-scale macro-groupings must be equivocal. At the very best they might be conceived as theoretical entities whose existence and whose non-dispositional attributes must be hypothetical. Is this an adequate explanation of the appearance of *words* for macro-collectives and their properties in the speech of sociologists, politicians and even ordinary folk? Suppose we examine the way some macro-concepts are used in everyday life, by looking at the uses of words like 'France', 'working class' and 'economic depression'. On the face of it the most convincing exegesis of the uses of the word 'France' is a taxonomic term, a way of speaking about the French and their geographical location. While everyone who is French must share some attribute with every other there need be no suggestion that the collective so formed is structured sufficiently to be properly considered a supra-individual. Just the same possibility exists for the exegesis of 'working class' and 'economic depression'. But will this exegesis explain how these words are used in everyday life? Do they imply anything more than taxonomic collectivity?

In phrases such as 'the true interest of the working class' and so on there seems to be a clear implication of macro-status, at the very least as a structured collective, and perhaps as a supra-individual. But if we look at the micro-interaction in which these uses occur, it seems that their main context is that of discussion, argument and persuasion. In short the supra-individual implications are rhetorical rather than ontological. Why offer this more complex exegesis when the obvious implications suggest something else?

The arguments for a rhetorical interpretation are essentially epistemological. If we take seriously the idea that *the* working class is a structured collective we should expect to be able to find some kind of empirical test or proof for this suggestion. In particular there must be real relations obtaining between its members, in terms of which it is constituted as an entity, while it constitutes its members. Commonplace, commonsense knowledge about the social world suggests that no such relations exist. In critical discussions of a recent work by Halsey *et al.*,[4] commentators drew attention to the unsubstantiated use of terms like 'class' to analyse the structure of a national social order through an alleged empirical system of classifications. Critics urged that the criteria by which we actually classify each other which are relevant to social issues such as respect, right to certain categories of work and so on, lead to a conception of a nation as a mosaic of overlapping groupings which, considered on a macro-scale, can be no more than what I have called 'taxonomic'. There can be no presumption of an ordered hierarchy. As one commentator put it: 'What has a

Cornish miner in common with a Hull fisherman?' And the answer is: 'Very little'. So the idea that they both belong in the same layer of an ordered hierarchy is wildly implausible. It is by no means clear that there is any set of relations in terms of which an individual typical of either of these groups could stand in relation to a Glaswegian professor or an East Anglian accountant.

What then is the role of a concept like 'working class' as it appears in the talk and the writing that occurs in social life? One answer might be, as I have suggested, that it is not functioning as a term with an empirical referent but as a device for making points, taking up a stance and so on; in short that it forms part of the apparatus of the expressive order. It is one among many devices for dealing with the respect–contempt hierarchies within which one moves, in the belief system that makes up the psychological basis of one's society. Think of the ways claims to be French or accusations of being Anglo-Saxon function in the expressive rhetoric of talk within the EEC. This is not to deny that terms of this sort have an empirical edge to them. But I want to insist that if there is any claim to their having more than merely taxonomic import, that claim would have to be substantiated by extensive and very difficult empirical demonstration. In the absence of such demonstration we must assume that their status is conceptual and their uses rhetorical.

3   The epistemology of groups

So far in this discussion I have been dealing only with claims about the existence of groups, and discussing the status of the macro-micro distinction in terms of its extremes. My conclusion has been that while there can be little dispute that there are taxonomic macro-groups on the largest scale, it is also clear that only relatively small-scale micro-groups can be unproblematically identified as ordered entities, that is as relational, structured and, in some cases, supra-individuals. But why couldn't one set about finding out whether a nation or an alleged social class, or whatever, was a structured and ordered system? To answer this question I shall turn to a brief exposition of the epistemological problems that beset the study of groups. It might be argued that it is obvious that any large-scale macro-group could be no more than a human construction, a taxonomic grouping, because we could know nothing else about larger groupings than whether or not their proposed membership of individuals did or did not have any common properties. The use of a macro-terminology could not be other than rhetorical. It might be that there were techniques by which something more could be found out about alleged macro-groupings, to test hypotheses about structure, internal relations and the like. A very similar issue has been discussed in the greatest detail in the recent past, namely Popper's thesis of methodological individualism.[5] That debate was notable for its abstract and theoretical character. The considerations to which I want to draw attention are somewhat obliquely related to the individualism issue since they concern actual studies and real methods in use by sociologists. I want to show that none of them has any claim to our allegiance when applied to larger-scale macro-groupings of men.

My argument turns on showing that there exists a proper micro-methodology, but that by its very nature it cannot be generalized to the extremes of the macro-pole of the spectrum of collectives.

The study of the structures and attributes of small-scale collectives such as families and modest institutions has been much facilitated by the development, from various sources, of the *ethogenic* methodology. It involves assembling members' understandings and interpretations of the institution and the events which make up its life, and negotiating these with an outside observer's ethnography. To call this methodology 'ethogenic' is to emphasize the normative character of the knowledge and systems of belief used by members to act in accordance with rules and interpretations, adherence to which generates the collective. This normative character is further emphasized in the way members demonstrate their expressive loyalty by the rhetorical deployment of the very rules and interpretations in the talk which sustains the collective and their own self presentations against the threat of actual or potential violations and disruptions. The central methodological point follows from the theory that it is acting in accordance with a belief-system which creates a micro-collective, so the form of that collective can be grasped by discovering what is the belief-system and its associated conventions.

On this view even such apparently biological groupings as nuclear families are not natural objects. The members must believe that they stand in certain relations, some no doubt biological, but they must also believe that there are culturally prescribed ways in which those relations are to be realized in the expressive order. Only in these prescribed ways do their actions serve as vehicles for the acts of respect, deference, and so on which maintain the group as a structured collective. This constructive quality of social action is even more clearly visible in those collectives which have no obvious biological foundation, such as business firms, fan clubs and the like. Ethogenic methods have proved very powerful in empirical application.[6] The methodology as briefly outlined and its relation to the way in which micro-collectives are actually brought into being and maintained can be illuminated by relating it to an important methodological distinction, similar to that used by linguists. It is important to distinguish studies directed to building up a theory of competence, that is a theory of the knowledge that members have to be able to act in ways recognizably appropriate to, and constitutive of, the collectives to which they belong, from studies directed to a theory of performance, that is a theory of how on particular occasions an individual actor draws on the corpus of knowledge relevant to the occasions in question to control his or her contribution to the social fabric. Since performance is necessarily individual while competence might involve a social distribution of a corpus of knowledge, from the point of view of micro-sociology it is the competence theory that counts. It is that theory that represents the body of knowledge and belief that must be shared and shared out among the members. Sociologists, using ethogenic methods, can come to know what the folk know, including both tacit and explicit social knowledge, individually located and socially distributed elements of the corpus. The development of role-play methods and particularly of scenario-reconstruction,[7] has allowed for the possibility of tests for hypotheses about members' knowledge. Proposals as to the local rule-systems and interpretative categories can be used to construct scenarios for the simulation of various activities of micro-collectives, and members' intuitions as to the propriety of these performances used as a check on the accuracy of the competence theory. There has been some confusion in the discussion of role-play methods, as if they were a way of formulating and testing performance theories. But there is no evidence that real people really acting perform their actions like stage players imitate, quote or simulate the actions of real people. A performance psychology, even for micro-collectives, is still in its infancy and I shall say no more about it here.

One might be tempted to generalize the successful ethogenic methodology, if one saw it as a realization of the Weberian idea of ideal types, to formulate an epistemology for the study of macro-collectives, nations, economic systems, social movements and so on. It would involve collecting many more accounts and negotiating them within the context of a bolder ethnography. There is an obvious theoretical objection to this. While there is every reason for thinking that micro-collectives are constituted by folk acting in accordance with their beliefs about proper and improper conduct, etc., the folk neither have, nor could have, beliefs about the *conduct* which would be constitutive of macro-collectives of any scale, since it is a central doctrine of the macro-collective approach that there are *ramifying systems of unintended consequences*, and that it is these that, as systems, are constitutive of the non-taxnomic aspects of a large-scale collective. So any route from people's declared norms of interpretation, maxims and so on is blocked by this consideration. On the other hand the second requirement, that there be an ethnography of the social order from which to negotiate with the folk about their theories and interpretations about that order, can hardly be met without circularity, since to have such an ethnography would presume an overall grasp of the structure and so on of that collective, which is just what the methodology is directed to achieving.

Of course we all know that none of this has stopped sociologists going on with their activities; in particular going on distributing questionnaires and then working up the results with the help of various mathematical techniques. I shall not retraverse the well trodden area of methodological criticism of naive sociological technique,[8] but merely sum up the main lines of criticism as reminders.

Criticism has turned on three main points. First of all, there is the problem created by the fact that asking anyone a question, in whatever circumstances, is an invitation not only to answer the question, but to use the fact of answering that question one way or another as an occasion for an act of *self-presentation*. Careful ethogenic style studies have shown that this phenomenon occurs even when the questionnaire is being administered by a machine. The second line of criticism turns on the problem of the extreme *context dependence* of the interpretation given to apparently straightforward questions. Demographic surveys are least affected by this phenomenon, for instance census returns on sex ratios, such as those used by Secord and Guttentag.[9] But, as is nicely illustrated in a Doonesbury cartoon (14 September 1980), the question of whether you like or dislike a President is not an unequivocal question. Disapproving of President Carter is quite a different thing from disapproving of President Nixon. This problem is exacerbated by the well-known distinction between the attitudes and opinions one avows in talk and those one evinces in action. In general these are likely to be rather different. The third criticism turns on something more subtle. It has been pointed out that, in some cases at least, propositions that look like and are presented as empirical sociological generalizations, on closer scrutiny turn out to be necessary truths, reflecting some *conceptual relation*. Some recent studies of the social conditions that engender personal popularity have been shown to be seriously confused, setting about empirical studies to verify statements that simply define 'popularity'.[10]

If all this amounts to a breakdown of a methodology which presumed that macro-social concepts had macro-social referents, the best solution would be to abandon the presumption. Suppose macro-social concepts do not in general have macro-social referents, what is their role in social talk? I have already sketched an answer: the role of macro-social concepts is rhetorical, not referential. But to secure a measure of conviction, I shall try to illustrate what is meant by making that step with an example, the vexed problem of how we should understand the term 'social class'.

4   'Social class', a misleading concept

The first hint that this concept may not be as simple in its uses as appears comes from noticing how it came into English in a social context. In origin 'class' is a term of art, having a technical sense in logic. Before the importation of the term into the social context in the course of the nineteenth century, the vocabulary with which the larger structural groupings of society were discussed consisted of terms like 'order', 'estate' and 'station'. It was almost impossible to formulate a theory involving gross macro-hierarchies with this vocabulary. For instance the use of the term 'station' suggests a network of relations rather than any simple hierarchy. By the 1820s the simple hierarchical conception was beginning to gain ground and the phrase 'higher orders, lower classes' began to appear. The first use of 'class' in any social sense in English goes back to 1656, but the qualifications are fairly modern. Thus the first use of 'lower class' seems to have been in 1772, and the distinction between 'working class' and 'leisure class' seems to have been introduced by Owen in 1816. How far a changing organization of society was reflected in the changing uses of the term is hard to say, of course. I will resist any speculations on that point.

These uses of 'class' are one and all extensional. The 'lower classes' are groups of people. But taxonomic terms can also be used intensionally, to refer to the attributes that individuals must display to be counted as members of such and such a group. In modern usage 'class' is often used in an intensional way, in such a phrase as 'his class'. The first use in this sense is credited to Disraeli in 1863.

The pejorative, extensional use with its implications of low prestige, manual labour and the like apparently derives from Macfarlane's translation of the Communist manifesto, published in 1850. I take that use to be transparently rhetorical.

It is not surprising that with such an ancestry the usage in modern English is thoroughly equivocal. In many cases 'class' is used taxonomically, that is for referring to a group brought into existence by the conceptual activity of the sociologist through the choice of certain membership criteria. The question of whether there is a collective *in rerum natura* remains open. But cross-cut with this is a use which suggests that the referent is a structured collective, having distinctive properties and causal powers. For instance, attributes like 'influence' and 'privilege', and even 'power' have been predicated of 'classes'. If the term is being used distributively then to say that a class has power is just an obscure way of saying that certain people have power, though why that method of expression is chosen would need an explanation in terms of rhetoric and indeed mystification, particularly if it appears in some form of political discourse. If the term 'class' is meant to imply a structured collectivity then this radically alters the sense in which the quality 'power' can be attributed to it. The confusion is further confounded by failure to distinguish ways in which people are located in the practical order (for example relative to the social organization of material production) and the ways they are located in the expressive order (the social organization of hierarchies of respect and of contempt). Some sociologists have suggested using 'class' for the former and 'status' for the latter. But the trouble with that suggestion is that while 'class' is equivocal and can be used distributively and collectively, it is very hard to see how 'status' could possibly be used collectively. The only resolution that seems to me to make sense is to abandon the idea that this kind of talk (even when backed up by a mathematical rhetoric of statistics) is empirical and to treat it as rhetorical.

In sum, then, the attempt to take the notion of 'social class' literally as unequivocally referring to a distinctive kind of macro-entity is implausible, either tacitly treating an analytical or criterial proposition as if it were empirical, or, on the other hand, treating a distributive proposition as if it were collective. In either case there is no empirical 'macro' use for the term. Is 'class' typical, and must we abandon all hope of an empirical macro-sociology? In the sense of traditional macro-sociology I am afraid little can be rescued; nevertheless, I do want to argue for a distinctive and ineliminable use for the idea of an autonomous macro-order, though in my application of this notion there will be no suggestion that we could possibly know its occurrent properties.

5   The uses of the macro

It does not follow from any of the above arguments that there is no place for hypotheses about the existence of macro-social orders, having emergent properties by virtue of some structural feature of the total flux of intended and unintended consequences of interpersonal social actions. The above arguments forbid any empirical claims about the nature of such properties. But though there may be a prohibition on such claims it is still open to a sociologist to hypothesize that there are macro-structures with certain generalized dispositions, through which influences are exerted on the flux of daily action. To avoid slipping into the same errors I have identified in the earlier sections of this chapter I begin with a brief examination of the notion of social power. Consonant with the micro-macro confusions in other areas of sociology there are characteristic equivocations in the way the concept of 'power' is used. Generally our idea of power suggests that it stems from some identifiable source and that it is focused upon a patient. In this usage only individuals (they need not be only at the level of human beings) can exercise power. This is not a matter of fact, but a reflection on the rules according to which we use the notion. In this sense power is usually taken to imply responsibility since the source of power is taken to be an agent. There is a temptation to use 'power' for the way macro-entities can exert influences of one sort or another. I take this usage to be transparently rhetorical since it is clearly involved in exploiting the responsibility implications of that use, so that a class which is said to have power is thereby implied to have responsibility. Once this kind of loose talk is allowed we are well set on the way to the mystifications of macro-politics. But none of the moral implications can really be drawn. The illusion that there are such implications stems from swallowing an equivocation between collective and distributive, micro and macro uses of a concept. By reserving, say, 'influence' for the causal efficacy of large-scale macro-collectives we cannot exploit the conceptual connection between 'power' and 'responsibility', and an independent argument would have to be built up to show that there could be macro-responsibility.

An argument to support the distinction between focused agency and diffuse causal influence can be developed by considering how role position is related to power, in the strict acceptance of that term. The point has been nicely made by Stephen Lukes.[11] Power, he argues, stems from the intersection between individual capacities for focused action and 'opportunity', where opportunity is determined partly by macro-structural properties, whether they can be known or not, and by the individual's capacity to see that there is an opportunity, also seen by Lukes as something of essentially social origin. In short the macro-structure provides necessary but not sufficient conditions for the exercise of power. I can illustrate the point with what I shall call 'the Rasputin effect'. Tsar Nicholas as the legitimate occupant of the Russian Imperial throne was thereby presented with the necessary conditions for the exercise of power, that is, in Lukes's term, he had the opportunity. In order for us to accept this proposition we do not need to know what were the structural and/or emergent properties of the social organization of the Russian state by virtue of which that opportunity existed. But Nicholas lacked personal efficacy, a personal capacity for the exercise of power, that is focused agency, with which Rasputin was endowed in more than sufficient measure.

Opportunity, I would like to emphasize, is one of a number of specific concepts in the genus 'influence', the common characteristic of which is the macro-social origin and unfocused form of the causal influence to which the term refers. I will round off this paper with a brief sketch of a theory of social change in which the notion of diffuse social influence from unknown structural properties of a macro-order plays a part. For a fully detailed exposition of this theory see my *Social Being*.[12] If there is no way in which we can know what are the macro-properties of social orders then hypotheses about those properties cannot play a leading empirical role in our account of social change. The solution to the problem this poses for the theorist of social change is to propose some version of a populational or mutation/selection theory of that change, in which mutations occur in micro-social practices and these spread or fail to spread through the society by virtue of some diffuse influence exerted by the macro-social order, whatever that might be. We can admit some measure of Lamarckism in the relation between selection environment and mutant practice, mediated by growing but imperfect social knowledge, without being tempted into any extravagant claims about social causation. The Lamarckian relationships are likely to change, becoming stronger as more anthropological and historical knowledge becomes part of the culture.

But this leaves the sources of mutation largely unspecified. This problem can be partially solved by returning to the distinction between practical and expressive social orders, a distinction that can be empirically established within collectives of a scale towards the micro-end of the spectrum. The social organization of a hospital that is concerned with cure is readily and empirically differentiable from the social organization that is concerned with reputation, honour and the like. Of course these orders interact, but it is clear from ethogenic research that they are distinct.[13] Felt disparities between one's location in one of these orders and one's location in the other provides some motivation towards efforts to better one's position in one, but it may, in case there are many like oneself, lead to attempts to reform and promulgate novel social practices (students and faculty sharing lunching facilities) which redress the balance. Will they or will they not 'take'? It depends on the macro-order or orders. But all we can say of them is that by virtue of some properties or other macro-orders have a disposition to filter out some novel practices but not others. In short the macro-orders serve as selection environments exerting a diffuse influence upon the course of life.

How can this theory be defended against a charge of empty rhetoric? It is clearly germane to a defence of anarchistic against socialist radical politics. Happily there is a simple defence to hand. As I argued at the beginning of this paper there are some macro-properties which are not susceptible to the standard epistemological criticisms. Since there is little that is negotiable about whether a human being is male or female (borderline cases must surely be a very small element in the matter) demographic properties of collectives are reliable and transparent in ways that other alleged properties are not. If, then, a convincing example of the mutation/selection format in use can be found, in which the selection environment is defined by a demographic macro-property, the case is made for the intelligibility and propriety of that format for explanations of social change. In their recent *Too Many Women* Secord and Guttentag[14] have shown how changed social practices, conceived in a dialectic tension between women's felt position in the practical order and their felt position in the expressive order, spread or fail to spread by virtue of a diffuse selective influence exerted by the demographic structures of certain social collectives.

Notes

1 H. Tajfel, *Differences between Social Groups* (London: Academic Press, 1978).
2 R. Bhaskar, *The Possibility of Naturalism* (Brighton: Harvester Press, 1979).
3 I. M. Wallerstein, *The Modern World System* (New York: Academic Press, 1976).
4 A. H. Halsey, A. F. Heath and J. M. Ridge, *Origins and Destinations: Family, Class and Education in Modern Britain* (Oxford: Clarendon Press, 1979).
5 K. R. Popper, *The Poverty of Historicism* (Boston: Beacon Press, 1957). For a discussion of methodological individualism, see J. O'Neill (ed.), *Modes of Individualism and Collectivism* (London: Heinemann, 1973).
6 See for example P. Marsh, E. Rosser and R. Harré, *The Rules of Disorder* (London: Routledge & Kegan Paul, 1978): and M. Kreckel, *Implicit Social Knowledge* (London: Academic Press, 1981).
7 G. Ginsburg, *Emerging Strategies of Social Scientific Research* (Chichester: Wiley, 1979).
8 For this criticism, see for example M. Brenner, P. Marsh and M. Brenner (eds), *The Social Context of Method* (London: Croom Helm, 1978).
9 P. F. Secord and M. Guttentag, *Too Many Women* (forthcoming, 1981).
10 M. Gilbert, 'On Being Categorized by Others', in R. Harré (ed.), *Life*

Sentences (Chichester: Wiley, 1979).

11 S. Lukes, *Essays in Social Theory* (Columbia University Press, 1977).
12 R. Harré, *Social Being* (Totowa: Rowman-Littlefield-Adams, 1980), particularly chapters 15 and 16.
13 E. Goffman, *Asylums* (Garden City: Anchor Books, 1961).
14 P. F. Secord and M. Guttentag, *Too Many Women.*

5 Agency, institution, and time–space analysis

Anthony Giddens

[*Chapter 5 conceives of the existing micro-macro problem as a problem of the gap between action theory and institutional analysis: in institutional analysis, agents are 'written off' as capable and knowledgeable actors, and action theory neglects the temporal and spatial extension and stability of structured social action.*

Giddens proposes to overcome the gap by means of his concept of the duality of structure. *Structure is seen to consist of the rules and resources which are instantiated in social systems. In social life, actors draw upon these rules and resources, which thereby 'structure' their actions. At the same time the structural qualities which generate social action are continually reproduced through these very same actions.*

However, like Harré, Giddens argues that the knowledgeability and capability of social actors is bounded by the unintended consequences of social action which condition social reproduction. By drawing upon their knowledgeability and capability, actors reproduce the structural qualities of the system limited by the constraints posed by the unintended consequences of previous social actions.

It is clear that the unintended consequences thereby adopt a key role in the explanation of social change, since it is they which presumably may decisively 'divert' social action from a structured course. Note, however, that the macro emerges from this chapter perhaps not so much a level of unforeseen effects of micro-action as a level of presumably shared structures of rules and resources continually reinstantiated in social action.]

1 The gap between action theory and institutional analysis

It is not difficult, I think, to see that the differentiation between so-called micro- and macro-sociological analysis has tended to coincide with a strongly embedded dualism in social theory and philosophy. This dualism has gone under various names and has taken various guises. In sociology, it has taken the form of an opposition between theories which emphasize human agency or 'action' on the one side, and theories which emphasize 'institutional analysis' or 'structural analysis' on the other. In philosophy, it has normally taken the form of a contrast between those conceptions which emphasize the primacy of the 'subject' (the knower or the locus of sense-experience) and those which take their point of departure from the 'object' (the social or natural world that shapes the experience of the human being).

When we look at the development of the major traditions of social theory, we can set up a theorem which, broadly speaking, summarizes the division I have in mind. The theorem is: 'strong on action theory, weak on institutional analysis'. The reverse also holds: 'strong on institutional analysis, weak on action theory'. That is to say, those traditions of thought which have attributed some importance to human action – to the everyday phenomenon that we have reasons for what we do, and that those reasons in some way enter into the very nature of what we do – have on the whole not provided sophisticated treatments of the overall institutional structuring of societies. On the other hand, most traditions which have placed their main emphasis upon institutional or structural analysis have not made adequate recognition of the significance of human agency. Rather than attempting to provide a general classification of social theories in respect of this dualism, let me mention two particular examples of eminent sociological authors whose writings can serve to illustrate what I have in mind: Erving Goffman, on the one hand, and R. K. Merton, on the other. Goffman's writings, I would say, do give centrality to the notion of action: not as an abstract concept, but as exemplified by his style of sociological work. Those of Merton – and I am thinking here primarily of Merton's by now classical essays on functionalism in sociology – fall into the opposing category I have mentioned above.

First of all it is important to define 'action' and 'institution'. The notion of human action has been much debated by philosophers, and has given rise to some considerable controversy. I shall understand 'action' here, however, to refer to two components or aspects of human conduct, which I shall refer to as '*capability*' and '*knowledge-ability*'. By the former of these I mean that, whenever we speak of human action, we imply the possibility that the agent 'could have acted otherwise'. The sense of this well-worn phrase is not easy to elucidate philosophically, and I do not propose to attempt to spell it out in any detail here. Its importance to social analysis is nevertheless very substantial indeed. By the second term, 'knowledgeability', I refer to the fact that the members of a society know a great deal about the workings of that society, and must do so if that society is recognizably a 'human society'. 'Capability' must not be identified with the ability of human beings to make 'decisions' or 'choices' – as is posited in 'utilitarian' social theory and also in most forms of game theory. 'Decision-making' is a sub-category of capability in general, if it refers to circumstances where individuals consciously confront a range of potential alternatives of conduct, and make some choice among those alternatives. The vast bulk of day-to-day social activity is predicated upon capability, the possibility of 'doing otherwise', but this is exercised as a routine feature of everyday behaviour. Much the same applies to knowledgeability: it is a basic mistake to equate the knowledgeability of human agents with what is known 'consciously', or 'held in mind' in a conscious way. The knowledgeable character of human conduct is displayed above all in the vast variety of tacit modes of awareness and competence that I call 'practical consciousness' as differentiated from 'discursive consciousness' – but which actors chronically employ in the course of daily life.

Goffman's writings display a strong awareness of each of these features of human action. In this sense, in my opinion, they are superior to those of many philosophers who have analysed problems of action theory in a more abstract way, but who have conceptualized action in a 'voluntaristic' manner, in terms of decision-making. Goffman treats human beings as capable and knowledgeable agents, who employ such capability and knowledgeability routinely in the production and reproduction of social encounters. The subjects Goffman portrays for the most part know what they are doing and why they are doing it: but much of this knowledge does not operate at an immediately 'conscious' level. Goffman's writings have an appeal for those unacquainted with the literature of sociology which many other sociological writers do not. The reader of Goffman also often experiences a feeling of illumination of his or her conduct that appears relatively rarely in other types of sociological writing. Why this is so is not simply the result of Goffman's own writing skill, however significant this may be. It is, I think, because Goffman shows us many of the things we 'know' about social conventions, and other aspects of society, but which we 'know' in a tacit rather than an explicit sense. They become clear to us only when he points them out, but nevertheless we do already know them: and very dazzling and complex these forms of tacit knowledge turn out to be, however much we ordinarily take them for granted as members of any given society. Consider what is involved in knowing a language. To 'know English' is to know a vast variety of syntactical and semantic rules and the contexts of their application. But linguists have to work very hard to elucidate what it is we already know, for if an ordinary English speaker is asked to actually spell out the rules and the pragmatics that he or she knows in order to speak the language, he or she is very unlikely to be able to identify more than a few of them. Goffman, in my view, is interested in laying bare the *tacit rules* and *resources* which competent social actors employ in the course of day-to-day life in much the same (although not exactly the same) sense as a linguist might be interested in specifying 'what we already know' when we speak a particular language, or language in general in so far as all tongues share common characteristics. Of course, this is not to say that Goffman is only concerned with tacit knowledge or practical consciousness; rather, he shows how the tacit and the explicit are interwoven in the texture of everyday social activity.

The theorem 'strong on action, weak on institutions' seems to me to apply with some force to Goffman's writings. Let me specify at this point how I want to use the term 'institution'. By institutions I mean structured social practices that have a broad spatial and temporal extension: that are structured in what the historian Braudel calls the *longue durée* of time, and which are followed or acknowledged by the majority of the members of a society. It is a banal enough criticism of Goffman's work to say that he does not explain, or seek to explain, the long-term development of the institutional frameworks within which his actors carry out the routines of their lives; but it seems to me one which is essentially correct. Just as, on a more philosophical plane, the forms of life within which Wittgenstein attempts to elucidate human action are taken by him as 'givens', so are the institutional backdrops which Goffman presumes. He has not elucidated an institutional theory of everyday life: rather, the institutional properties of the social systems within which his actors find themselves form an 'environment' of their action. This judgment, I consider, is not affected by Goffman's more recent work on the 'framing' of social interaction, since what is at issue is the absence of an attempt to explain how it is that 'frames' originate in the overall institutional context of societal development.

Goffman's predominant concern is with how social interaction is organized in and through the capable and knowledgeable conduct of human actors (and the strains and tensions in which such actors are involved). I want now to try to show that the reverse theorem, 'strong on institutions, weak on action' applies to Merton's codification of functionalism in what surely remains the most cogent presentation of functionalist theory to be found in the sociological literature. In his discussion of functionalism, Merton is certainly occupied mainly with what I have earlier identified as institutional analysis: with how the sociologist explains overall features of the organization and development of societies. Rather than concentrating his attention upon 'action', he is primarily concerned with how social forces operate 'behind the backs' of members of society so as to effect specific outcomes either stabilizing society or leading to social change.

Merton's now famous distinction between 'manifest' and 'latent functions', I shall try to show, fudges over some major characteristics of human action: in fact, precisely the two elements I have talked about above. I shall later want to say that the concept of function *en gros* is a redundant one in sociology – while accepting that functionalist authors have diverted attention to some fundamental exigencies of social analysis. But at the present juncture what is relevant are the deficiencies of the notion of 'manifest function': an aspect of Merton's analysis that has been much less discussed in the sociological literature than other of his concepts and arguments. Perusal of what Merton says indicates: (a) that 'manifest function' is ambiguous in respect of to whom it is manifest and in what way; and (b) that it is not at all clear what relation it bears to the capable and knowledgeable features I have held to be intrinsic to human action. These points can perhaps be most effectively demonstrated by reference to an example Merton himself uses. At one point in his articles he refers to the Hopi rain ceremonial as an illustration of the distinction between manifest and latent functions. The manifest function of the ceremonial, he says, is to produce rain. We know that it does not produce this result, and hence as sociologists we may enquire what accounts for its long-term persistence. Why does the institution of the rain ceremonial persist if it does not achieve its 'manifest function', that of bringing about rain? Merton's answer is to appeal to the 'latent functions' of the ceremonial in fostering group cohesion.

There are quite a number of critical points that can be made about this analysis, but I shall only concentrate upon those relevant to the present context. The 'manifest function' of the ceremonial is to produce rain. But what relation does this 'manifest function' bear to the reasons the participant actors have for enacting, and continuing to enact, the ceremonial? Is 'manifest function' equivalent to 'reason' (or perhaps 'purpose')? If it is, it is certainly a deficient idea, for it is evident that the reasons people have for engaging in a particular activity are not necessarily equivalent to the 'official charter' of that activity, and that reasons for participation may vary between individuals. Merton provides no analysis at all as to how the Hopi perceive the nature of the ceremonial: they are, as it were, 'written off' as capable and knowledgeable actors by the sociologist. Notice how different Merton's solution to the question of why the Hopi rain ceremonial persists is from that offered by Evans-Pritchard to a very similar problem. One of the issues Evans-Pritchard posed in his *Witchcraft, Oracles and Magic among the Azande* was the following. Why do the Azande go on believing in and practising sorcery (when we, as Western observers, know that it does not produce the results that the members of that society think it does)? Evans-Pritchard's answer, however, is quite different from Merton's, and does not disregard the capable, knowledgeable character of the conduct of his Zande subjects. What might initially appear to the outside observer as an 'irrational' cluster of beliefs and practices turns out to be a mode of behaviour which, if one is a member of Zande society, there are good reasons for continuing to accept. If one is 'inside' the system of belief upon which Zande sorcery is based, there is no difficulty in explaining events which seem to the Western observer to contravene the ideas to which the Azande adhere; moreover there are sceptics in Zande society as elsewhere.

Evans-Pritchard's portrayal of Zande witchcraft has figured prominently in debates about the universality or otherwise of 'rational belief', but it is not my intention to pursue the implications of these debates here. I wish only to point to the contrast between Merton's discussion of the Hopi ceremonial and Evans-Pritchard's view. My point is that what Merton talks of (ambiguously) as the 'manifest function' of the practices in question, Evans-Pritchard shows to be comprehensible in the light of treating the Azande as capable agents who know (tacitly and explicitly) a good deal about what they are doing. In saying this, I do not however want to suggest that the sort of analysis Merton pursues is without value, or that we should simply grasp the capable/knowledgeable character of human action and leave it at that. To do so would be equivalent to endorsing some sort of action theory without taking up the problem of how action analysis connects to institutional analysis. I want to propose that there are valid elements in the types of approach adopted by both authors, and that – appropriately explicated – they are not inconsistent but (in principle) complementary.

At this juncture what I have argued so far can be connected to the relation between so-called micro- and macro-sociological analysis. I repeat 'so-called' because I want to place the distinction in question, at least as it is ordinarily understood. One might perhaps suppose that the dualism between action and institutional analyses – which I have attempted to exemplify by particular examples but which I claim to be deeply embedded in sociology generally – is simply an expression of two perspectives in social analysis: the micro- and macro-sociological perspectives. Indeed, I think this is a view either explicitly adopted by many authors, or implicitly assumed to be the case. The origins of such a view can be traced in some part to specific developments within American sociology since the Second World War. One major theoretical tradition within American sociology, symbolic interactionism (to which one might claim Goffman's writings have a fairly strong affiliation), has generically embodied notions of human agency such as I have formulated it in this paper. The territory that symbolic interactionism has staked out has been mainly that of 'social encounters' in Goffman's sense: face-to-face interaction between individuals. A second, vying tradition, function-alism, has claimed the domain of institutional analysis, in the sense in which I have employed that term above. The two traditions of thought, of course, have been in some competition with one another; by and large, however, each seems to have respected the domain of the other. The result has been a sort of mutual accommodation, organized around a division of labour between micro- and macro-sociological analysis.

2   Structures as rules and resources

I do not think that the dualism I have described between action theory and institutional analysis can be resolved merely by declaring that there can be a sort of sharing-out of the tasks of sociology. The problems involved lie at a much deeper level than that. Micro-sociological analysis cannot be identified *ipso facto* with action theory, or macro-sociological analysis with the theory of institutions. I want to suggest here the outlines of a theoretical scheme which I have developed in more detail elsewhere.[1] It involves providing a conceptualization of the notions of 'action', 'institution' and 'structure', and indicating that there is a relation between these notions of rather profound importance for social analysis. I have already described in this paper, at least in a general way, how I wish to understand the concepts of action and institution. But I have not so far discussed the idea of 'structure', which has generally loomed large in those traditions, including functionalism ('structural functionalism') which I have associated with a predominant emphasis upon institutional analysis. In the English-speaking sociological world at least, I think it would be true to say that the concept of structure has operated largely as a received one, and one which has not been subject to detailed examination. We have only to think, for example, of the controversies surrounding functionalism to see that this is so. While the notion of function has been debated almost *ad nauseam*, the concept of structure, which is used at least as often in a great deal of sociological literature, has received far less attention. It seems to me that when most sociologists speak of 'structure', or 'social structure', they have in mind a 'patterning' of social relationships: they have in mind something like the girders of a building or the anatomy of a body. Moreover, they also tend to identify 'structure' with 'constraint'. The *locus classicus* of this second aspect of the idea of structure is of course Durkheim, even if he himself rarely used the term itself. I do not want to discard the conception that it is useful and indeed necessary to think of social relationships between individuals or collectivities as 'patterned' – which in my view means reproduced across time and space. But I do not propose to use the term 'structure' to refer to such patterning, nor do I wish to link structure only with constraint. The equation of structure with constraint, in fact, is one of the major elements creating the dualism between action and institutional theories. If structure is conceived of as merely 'external' to human action, it becomes regarded as a sort of autonomous form, independent of such action: or worse, as determining such action wholly through 'social causes'.

To consider how the concept of structure might usefully be reconceptualized in social analysis it is necessary to refer briefly to yet another popular sociological notion, that of 'system'. Most functionalist authors, and many others besides, employ both terms in their writings, and take the view that social systems *are* structures. The conception I want to propose, by contrast, is rather that social systems have *structural properties*, but are not as such structures – in the sense which I wish to attribute to that latter term. Most functionalist authors who have used the concepts of structure and system have thought of them as being distinguished from one another in the following way, whether or not they have employed direct organic analogies. The structure of a society is like the anatomy of a body, so the reasoning runs: it is the morphology, or 'patterning of parts'. If we inject the 'functioning' – if, in other words, we think of a living body – we have a system. A system is a 'functioning structure'. But however valid this may be in the case of a biological organism, it is inapplicable to a society. While one might (perhaps) accept that the anatomy of a body can be examined independently of its 'functioning' – as in the case of dissecting a corpse, which has stopped 'functioning' – such a separation has no sense when applied to a society. A society which ceases to 'function' – to be reproduced across time and space – ceases to be. Hence it is not surprising that the distinction between structure and system tends to collapse, so that the two become used more or less synonymously.

I want to propose that what most sociologists have thought of as 'structure', the 'patterning' of relationships between individuals or collectivities, can be best dealt with by the notion of system. Social systems (and overall societies, as encompassing types of social system) consist of reproduced relationships between individuals and (or) collectivities. As such, social systems have always to be treated as situated in time–space. If we understand 'system' in this way, we can free the concept of structure to perform other conceptual tasks.

English-speaking sociologists can learn a good deal here from a general tradition of thought which has until now remained largely alien: the French tradition of 'structuralism' (which, of course, like 'functionalism' is internally diverse). Although I think there are several important contributions which structuralist thought can render to Anglo-Saxon sociology, I shall confine my attention here to the concept of structure itself. The best place to locate a discussion of this is at origin, in the work of Saussure, by general agreement the founder of 'structuralist linguistics'. Somewhat confusingly, Saussure used the term 'system' rather than that of 'structure', but this is not relevant to my argument at this point. The notion of structure in structuralist linguistics has reference to a part/whole relation of a different kind to that expressed by the 'patterning' of social systems as described above. When I speak a sentence, the sentence is generated by, and understood by the listener in terms of, an 'absent totality': that 'absent totality' is the rest of the language, which has to be known for the sentence to be either spoken or understood. The relation between the speech act and the rest of the language is a moment/totality relation between 'presences' (the spoken words) and 'absences' (the unspoken, taken for granted knowledge of the rules and resources that constitutes 'knowing a language'). This is a structural relation, where 'structure' refers to the 'structured properties' of a language. One should notice that in this sense structure does not exist anywhere in time–space – as speech acts do – except in the form of memory-traces in the human brain, and except in so far as it is instantiated in speech acts, writing, etc.

I suggest that the concept of structure can be applied in sociology in a sense which is formally parallel to, and substantively in some part includes (since language-use is intertwined with social practices), the Saussurean conception of the structural properties of language. 'Structure' then refers to rules and resources instantiated in social systems, but having only a 'virtual existence'. The 'rules' involved here are social conventions, and knowledge of them includes knowledge of the contexts of their application. By resources I mean 'capabilities of making things happen', of bringing about particular states of affairs. There is a great deal more that can be said about the significance of resources than I shall be able to discuss in this paper, since the notion of resources can be applied to connect the structural study of domination with the analysis of the *power relations* involved in social systems.

To conceptualize structure as rules and resources (or structures as rule/resource sets) is to acknowledge that structure is both enabling and constraining. The one, so to speak, is the price of the other. This can again be illustrated by reference to the example of language. Every language involves relatively 'fixed' categorizations that constrain thought at the same time as they make possible a whole variety of conceptual operations that without language would be impossible.

3 Overcoming the dualism between action and institution: the duality of structure

This discussion of structure and system can now be connected to what I have remarked earlier about human agency. The structured properties of society, the study of which is basic to explaining the long-term development of institutions only exist (a) in their instantiation in social systems, made possible (b) by the memory-traces (reinforced or altered in the continuity of daily social life) that constitute the knowledgeability of social actors. This brings me to an essential part of my analysis, which consists in the thesis that the properties of society are fundamentally *recursive*. The recursive nature of the structural properties of social systems has to be understood as presuming what I call the *duality of structure*. The scheme I am putting forward here involves the claim that the traditional dualism of action theories and institutional theories can be avoided by the emphasis that action and structure – as I have formulated the notions – form a duality. That is to say, action and structure stand in a relation of logical entailment: the concept of action presumes that of structure and vice versa. I use the phrase 'duality of structure' to mean that structure is both the medium and outcome of the social practices it recursively organizes. The sense of this can be illustrated by Saussurean linguistics, so long as one keeps in mind the proviso noted above. In using examples drawn from linguistics I do not mean to imply that society is a language, or can be studied as a language – the characteristic error of structuralism, in fact. So this example should be treated cautiously, but none the less helps indicate clearly what I mean by the 'duality of structure'. When I utter a grammatical sentence, I draw upon various syntactical rules of the English language in order to do so. But the very drawing upon of those rules helps reproduce them as structural

properties of English as recursively involved with the linguistic practices of the community of English language speakers. The moment
(not in a temporal sense) of the production of the speech act at the
same time contributes to the reproduction of the structural qualities
that generated it. It is very important to see that 'reproduction' here
does not imply homology: the potential for change is built into every
moment of social reproduction (as a contingent phenomenon).

I can represent formally what I have been arguing as below:

Structure	Recursively organized rules and resources, having a virtual existence outside of time–space.
System	Reproduced relations between actors or collectivities, situated in time–space.
Structuration	Conditions governing system reproduction.

The introduction of the term 'structuration' returns us to the problems
I raised in the beginning part of this paper. For, as I emphasized
there, we have to recognize that the issues theorized by functionalist
authors – especially the fact that there are social influences which
work 'behind our backs', and which are centrally implicated in the
long-term formation/transformation of social institutions – are of
integral significance to social theory. To talk of 'structuration', in the
context of my discussion here at any rate, is to say: (a) that social
systems are structured only in and through their continual and contingent reproduction in day-to-day social life; and (b) that the capa-
bility/knowledgeability of social actors is always *bounded* (although in
historically mutable ways). The boundaries of the capability/know-
ledgeability that social agents apply in and through the duality of
structure concern just those influences about which functionalist
theories have maintained a prime interest: the *unintended consequences* of
action. Such phenomena chronically enter into system constitution
and hence have to be analysed as fundamental features *conditioning*
social reproduction. But I do not think they should be regarded as
'functions', latent or otherwise. The concept of function, as I have
tried to show elsewhere, only has some plausibility as part of the
technical vocabulary of sociology if we attribute 'needs' to social
systems.[2] But social systems have no needs, and to suppose that they
do is to apply an illegitimate teleology to them. According to the ideas
I have tried to formulate above, 'social reproduction' is not an explanatory term: it always has itself to be explained in terms of the struc-

turally bounded and contingently applied knowledgeability of social actors. It is worth emphasizing this, not merely in respect of criticizing orthodox functionalism, but also in regard of the not infrequent tendency of Marxist authors to suppose that 'social reproduction' has magical explanatory properties – as if merely to invoke the term is to explain something.

Let me return again to the differentiation between micro- and macro-sociological analysis. It follows from the arguments I have advanced above that there can be no theoretical defence for supposing that the personal encounters of day-to-day life can be conceptually separated from the long-term institutional development of society. The most trivial exchange of words implicates the speakers in the long-term history of the language via which those words are formed, and at the same time in the continuing reproduction of that language. There is more than a fortuitous similarity between the *longue durée* of historical time of which Braudel writes and the *durée* of daily social life to which Schutz, following Bergson, draws our attention. Where the distinction between micro- and macro-sociological analysis, or something like it, is important is in respect of the time–space constitution of social systems as involving presences or absences. That is to say, the distinction can be treated as focusing upon the differences between social interaction where others are *present*, and social interaction with others who are *absent*. The conventional term 'face-to-face interaction' perhaps will do to refer to the former, but we have no established term to refer to the latter. It should be clear, however, that the differences between these can only be adequately expressed in terms of time–space analysis. 'Presence' – the presence of others in an immediate milieu of interaction – does not simply refer to the fact that there are people physically together in a room, shop or street where one happens to be. Or at least presence in this sense is sociologically uninteresting. What matters for purposes of sociological analysis is what might be termed *presence-availability*. Most face-to-face interaction, as ethnomethodological studies of 'turn-taking' have helped to point out, is serial. At a cocktail party, there is a large amount of face-to-face interaction, but everybody does not talk to everybody else at once. What matters is that the interaction is characterized by what, for want of a less cumbersome phrase, I should call 'high presence-availability'. Others are 'there' in the sense that they are available, they *can* be talked to directly. There probably are cocktail parties where everybody is expected, and does, at some point talk to everybody else.

Notes

1 A. Giddens, *Central Problems in Social Theory* (University of California Press, 1979).
2 A. Giddens, 'Functionalism: après la lutte', in A. Giddens, *Studies in Social and Political Theory* (London: Hutchinson, 1977).

6 Social ritual and relative truth in natural language*

Gilles Fauconnier

[*Sophisticated 'micro-analysis' of linguistic structures leads to compartmentation and development of 'autonomous' theoretical components. The paradoxes generated internally by this methodology force us to reconsider the 'macro' organization of language, in particular discourse construction, the role of background knowledge and the social setting in which language is actually 'used'.*

The present paper shows how superficial speech act phenomena are deeply rooted in more fundamental, potentially language-independent principles of social interaction. It argues that the linguistically relevant notion of 'truth' is itself socially relativized to rituals and contexts.

These theoretical points are illustrated by the analysis of the Jesuit casuists' view of speech acts, 'lying', testimony under oath, and social conventions, in the second part (and last section) of the paper. Some readers may prefer to look first at the materials in that section, which have sociological relevance beyond the particular linguistic point of view adopted here.

Technical issues and arguments have been largely left out of this version of the paper. Their contents are briefly indicated at various points in the text.]

* The following remarks were strongly influenced by my reading of B. de Cornulier, 'La Notion d'auto-interprétation', *Études de linguistique appliquée*, 19 (1975), pp. 52–82; B. de Cornulier, 'Le Détachement du sens', in H. E. Kiefer and J. Searle (eds), *Speech Act Theory and Pragmatics* (Dordrecht-Boston: D. Reidel, 1978); P. Bourdieu, 'Le Langage autorisé', *Actes de la recherche en sciences sociales*, 5–6 (1975), pp. 65–79. They were also strongly influenced by discussions with T. Huynh, O. Ducrot, C. Grignon and B. de Cornulier. A more thorough technical treatment of the matters discussed here can be found in G. Fauconnier, 'Comment controler la vérité: remarques illustrées par des assertions dangereuses et pernicieuses en tout genre', *Actes de la recherche en sciences sociales*, 25 (1975), pp. 3–22.

1   The autonomy and the social dependence model of speech acts

Autonomy is at the heart of much work in contemporary linguistics and philosophy of language. It is assumed, sometimes tacitly, that the organization of language divides neatly, both at the empirical level of observation and classification and at the theoretical level of explanation, into autonomous components which are best studied independently of one another and according to specific techniques. Thus form, meaning, use are envisioned as separate fields of study approached respectively in terms of the conceptual tools offered by syntax, logic and pragmatics and those fields are in turn and *a fortiori* viewed as formally independent of other domains of social interaction.

Remarkably, the autonomy thesis, although initially accepted without question as sound scientific methodology has brought about its own demise: as the study of autonomous components developed more and more extensively, with greater rigour and with technically more sophisticated means of investigation and theorization, it became apparent that all aspects of language were heavily dependent upon each other in deep, non-trivial ways: logic was at work in syntactic organization, pragmatic principles were responsible for logical phenomena, syntax accounted for pragmatic possibilities, and furthermore social variation was pervasive everywhere.

This conceptual evolution has had far-reaching consequences: for example, if the innovative trend represented by generative grammar in the late 1950s was once heralded as an anti-structuralist revolution, it is now perceived on the contrary as the last, and natural, step in the structuralist conception of social science and linguistics in particular, because its overwhelming characteristic is precisely the emphasis on autonomy and the primacy of form. This is not to say that such approaches were without merit: their sophistication and thoroughness played an important part in making possible the transition that we can witness today.

The new outlook mentioned above and justified by results internal to linguistics opens up a larger and perhaps more exciting field of inquiry: if many logical properties of natural language and their syntactic reflexes follow from well-articulated pragmatic principles and if these principles are themselves special, i.e. linguistic, instances of social interaction, then a number of essentially linguistic properties will result, at least in part, from more general *language independent* characteristics of *social organization*. Linguistic theories, in order to achieve maximum explanatory adequacy, must then take such principles into account, in the same way that thermodynamics for example ultimately rests on kinetics. Correlatively linguistic facts will then come to bear on matters of wider sociological relevance.

The present paper illustrates this possibility in the domain of speech acts by showing how properties of *social rituals* interact with language to determine illocutionary force. Such an account differs sharply from autonomous speech act theories proposed by some philosophers[1] or from linguistic structural analyses involving abstract levels at which illocutionary aspects are represented.[2] The thesis is illustrated by a series of quotes from the seventeenth-century Jesuits, who by an implicit, but very literal, application of the autonomy thesis to linguistic structure and social interaction, including pragmatics, were able to defend 'extravagant' positions.

This extravagance, it turns out, is a particularly neat indicator of crucial social principles of language use and interpretation which might otherwise go unnoticed because their universality makes them appear (to us) incredibly obvious.

2 Verbal magic

True or false? If I declare: (1) The San Francisco Giants won last night by three to nothing, one may ask if my statement corresponds to what actually happened, that is if it is true or false. Similarly, if I watch the battle of Alesia and report: (2) Cesar orders his troops to charge, my words will be a description, apt to the extent that it relates to a situation, an action, an event, of the 'real' world: Cesar giving his troops the order to charge. I will then have said the truth.

On the other hand, if I say:

(3) Get out
(4) What time is it?
(5) Thank God!
(6) Shit
(7) Watch out for the Martians

    (8) Onward
    (9) Attention!
  (10) Time out
  (11) *Gesundheit*

the true/false distinction cannot apply even though the words in question are not without information.

It might be thought that language marks such differences grammatically, for example, by means of the indicative and a subject-predicate form in (1) and (2) and by means of imperatives, subjunctives and truncated forms in (3)–(11), which explicitly indicate their illocutionary force. This hypothesis would lead naturally to question the status of examples like the following:

  (12) I advise you to leave
  (13) I warn you that the Martians are coming
  (14) I ask you to tell me the time

Grammatically, such sentences are constructed like (2), and nevertheless their value is closer to that of (3), (7) and (4): for instance, (14) can be a request similar to (4) and as such will escape the logical necessity of being true or false. It is customary[3] to call 'performative' expressions which are not used to transmit a simple information or to describe an event or state of affairs, but rather to accomplish some determined social act: order, advice, request, promise, etc.; and the verbs (advise, warn, ask) which indicate the nature of the act are also christened 'performatives'. If a performative verb explicitly indicates the nature of the act performed, as in (12), (13), and (14), the utterance is an 'explicit performative'. In contrast, 'ordinary' utterances like (1) and (2) are labelled 'constative'.[4]

Explicit performatives may be singled out for their lack of truth value;[5] or, according to a different interpretation, they do have a truth value, namely '*true*', which is conferred upon them simply by uttering them.[6] Indeed, merely from my saying: 'I ask you to tell me the time,' it becomes true that I ask you to tell me the time. My saying 'I promise to come back,' makes it the case that I promise to come back. Simply uttering an explicit performative, then, is enough to make true the corresponding description, conveyed by the same sentence. This is the sense in which such expressions have been called self-verifying. From this point of view, assertions divide into two classes: on the one hand, those for which the utterance is not linked to the realization of the event described – it is not enough to say 'I wash the dishes' for the dishes to get washed; and, on the other, those which guarantee the realization of the event by virtue of being uttered: to say 'I accuse Brutus' is to make an accusation against Brutus. How can a language lend itself to this verbal magic?

Of course, this magic is not without constraints; in saying 'I crown you emperor of Annam,' it is improbable that I shall effectively crown you emperor unless I happen to be the person entitled to crown according to Annamite laws and customs.[7] On the other hand, if I declare 'I order you to leave the country,' but that I have in fact no business giving you orders, that nothing *gives me the right* to talk to you in this way, and that you have no intention of obeying, I will nevertheless have given you an order: however inappropriate, my utterance remains self-verifying. Thus, social conditions of use are not enough at this superficial level to account for self-verification.[8] But why want to account for it in the first place? After all, the use of the indicative in explicit performatives may be a simple convenience. One needs to indicate that an expression has a certain value: an order, a promise, a piece of advice, etc., and the indicative serves that purpose arbitrarily and conventionally; as a result, sentences like (12), (13) and (14) happen to be ambiguous, and the 'self-verification' property is only an amusing coincidence, a secondary effect of this ambiguity. Now this point of view is not necessarily implausible, given the examples surveyed so far. But its limits will become apparent if further data are examined.

Consider the utterance: (15) You will go to Timbuktu. This is a harmless indicative which may transmit 'pure' information: I am your travel agent telling you about your itinerary; or perhaps I have learned about your next assignment and wish to communicate this knowledge. But it is also clear that (15) may be 'performative' in many ways: if I am the judge talking to the prisoner, (15) may be the sentence handed down; if I am the colonel talking to the sergeant, (15) is an order; a state official to a subordinate, (15) is an appointment; a suitor to his love, (15) could be a promise; a clairvoyant in her crystal ball, (15) becomes a prophecy. If you are undecided, and ask for my opinion, (15) as a response will be taken as advice. But if you are the black knight, and I am begging you to rescue the diamond-eyed princess locked up in Timbuktu, (15) will of course become a request.

The various performative values of an utterance like (15) could easily be multiplied. It is clear that the *context alone* can signal such values. Clearly, too, the performative value can be made explicit:

(17) You will go to Timbuktu, { that's your punishment.
that's an order.
that's my decision.
that's a promise.
that's my suggestion.

One can also use an explicit performative verb:

(18) I { order
sentence
advise
beseech } you to go to Timbuktu.

(19) I { promise
predict } that you will go to Timbuktu.

And the various processes may be combined:

(20) You will go to Timbuktu, { I order you to.
I sentence you to.
I promise.
I beseech you.
I suggest.

Leaving aside for the time being examples (18)–(20), and 'explicit' performatives, consider once more the multiple values of an unmarked utterance like (15). Clearly, a very ordinary sentence, grammatically and lexically, is being used with a rich array of illocutionary values. In other words, the initial hypothesis – grammatical distinction between constatives ((1), (2)) and performatives ((3)–(11)) – is untenable at the most elementary level: the indicative subject-predicate construction does not mark constativity. It follows that the problem of explicit performatives like (12), (13) and (14) is altered, since their anomaly was precisely based on that initial hypothesis. Consider in this perspective the elementary and fundamental case of (15).

How can a banal five-word sentence take so many values? One might attempt to deal with this question in terms of ambiguity, for instance by saying that the grammatical *future* contains all the observed values: promise, order, request, etc. The use of a future in this perspective would be quite arbitrary for each case: there would be no more links between them than between two accidental homonyms. The non-explanatory character of this approach is obvious, but it does emerge in certain types of syntactic argumentation which are strongly influenced by a structuralist and representational methodology.[9]

Setting aside this kind of analysis, another classical view is available: a sentence like (15) has a meaning independent of context and present in all of its uses. Interaction with context adds to this meaning a particular illocutionary force. All we have to do is to determine how 'context' can interact with this unmarked, minimal, 'neutral' meaning. But in fact this is not so easy: the meaning of linguistic forms like (15) is viewed semantically to be a set of truth conditions. How does (15) relate to the true/false distinction which we took as a starting-point?

In the context of the travel agency, where the utterance is constative there is no problem:[10] either you will in fact go to Timbuktu and the statement will be verified, or you won't and (15) will turn out to be false. But suppose (15) is an order: the truth of (15) becomes irrelevant, since the utterance is equivalent to the imperative, 'Go to Timbuktu,' which we agree has no truth value. In other words if a counter-order voids (15), one cannot accuse the colonel of having lied or hidden the truth by saying (15). Similarly if a judge utters (15) as a legal sentence, and this sentence is later modified or annulled, say by a governor or higher court, the constative statement corresponding to the judge's words will of course be falsified, but once again the judge will not have said anything false: he will have condemned you and it will remain true that he condemned you to go to Timbuktu whether you go there or not in the end. In the same way, friendly advice (e.g. (15)) will not be labelled 'false' if it is not followed.

Thus it appears that a grammatically unmarked utterance like (15) can have many uses for which the notion of truth value is no more appropriate than for implicit performatives ((3)–(11)) or explicit ones ((12)–(14)). Still, the logical situation is different: examples (3)–(11) never correspond to a constative utterance: truth is not an issue. Explicit performatives like (12)–(14), on the other hand, always have a corresponding, identical, constative which is 'true' simply by virtue of the sentence being uttered performatively: they are self-verifying. And finally, 'ordinary' expressions like (15), when used performatively, also have a corresponding identical constative expression, but its truth value is unrelated to the meaning it has in the context in which it is uttered: there is no self-verification. In this respect, such expressions are different not only from the first-person indicative explicit performatives but also from the following:

(21)   You are fired [boss to employee].
(22)   The assembly is now in session [chairman to delegates].

In the appropriate situations (21) and (22) are performative: they are used to dismiss someone, and to start a meeting, and they are self-verifying – if you are told (21), then you are indeed fired. But in contrast to explicit performatives like 'I order you to leave' which, as we have seen, are self-verifying independently of the contextual situation, i.e. whether or not they are uttered felicitously, cases like (21)–(22) are narrowly constrained by social conditions of production: (21) is self-verifying only if the social relation between speaker and hearer allows the former to fire the latter.

To sum up: performative utterances can be related to the true/false distinction in various ways:

(i)   No truth-value
　　　　　　　　ex. Get out!, What time is it?
(ii)   The corresponding constative has a truth value, which is
　　　　　　　　(a)   undetermined
　　　　　　　　　　　ex. You will go to Timbuktu [as an order].

self-
verifying
$\left\{\begin{array}{l}\end{array}\right.$
(b)   Determined entirely by the performative value of the utterance
　　　　ex. I order you to leave.
(c)   Determined by the performative utterance in appropriate social conditions of use
　　　　ex. You are fired.
　　　　　　I crown you Emperor of Annam.

We have pointed out the inadequacies of an analysis in terms of 'ambiguity' or 'illocutionary force' conventionally superimposed on a primitive meaning. The next step is to propose another conception and approach for the observed phenomena.

3   The relativity of truth as a common social action

This notion of state of affairs and truth values independent of individuals and their language contrasts with a totally different social reality: either by virtue of her/his biological and psychological constitution, or by virtue of her/his position in the social system, an individual exerts decisive influence over the realization of events or states of affairs and consequently over the truth values of certain propositions. It is obvious, too, that the actions by which this influence is exercised may be purely symbolic: the signature of a bill triggers the construction of a dam, a pinch of salt baptizes a child, etc.

The testimony of the individual concerned can then lead to a confident assignment of truth values. Suppose a cabinet minister is asked: What will happen to the factories? and answers: (23) I've decided they would be replaced. The reporter may reproduce the gist of this exchange as *constative* information: (24) [headline] 'The factories will be replaced.' Nothing is performative here: the leap from (23) to (24) is the result of a straightforward logical progression: information (23) is acceptable since a person is capable of knowing and therefore of reporting her/his own decisions. It is therefore 'true' that the 'minister has decided X'. Furthermore it is considered natural to act in accordance with one's decisions, and since the minister's social position gives him the power to act, that is to make X or not X true, it follows that if he has decided X, he will do X, and hence that X will happen.

Thus (24) is felicitous. But suppose the government is suddenly overthrown; the decisions of the (ex-)minister no longer bear on the course of events. Evidently (23) remains true, but not (24). Yet in this case as in performative examples (cf. (15)) no one will accuse the reporter of having *lied* or 'spoken' falsely in writing (24): it is clear that truth is conceived as relative to a set of parameters implicitly determined by context.

Three ideas emerge:

> Truth values are not external to individuals and the course of events: on the contrary they are necessarily *linked to the action and power of individuals* belonging to a rule-governed social system.
> The testimony of those who hold social power may be the *only observable clue* as to the truth value of a proposition (ex. 23, 24).

The truth expressed is accepted as *relative to context* rather than absolute.

By controlling various types of actions, agents in effect 'control' the truth values of propositions. This is especially true of conventionally regulated social interaction: it is within social interaction and often through varied symbolic acts that control of truth values offers the most diverse forms. The truth value of 'Peter will do X' evidently depends on his position within social hierarchies and on the power which others may have over him: his captain in the army, his judge at a trial, his subjects if he is king, those who seek to persuade him, etc. Peter's boss may have control, sometimes total control, over the proposition 'Peter is fired,' in so far as its truth value is determined by his actions. And for the same reason Peter controls the truth value of propositions like 'Peter resigns,' 'Peter asks to be hired.'

But how is control over truth values actually applied? We noted it could be effected very simply by performing the corresponding acts: (raising one's hand) in order for 'I raise my hand' to be true; or (firing Peter) in order for 'Peter is fired' to be true; or again (ordering Peter to go to Timbuktu) in order for 'Peter will go to Timbuktu' to be true.

But it happens that in many cases the act which can make 'P' true consists precisely in saying 'P':

You will go to Timbuktu [order].
You are fired [firing].
I resign [resignation].
The assembly is (hereby) in session [opening].

In this perspective, the process appears to be circular: one controls truth values of propositions because one controls the acts which determine them, but the acts themselves reduce to the expression of the propositions in question. How can language, an objective vehicle of truth values, become the subjective basis for their determination?

This question is of course fundamentally the same as in section 2, but it is couched in different terms, truth values being not merely statable but also controllable. Much of social life, therefore, depends on our use and evaluation of speech acts as normative expressions of a system of social stratification as realized in textual statements (announcements, documents, etc.) and daily social interaction.

4   Language and ritual

In order to account for the paradoxical role of language within social acts we shall begin with those acts which are agreed to be rituals and then go on to claim that their formal and symbolic properties are shared by other much more 'ordinary' acts. The distinction between physical control and symbolic control of truth values will provide the answer to the problem of illocutionary acts.

So, consider baptism or any other initiation rite: the gestures, the location, the agents of the rite, historically necessary, are logically arbitrary – the rite does not aim to put salt on the child's tongue or to immerse him in water, but rather to make him enter a congregation, to confer upon him a symbolic property, a special social status. The priest, acting as a legitimate agent, controls the truth value of the proposition 'I baptize this child,' but this control is subject to specific constraints: the agent must perform the conventional physical acts which are part of the rite, in the place, at the time conventionally imposed by the rite, dressed in the conventionally prescribed manner, etc. Part of his control – gestures, prayers, choice of location – is physical; the other is social: he is invested personally with the symbolic power that legitimates the ritual act he can perform.[11] Suppose first that the ritual does not contain any spoken words; the agent remains free to describe the rite he is performing, for example by saying: (28) 'I baptize this child.' This is a banal constative which is true every time the physical and social conditions of the rite are met, just as (29) 'I run', is true when I am running. This kind of description may have a functional value, by specifying how the act performed is to be interpreted. Such descriptions are frequently added to purely physical acts, as for example in a cooking lesson: (30) 'I cook the pieces in sequence and return all rabbit and any juice to the pan. Now, I blend in 2 tablespoons Dijon mustard, 2 cups whipping cream and 2 tablespoons lemon juice.' But the ritual differs from the physical act in the following fundamental respect: the description of the rite, which can accompany it, may also conventionally become part of it (call this the *principle of incorporation*). In other words, while (30) cannot be used to cook the rabbit, the oral expression of description (28) 'I baptize you' can become one of the elements of the baptismal rite.

This possibility exists initially only by virtue of the arbitrary nature of symbolic acts: the description uttered at the time of the act becomes one more of its symbols. It seems rather natural to speculate that *incorporation happens as a reinterpretation* of the act. For example if during the first stage, the rite is accompanied by its description for functional reasons (as suggested above), a new 'generation' will perceive the original rite plus its description as a coherent whole, always repeated as such, i.e. as a rite in itself. This is, if you will, a Pavlovian aspect of symbolic acts: if an act S always co-occurs with a manifestation M, this manifestation is perceived as a symbol of the act S and therefore, since S itself is made up of symbols, M is perceived as one of the components of the act S.[12] I shall not pursue these considerations; they belong to a wider study of the evolution of symbolic acts and of changes that go from functional to symbolic.

The principle of incorporation automatically produces self-reference,[13] since the language of the description external to the act becomes by incorporation a full-fledged component of the act it describes: as soon as description (28) 'I baptize you' is incorporated in the ritual of baptism, then since it refers, as a description, to all the components of the symbolic act which constitute baptism, it refers also to itself, which has become one of these components. It is important to distinguish carefully this type of self-reference, which is a trivial consequence of incorporation, from self-verification, mentioned in section 2: saying (28) is only one of the components of the act and therefore not sufficient by itself to perform it, i.e. to make description (28) true.

Yet it is also clear that after incorporation the use of (28) is performative in so far as the ritual confers upon it part of the power of the symbolic act. Furthermore, it remains observationally true that the physical nature of symbolic acts linked to a ritual are perpetually modified. In particular, the symbolic act is liable to lose one or more of its components. Call *reduction* the corresponding process of modification.

Now suppose that after incorporation a symbolic act linked to a ritual loses all its arbitrary components except D, the constative description incorporated in the ritual.

Ritual R: Symbolic act S   Constative description   Precondi-
                                of the act (optional)   tions
              (A, B, C,. . .) +   D   /   U
                      ↓   Incorporation
              (A, B, C, . . ., D)   /   U
                      ↓   Reduction
                    (D)   /   U

Such a process would have a special logical consequence: expression D, which states that ritual R is being performed, would become the only component of act S; in other words, under appropriate conditions U, the mere utterance of D would be sufficient to perform ritual R, and therefore to make D itself true. This would lead not only to self-reference but also to self-verification. But this self-verification would not count as a logical or linguistic paradox: it would only be a relatively direct consequence of the interaction of two independently motivated sociological principles linked to rituals, incorporation and reduction.

The preceding discussion shows that self-verification may appear in language use, not as a fundamental property of language, but rather as a *by-product* of more general principles linked to symbolic acts. A stronger claim remains to be defended: that *all* cases of self-verification linked to performatives are essentially of this type.

5   Orders and promises: an illustration

It is banal to note that an order given by A to B involves a social hierarchy where A would have the power to determine some of B's actions (and therefore to control the corresponding truth values). In social situations for which ordering is institutionalized – army, family, factory – the conditions under which an order may be given, and the manner of giving it, may be determined with as much conventional precision as a christening or a wedding: uniform, expression, location, seals and attitudes, authority has its symbols. Yet, to treat ordering as just another rite would not clarify all its linguistic features. Consider instead a larger unit: the order given and executed (OGE).

Agents $\left\{ \begin{array}{l} \text{I : inferior – receives and executes the order} \\ \text{S: superior – gives the order} \end{array} \right.$

Key act A   to execute the order is to perform act A, which may be
specified as to time, location, manner, etc.

Time $\left\{ \begin{array}{l} t_0 \text{ : at which the order is given} \\ t \text{ : at which the order is executed} \end{array} \right.$

Symbolic act O : S orders I to perform A verifying propositions:

P : 'I perform A at t' (if P is true the order is
executed)

Q : 'S performs O at t_0'

Conditions U :

Social conditions which define the relative hierarchical positions of I
and S with respect to some institution; conditions which determine
(for a given institution) the nature of the acts A which may be
'ordered'; symbolic conditions of authority (location, tone of voice,
appropriate clothes, insignia, language), etc.

Psychological conditions: I and S must believe that the above
conditions are satisfied (or, at least, I believes they are satisfied and
S believes that I has this belief).

The social ritual OGE involves two actors, I and S, includes two
distinct parts, the symbolic act O and the key act A, and is subject to
multiple social and psychological conditions, U. This characterization is at best a 'prototype' of given and executed orders; real
situations may involve other complications.

Note that *within* the ritual OGE, the agent S controls the truth
values of the two propositions P and Q: S is the one who initiates the
ritual with act O and the one who determines key act A and therefore
proposition P.

Of course the ritual OGE may also be *interrupted* in many ways
(institutional: counter order, incompatibility with a higher order,
challenge of conditions U; physical: death of I, or any other destruction of the conditions of applicability). In this perspective, the
symbolic act O does not constitute a whole ritual, but rather only a
subpart of OGE. As such it shares the properties of symbolic acts
noted in section 4: it may incorporate its own description (incorporation), i.e. proposition Q, and then reduce to the expression of that
proposition (reduction). There is a difference between acts of type O
and more 'purely' ritual ones: the expression of O is not quite as

logically arbitrary, since it must in general specify the key act A. The operation of reduction is therefore limited *a priori* by this constraint. But since the description by means of proposition Q specifies the agents and the key act A (this is a *semantic* property of the verb *order*), reduction remains possible.

This analysis of ordering as a symbolic act belonging to a larger ritual (OGE) is especially simple (and perhaps overly so). But, coupled with the independently motivated principles of incorporation and reduction, it will account directly for less trivial logico-linguistic phenomena. First, the performative value of constative statements 'I order that X' is an immediate consequence of reduction as in the case of 'full' rituals (section 4). But also, since ordering is only a subpart of OGE, the description applies only to O and not to the entire ritual: it does not indicate that the ritual has been performed and therefore does not imply that the conditions of the ritual (e.g. relative hier- archical positions) are satisfied. This point has its importance, for in the schema above we lumped under U all the social and psychological conditions linked to OGE. But it is clear that these conditions apply in different ways to the subparts of OGE: for S to give an order it is sufficient that S *believe* that conditions U are satisfied; for the entire ritual OGE to be performed, it is necessary also, *inter alia*, for I to believe that these conditions are met. It follows that subpart O can perfectly well be performed without conditions U being satisfied, and therefore without any ensuing ritual. This clarifies the difference noted in Section 1 between:

(31) I crown you Emperor of Annam; and
(32) I order you to leave the country.

Both are cases of incorporation, but (31) as a *description* refers to the entire ritual (crowning) and can only be true if the ritual is actually performed, i.e. in particular if all the conditions U are satisfied; (32) on the contrary refers to a symbolic act O (subpart of a ritual) which can be initiated freely by the speaker, who is habilitated to open the ritual on the basis of his own beliefs, but not to complete it. Conse- quently, utterance (32) is self-verifying independently of its con- ditions of use: as soon as (32) is uttered, symbolic act O subpart of OGE, is performed, and it is performed as an opening to OGE; conditions U and physical conditions of execution will determine whether OGE can actually be performed or not.

Consider finally the example of promises. As before, a promise is held to be not a ritual in itself but rather a symbolic act, subpart of a full ritual: 'promise made and kept' (PMK). Two acts are involved: the symbolic act by means of which the promise is made, P, and the key act by means of which the promise is kept, A. As in the case of ordering, the symbolic act P must specify the key act A. The symbols of promising are arbitrary: it may be agreed that crossing one's fingers, placing one's hand on the Bible, or writing in blood, etc., are taken to mean that one's utterance is within the ritual PMK. Moreover, in this case the same agent (author of the promise) controls the truth values of the propositions corresponding to the symbolic act and to the key act. The restrictions on the symbolic act P are the same as for ordering and therefore incorporation and reduction are possible here, too, which accounts directly for the performative and self-verifying value of expressions like 'I promise to,' 'I promise you that,' etc.

Notice incidentally that in institutionalized promises, there is usually incorporation but seldom reduction: a promise to sell (e.g. a real estate purchase contract) has no legal value when reduced to the corresponding simple constative utterance: it must have other symbolic features such as a conventional formulation, the agent's signature, fiscal stamps, etc. The corresponding formula which may be part of it, 'I, John Doe, promise to X' is neither self-verifying nor fully performative since it is not sufficient to perform the act. All of this is an immediate consequence of the principle of incorporation, but is not accounted for by logical analyses with only the concept of self-reference, or by analyses which treat performatives as primitive.

6   Extreme relativization of truth: a historical example

Linguistic observation of speech acts leads to semantic questions pertaining to performative verbs. If (33) Theseus promises to go to Crete, does it follow that Theseus has the intention of going to Crete? That Theseus has committed himself to going to Crete? That Theseus is obligated to go to Crete? That Theseus 'must' go to Crete? That Theseus thinks he will go to Crete, etc.[14] Such questions have little meaning, *semantically*, in the present perspective. By (33) it is indicated that Theseus takes part in the ritual PMK and this ritual will be completed if the corresponding key act is performed. The notion of obligation is introduced here by the sanctions, symbolic or material, which apply to the interruption of the ritual and which are defined conventionally, but differently according to the social situations in which the ritual 'promise' is used. Thus symbolically: dishonour, sin, bad conscience, blame etc.; materially: sum to pay, addressee's vengeance, legal punishment.

Such sanctions are in principle independent of each other. It may for example be perfectly honourable not to 'honour' a promise to buy if a certain, agreed-upon, retainer is paid. One may therefore legitimately infer from (33) that Theseus intends to go to Crete from general pragmatic suppositions (e.g. everyone wishes to avoid social sanctions, or one usually initiates a ritual with the intention that it will be completed). Similarly, one can probably say that he 'must' do it or that he is committed to doing it if this marks a *conditional social necessity relative to sanctions of all kinds*. Clearly, the implications are not absolute and semantic but *pragmatic* and relativized.

This aspect of the nature of speech acts exposes them to a subversive use cleverly defended by the Jesuit 'casuists' of the seventeenth and eighteenth centuries.[15] By playing upon the principles of incorporation and reduction and the possibility they imply to attach truth value only to subparts of the ritual, by relativizing the truth of speech acts to a *private and implicit context* which does not correspond to the socially presupposed context within which the speech act is conventionally understood, the Jesuits provide us with a *historical example* of the social control and relativity of truth postulated here. The fact that the Jesuits' manipulation of context-relativity remained unilateral implies a *reductio ad absurdum* of this feature of speech acts. Consider for example this passage from Suarez (1614):

Si quis promisit, aut contraxit exterius, sine intentione promittendi & interrogatur à Judice sub juramento, an promiserit, vel contraxerit; simpliciter negare potest: quia habere potest legitimum sensum, scilicet non promisi promissione me obligante.

[If someone has promised or contracted externally without the intention to promise, and is questioned by the judge under oath as to whether he promised or contracted, he may simply answer that he didn't: for this may have a legitimate meaning, namely: I did not promise by a promise which obligates me.]

The first instance of 'promised' refers to the subpart of the ritual which initiates it; 'promise' below (without the intention to *promise*) refers on the contrary to the whole ritual and the apparently contradictory formula, 'I did not promise by a promise which obligates me,' indicates the difference between initiating the ritual (to promise), and feeling compelled to complete it. The fact that these words are not actually spoken out loud means of course that the obligation is not the same in the eyes of the judge and of the author of the promise.

This relativization of controlled 'truths' is displayed in the following instruction for priests by François Tolet:

Tamen cautus debet esse reus, ut talia verba proserat juxta suam intentionem in sensu vero, puta ut intendat dicere, non feci, puta in carcere, & non habui complices, in aliis criminibus, vel aliquid simile, alias esset mendacium; non autem illo modo; quia verba in tali casu, non sunt consideranda juxta judicis intentionem, sed ipsius rei.

[However, the guilty party must be extremely careful to say these words only in a sense which is true and in conformity with his intention. For example if he answers 'I didn't do it', his intention must be to say that he didn't do it during the time he was in prison. If he answers 'I had no accomplices' he must conceive this answer with respect to other crimes than the one he is being questioned about, or have some similar intention; otherwise he would be lying, whereas in this manner he is not since the words must be considered not according to the Judge's intention, but according to the accused's.]

The lie is 'avoided' by relativizing the proposition 'I didn't do it,' not to the obvious context presupposed by the judge, but to another context ('during the time I was in prison') chosen by the speaker. It must be understood that the possibility of this ambiguity (*equivoca*) is linguistic: the answer suggested by Tolet, which may seem extravagant given the most obvious conventions governing dialogue, is not different logically and grammatically from the answer 'no' to someone who asks 'Have you had lunch?' The answer 'no' evidently does not mean that you *never* had lunch, but rather, usually, that you haven't had lunch *today* or *since this morning*, etc. Therefore, language allows truth to be relativized to a particular context, as we already observed for rituals; but society usually discourages *unilateral* choice of such contexts.

What the Jesuits question is implicitly the validity of the social sanctions (including religious ones) linked to various actions (unkept promise, homicide, etc.) and therefore explicitly the pragmatic conditions on the rituals which can lead to such sanctions. J. de Dicastille (1641) expresses clearly this difference between, on the one hand, the roles of the judge and the accused in the trial ritual, which define certain 'rights', and, on the other hand, the perlocutionary effects that certain parts of the ritual aim to achieve ('forcing the accused to answer'):

Ex his jam omnino liquet, non esse bellum inter utrumque jus, rei & Judicis. Nam jus Judicis est interrogare, non vero obligare, praecipiendo, ad respondendum: jus autem rei, est non respondere, vel non fateri veritatem; sed libere posse illam celare: quod jus non est oppositum juri interrogationis quod habet Judex, sed est oppositum potestati obligandi, quod jus obligandi hic & nunc, ut probatum est, non habet Judex. Ergo non est bellum proprie ex utrâque parte, cum non sint opposita jura.

[Accordingly, it is clear that there is no contradiction between the right of the Judge and the right of the Accused. For the Judge's right is to question the Accused, but not to force him imperatively to answer. The right of the Accused is to give no answer or not to confess the truth, but to have the freedom to hide it; and this right is not opposed to the right the Judge has to question, but to the power to force an answer; and this is a right which the Judge does not have, as we just proved. Therefore, since the rights of the Judge and the Accused are not opposed, they do not conflict.]

If this interpretation seems subversive, it is precisely because it separates the components of the ritual: illocutionary act of the judge, illocutionary act of the accused, perlocutionary aims, allowing each component to be *relativized to a different context*. The relativization of truth is also expressed with limpidity in the following passage from Reginald (1620):

Ambiguitas autem qua celatur veritas sine mendacio, contingit, quando id quod quis dicit, verum est secundum suam intentionem, licet falsum sit secundum intentionem audientis, & communem intelligentiam.

[The case when truth can be hidden by an ambiguous discourse without lying is when what a man says is true, according to his own intention, even though it is false according to the hearer's and according to the common interpretation.]

By not interpreting *lying* as the general violation of communication rituals, but rather only as its most frequent cause, namely 'to speak against one's mind', the Reverend Fathers can let the ritual be violated *de facto* without any ensuing lie, as is clearly shown by the last part of the first paragraph of the following text by André Eudemon-Jean:

Nam aequivocationem vel ideò damnant, quia mendacium esse putant; vel quia etsi mendacium non est, tamen auditorem fallit; vel quia tollit commerciorum atque humanae societatis fidem; vel quia nonnullus aliquandò abusus est. At haec, & quae sunt hujusmodi nihil efficiunt. Nam ut ordiamur à primo: qui potest esse mendacium? Cum mentiri fit enunciare contrà quàm fentias; qui autem utitur aequivocatione, eam omninò verbis fuis sententiam subjiciat, quam conceptam tenet animo, quamque verba ipsa significare possunt? quamvis auditor in aliam partem interpretaturus existimetur?

Quod verò aequivocatio auditorem plerumque fugiat, eâque ratione fallat, non video quid istos juvare possit, nisi axiomatis instar assumpserint: nemini, ne bonis quidem artibus, unquàm licere quemquam fallere.

Quid autem humanae Societati pernicionus, quaeve capitalis adeo pestis humano convictui excogitari potest, quàm cùm arcanorum jure sublato, nihil cuiquam rerum suarum apud se habere licet; atque ut quisque importunissimus est, ita potest aliena omnia facta, dicta, consilia rimari, atque investigare; cùm interim

viris bonis non respondere ad interrogata, hoc est, sua omnia non
prodere religio fit. Nam ut sermonum & commerciorum fidem
exigit humana societas, ut si hanc tollas, convictus constare non
possit: ita etiam si privatarum cuique rerum consiliorumque
postestatem adimas, ut ea vel esserre in vulgus, vel tegere arbitrio
suo possit, humanam profectò societatem sustulisti.

[For ambiguity will be condemned, either because it is considered
to be a lie, or because if it is not a lie, it still deceives the person
before whom it is used. It will be condemned either because it
eliminates good faith from commerce and human society, or
because some people have made bad use of it. But all these reasons
and other similar ones carry no weight. For, to start with the first
objection, how could ambiguity be a lie, when lying is to speak
against one's mind and when he who makes use of ambiguity gives
to the words he utters the full meaning of the thoughts he withholds
in his mind, and which these same words can express, even though
he believes that the person he is talking to will interpret them
differently?

But from the fact that ambiguity usually eludes the addressee
and thereby deceives him, I do not see what advantage can be
claimed by our Adversaries, unless they make an axiom out of the
maxim that no one is ever allowed to deceive anyone else, even if his
means of doing so are good.

But what would be more pernicious for human society, what
would be a worse plague in the commerce of life than to deprive
everyone of the freedom to keep their belongings, by depriving
them of the right to keep their secrets – so that misplaced curiosity
could discover and follow all the actions, all the words, and all the
intentions of others; while honest people would feel obligated to
answer every question, i.e. to reveal their deepest secrets? Indeed, if
human society demands good faith in speech and social exchange,
so that without this good faith, society is threatened, by the same
token, depriving each individual of the right he has over his
possessions and over his thoughts, and suppressing his free choice
to let them be known to others or to hide them, is also to destroy
society.]

The text is important because it answers the fundamental objection against ambiguity, 'amphibology', mental restriction, etc. (viz. that they prevent any good faith in human exchanges: the social dynamics which depend on the operation of rituals are threatened if the functioning of these rituals is subverted). Eudemon-Jean's defence is an attack based on the principle of private property applied to 'thoughts' as well as to other goods, and which is directed against any ritual which might force an agent to give up the *control of truth values* which he or she 'possesses'. As to possible misuses of ambiguity he adds:

Quid est enim é rebus omnibus adéo bonum, quo abuti non possis, si velis?

[Is there anything so good in all of Nature, that it cannot be misused?]

After condemnations by Pope Innocent XI, mental restriction is no longer a safe instrument, but perjury can still be avoided by distinguishing the sincere intention linked to a promise (Searle's felicity condition) from the actual keeping of the promise.

Probabile tamen est . . . tunc tantum obligare sub veniali. Ratio est, quia qui ita jurat, non invocat Deum proprié in testem future executionis, sed tantum in testem promissionis, seu praesentis propositi; quod propositum, si tunc non habeat, peccat mortaliter, & est perjurus.
　　Deinde intuitu nominis Dei intendit se formare ad non mutandam voluntatem, sed proportionaté ad exigentiam materiae. Unde si postea non exequatur istam voluntatem, non est proprié perjurus, nec mendax, sed infidelis [Jean-Baptiste Taberna (1736)].

[However, an oath in this second case is only weakly binding. The reason is that whoever swears in this way does not actually take God as a witness of his future act ['keeping the promise'] but only of his promise and his present intention. If he does not have this intention he commits a mortal sin.
　　Later he has the intention, out of respect for the name of God, to try not to change his will, but in proportion to the pressures of the

object of his promise. This is why if he does not keep the promise later on, he is not, strictly speaking, a liar or a perjurer, but a man who is unfaithful to his promises.]

In contrast to the passage from Suarez, above, this one emphasizes the truth of the *intention* at the time of the promise. In saying 'I promise', one cannot lie since one is effectively promising and has the intention of keeping the promise. The words uttered express a truth which can only be measured in terms of the situation *at the time* of the speech act. Later events cannot modify this truth retroactively and whether or not a promise is kept becomes independent of the 'truth' of the utterance used to formulate this promise. *Lying*, an absolute notion, is sharply distinguished in this way from *breaking rituals* (not keeping promises etc.) which remain minor sins: lying is unforgivable, because it is directed against God; infidelities are directed against men and their society and may be justified by the course of events and by virtue of higher considerations (defending one's belongings, one's life).

The following passages show a certain hesitation on the part of the Jesuits as to the status of the intention linked to a promise:

Sequitur 5°, quando sicté promittens immunis est à matrimonii obligatione . . . posse rogatum sub juramento à judice, negare se matrimonium promisisse ne, si fateatur promissionem, cum in foro externo & coram judice intentionem & fictionem probare nequeat, cogatur ad matrimonium [Etienne Fagundez (1640)].

[5° It follows that someone who has made only a feigned promise of marriage need not keep it. He may, when questioned about his oath by the Judge, deny that he promised; for fear that if he acknowledged the promise he made, and were not able externally in front of the Judge to prove his actual intention and deception, he might be forced to marry.]

fictum promissorem (Matrimonii) dum non tenetur ducere, nec resarcire damnum, posse negare promissionem, rogatum à judice; quia, cum judex roget ut cogat ad matrimonium debitum, sensus interrogationis est: promisisti matrimonium, ita ut tenearis? Cui vere respondet, non promisi, sine restrictione mentali [Jean Marin (1720)].

[Someone who has made a deceptive promise of marriage is not
obligated to marry or to pay and, when questioned by the Judge,
he may deny the promise, for the Judge, who questions him in order
to force him to marry, intends to ask: did you make a promise
of marriage with the intention of keeping it? He may therefore
answer truthfully: I did not, and this involves no mental
restriction.]

The recourse to mental restriction, which was already condemned
at this time, is avoided in the previous passage by incorporating the
restriction in the judge's intention, rather than in the accused's.

The Jesuit analysis is especially interesting in its *contempt for the
social conventions* which in fact govern the rituals considered, combined
with equal *respect for the linguistic rules* (pragmatic, semantic and grammatical) which operate out of social context on the sentences used in
these rituals (this was already noted in connection with the quote
from Tolet). The principle expressed by Fillucius in the form: 'everyone is free to express his thoughts in totality or in part,' allows the
following strategy:

cum incipit, v.g. dicere *juro*, interponere submissé restrictionem
mentalem, *ut me hodie* & deindé addere altà voce, *non comedisse rem
illam*, vel *juro*, & interponere, *me dicere*, tum absolvere altà item voce,
quod non feci hoc vel illud: Sic enim verissima est oratio tota [Fillucius
(1633)].

[when starting to say *I swear*, one must whisper the mental
restriction, *that today*, and continue out loud, *I did not eat such and such*;
or *I swear*, whisper *that I say*, out loud *that I did not do this or that*. For in
this way the whole discourse is true.]

licere juranti uti hac aequivocatione: *juro tibi me numeraturum
pecuniam*, intelligendo ut elle casus, tibi, regatur à verbo juro: ita ut
sit sensus, tibi juro, fore ut nemerem pecunias sive tibi sive alteri
[Sanchez (1614)].

[someone who swears may use the following ambiguity: 'I swear to
pay this sum of money' meaning: I swear to pay this sum, to you, or
to someone else.]

Note the semantic validity of Sanchez's argument: the sentence 'I swear to pay this sum' indeed specifies in no way the dative complement of *pay*. The argument operates by suppressing all social conditions of use.

Fillucius' trick reminds us of the self-reference paradoxes. To say 'I did such and such,' and to say 'I say that I did such and such,' are equivalent because *to say* is performative. But even though the two statements are equivalent, the two propositions are not mutually substitutable:

> *salva veritate* in the context 'I swear that'
>   'I swear that I did such and such'
>   'I swear that I say that I did such and such'

Speech act equivalence does not entail *logical equivalence*.

Another statement by Sanchez takes similar advantage of a feature of ordinary language:

> Undecimo deducitur, coactum aliquam accipere in sponsam,
> quam ducere non tenetur, posse jurare se accepturum, intelligendo
> intra se, si teneor, vel si postea placuerit mihi.

> [It follows, 11°, that someone who is forced to take a woman as his
> wife, without being obligated, may swear that he will take her,
> meaning implicitly, if I am so obligated, or if later on she appeals to
> me.]

Indeed, any ritual is constrained by innumerable unexpressed conditions, as noted before: if I promise to climb the Eiffel Tower next year, this holds under the implicit (and 'obvious') conditions, that the Tower will not have been destroyed in the meantime, that I will not have become paralysed, or been sent off to war, etc.

Such restrictive conditions are socially recognized. By instead treating the phenomenon as a sort of inherent multiple ambiguity, Sanchez is able to present such restrictive conditions as totally *arbitrary*.

The pragmatic ambiguity inherent in deictic expressions allows an extensive use of the procedure, without any mental restriction:

> Sic qui tenetur celare veritatem, & interrogatur, an fur istà vià

transierit, potest, sigendo pedem super uno lapide, dicere, non transivit, nempe per istum lapidem [Fegeli (1750)].

[A man who must hide the truth is asked, for example, if the robber came this way. He may place his foot on some cobblestone and answer: he did not come here, meaning on this cobblestone.]

For, as Fegeli also writes:

licité adhibentur, non intendendo, sed solum permittendo aliorum deceptionem.

[it is permitted to use all these ways of hiding the truth, not with the intention of deceiving others, but only of letting them deceive themselves.]

Conscious of the practical difficulties involved in applying their analyses in the face of the obsessions of ordinary usage, the Jesuits set up admirable principles of universal application:

Quod si forté quis rudis sit, & nesciat in particulari amphibologiam concipere, consilium erit ut intendat negare vel affirmare in sensu qui veritatem reipsà contineat. Ad hoc autem necesse est, ut saltem in genere sciat, & sibi persudeat, in aliquo vero sensu posse se negare quod revelare non tenetur, quamvis in particulari nesciat modum. Nam si hoc etiam generaliter ignoret, nullo modo poterit in vero sensu loqui nisi plané & simpliciter loquatur, pejerabit [Suarez (1614)].

[If someone is so gross that he cannot conceive for himself an appropriate ambiguity, he will be advised to have the intention, in answering, of denying or asserting in a way that contains the truth. But for this, he must know, at least in general, that he can deny in some true sense what he is not obliged to reveal, although, specifically, he may not know how to do it: for if he does not know this in general, he will in no way be able to talk in a true sense. This is why, unless he talks plainly and simply, he will be lying.]

For indeed, as Casnedi (Crisis Theologica) aptly puts it: 'everyone must have access to the ways of hiding the truth'.

6　Conclusion

To conclude, let me single out the main themes dealt with in this study:

(1) There is no way neatly to separate structural, internal rules of language organization from the social conventions that govern language use; as the Jesuit examples demonstrate by *reductio ad absurdum*, the social conventions are inextricably bound in non-trivial ways to any elucidation of meaning.

(2) The linguistically relevant notion of truth is a social one, relativized to highly structured background assumptions about the organization of social life.

(3) Autonomizing bodies of data and corresponding theoretical components can be heuristically useful at specific stages of theory construction, but may also in the end hide broader and more perspicuous generalizations. An autonomous account of speech acts stumbles on anomalies and paradoxes by failing to relate to independently motivated sociological principles, here illustrated by the principle of incorporation and the principle of reduction.

Notes

1　E.g. J. Searle, *Speech Acts – An Essay in the Philosophy of Language* (Cambridge University Press, 1969).
2　E.g. J. Sadock, *Toward a Linguistic Theory of Speech Acts* (New York: Academic Press, 1974).
3　Cf. J. L. Austin, *How To Do Things With Words* (Oxford: Clarendon Press, 1962); E. Benveniste, 'La Philosophie analytique et le langage', *Problèmes de linguistique générale* (Paris: Gallimard, 1963).
4　Under this terminology, (3)–(11) are implicit performatives.
5　The grammatical form of (12)–(14) is the same as for 'true or false' examples like (1) and (2).
6　Cf. E. Benveniste, 'La Philosophie analytique et le langage', and B. de Cornulier,' 'La Notion d'auto-interprétation', *Études de linguistique appliquée*, 19 (1975), pp. 52–82.
7　Moreover, the time, circumstances, etc., should be appropriate.

202   *G. Fauconnier*

8 Self-verification differs from the success of the perlocutionary aims of the utterance. Cf. P. Bourdieu, 'Le Langage autorisé', *Actes de la recherche en sciences sociales*, 5–6 (1975), pp. 65–79: 'a performative utterance is doomed to fail every time it is not expressed by a person who has the power to utter it . . .'

9 Cf. J. Sadock, *Toward a Linguistic Theory of Speech Acts*, and the review of this work by J. Searle, 'Review of J. Sadock, *Toward a Linguistic Theory of Speech Acts*', *Language*, 52 (1976), pp. 966–71. For a critique of representational methods in linguistics cf. G. Fauconnier, 'Is There a Linguistic Level of Logical Representation?'. *Theoretical Linguistics*, 5/1 (1978), pp. 31–49.

10 (15) as a constative, may be immediately falsified, e.g. by a 'more certain' affirmation; 'no problem' is an exaggeration here, since any information (especially in the future) is itself constrained by multiple conditions.

11 Cf. P. Bourdieu, 'Le Langage autorisé'.

12 Many non-verbal examples of ritual incorporation can be found. G. Bohas points out that choir boys used to carry candles to light the church – with the advent of electricity, the candles have remained as part of the religious rituals. Wedding rings, although formally not a part of the marriage ritual, have in practice been incorporated into the rite. The catholic priest's garments are an incorporated form of ordinary clothes of earlier times.

13 The term 'self-reference' is borrowed from E. Benveniste, 'La Philosophie analytique et le langage', but used in a wider sense. For Benveniste an utterance is self-referential if it refers to an act entirely constituted by this utterance itself. Here, 'self-referential' is applied to an utterance E which refers to an act of which E is a part (it may of course be the only part). Cf. O. Ducrot, *Dire et ne pas dire* (Paris: Hermann, 1972).

14 Cf. for example J. R. Searle, *Speech Acts – An Essay in the Philosophy of Language*, ch. 8.

15 The following texts are from P. G. Simon, 1762, *Extrait des assertions dangereuses et pernicieuses en tout genre soutenues et enseignées par les soi-disans Jésuites*, Paris, Imprimerie du Parlement, tome II , Parjure, Fausseté, Faux Témoignage.

Part 3

Toward a reconstruction of systems perspectives

7 Transformational theory and the internal environment of action systems[1]

Victor Lidz

[*The thrust of Lidz's contribution to this volume is that he attempts to combine a systems perspective as informed by Parsons's functionalist conception with a notion of transformational theory as informed by transformational grammar in linguistics, and thereby to overcome the consistent difficulty of social theory to account for the seeming stability and at the same time creativity of social life.*

To illustrate this, consider definitions of the situation negotiated in micro-social action as surface structures which assign variable rights and responsibilities to actors engaged in specific projects. And consider the institutionalized normative order postulated by functionalism as an underlying structure which has, like the structure of rules and resources proposed by Giddens in chapter 5, stability over time and across situations. It is the situated rhetorical judgments which rationalize choices among transformational alternatives within the normative order, and which hence command or reject a specific course of action.

The paper outlines how transformational concepts might be articulated with the theory of communicative media, and it illustrates the operation of these media which regulate system processes by the metaphor of the circulation of the blood. Note that there are dynamic *processes which are here invoked as the basis of the stability of the normative order, and which are congenial to the emphasis micro-sociologies have placed on the dynamic character of social action.*]

1 The reception of generative theory in sociology

For the discipline of sociology, the years since 1960 have been widely experienced as an era of intellectual fragmentation and of tense struggle among competing schools of thought. Over the past several years, however, a curious, if partial, basis for renewed agreement has emerged as proponents of several of the most actively competing schools have taken up work on a common theoretical problem. This problem may be called the reception of the theory of transformational grammars, developed in linguistics and secondarily in philosophy and psychology by Noam Chomsky and his followers, into the domain of sociological analysis. The sociological interest in Chomsky's work derives from its formal elegance and its originality in subjecting the creativity or generativity of human uses of language to rigorous analysis,[2] but also from the conviction of sociologists that it has systematically overlooked important social factors in linguistic communication.[3] The engagement between transformational theory and sociology has by now produced interesting new thought on the involvements of language in social interaction, on problems of apprehending, and giving disciplined descriptions of, the meanings exchanged in everyday social relationships, and on the actual workings of elements in normative orders. Issues utterly fundamental to sociological theory have been addressed in original ways, but with some bias toward micro-level problems relatively close to the sociolinguistic starting-point.

The specific studies that have contributed to the sociological reception of generative theory have been diverse in empirical focus and consideration as well as anchorage in established schools of thought. A selective listing of pertinent works may indicate the range, though hardly the full weight, of evidence and argument that has been raised in favour of transformational modes of analysis in sociology:

(1)   Labov has studied exchanges of ritual insults in the informal interaction of black inner-city youths, showing that the competence of participants to generate rhetorically effective insults involves standards concerning such matters as the status order of peer groups, avoidance of certain types of personal truths about the objects of insults, common understandings of the social structure of the urban lower-class environment, and a special rhetorical style as well as the grammar of the vernacular.[4]

(2)   Sacks, Jefferson, and Schegloff[5] have demonstrated that orderly turn-taking in informal conversation depends upon observance of several simple rules organized in a structural hierarchy. The different patterns of turn-taking found in classroom discussions, interviews, religious rituals, public debates, psychotherapy, and other types of verbal interchange might be treated as deriving from

transformations on the rule structure for informal conversation. Although the investigatory lead has not been pursued intensively since Sacks's death, it would appear that the capacity of interactors to co-ordinate with one another in creating orderly sequences of turntaking in a wide variety of different types of verbal exchanges cannot be understood without recourse to a model of a transformational competence.

(3) Habermas[6] has undertaken a study of illocutionary speech acts in order to extend transformational modes of analysis into the domain of pragmatics, which has long been residual to systematic research. Illocutionary speech has social force or achieves an overt social consequence through spoken words, as in the giving of advice. The category of illocutions includes socially formal performatives, such as swearing to the truth in court, disinheriting an heir, or sacralizing a ritual object, where observing certain standards of form imparts an objective validity to the action. Habermas emphasizes that the formal consequences of such performatives rest upon subtle normative presuppositions intricately interwoven with quite various institutional structures but also precisely articulated with transformational rules of grammar.

(4) Cicourel[7] suggested some years ago that the intersubjective sense of social structure, or certainty about the constraining facticity of normative arrangements in immediate situations, may be treated as a kind of generated surface structure in the specific usage of transformational theory. Several of the interpretive devices identified by ethnomethodologists as means for sustaining intersubjectivity of understanding, e.g. use of indexical expressions, attention to the reflexivity of talk, or resort to the '*et cetera* assumption', may then be regarded as transformational procedures for adapting the sense of social structure to the innumerable differences encountered by actors among the concrete situations in which they participate. By viewing interpretive procedures as transformational operations, the sociologist can gain a formal understanding of how actors process a limited set of normative rules to gain orientation to the open-ended, creative quality of social interaction.

(5) Goffman[8] has essayed the ways in which underlying presuppositions frame the purpose, type, and meaning of co-ordinated activities within particular social situations. Clarity about the framing presuppositions of a course of action is ordinarily an essential

prerequisite for contributing appropriately to it, even though actors often do not signal their presuppositions explicitly. Conduct oriented in terms of presuppositions conflicting with those expected by others may, depending upon circumstances, be embarrassing, humorous, uncanny, insane, criminal, dangerous, or nonsensical. The presuppositions framing activities for particular situations are generally transformations of presuppositions underlying the sense of activities in certain other situations. For example, historic events such as the Watergate crimes will be represented in systematically different ways in newspaper accounts, stage dramas, courtroom testimony, partisan political speeches, autobiographies, etc. Study of the transformations obtaining among presuppositions·framing different situations should carry our understanding of how creative social processes are ordered to a deeper level, more closely linked to macrosocial factors.

(6)   The present author has analysed the law as a set of generative procedures and underlying normative standards for securing definitions of the situation that are otherwise vulnerable to deviance, disavowal, or misinterpretation.[9] In this view, definitions of the situation are generated surface structures assigning rights and responsibilities to parties engaged in specific projects of action, while institutionalized normative orders, including the legal order, are underlying structures having stability over time and across situations. Situations become defined through processes of negotiation (entailing interpretive procedures in Cicourel's sense) that devise new means of normative governance by operating transformationally on underlying institutions in order to adapt to the interests of parties, the requirements of planned activities, and other contingent circumstances.[10] In so far as the generative negotiations proceed informally, resulting definitions are apt to be brief, partially explicated, ambiguous, casually supported, and thus readily manipulated. They may suffice where social trust is firm, but become vulnerable where impersonal relationships, strong material or moral interests, complex activities, or public accountability are involved. The formal language, codified norms, and rational procedures of law favour precision, refinement, flexibility, and security of interests in the defining of situations. Contracts may be taken as a prototype of creative, voluntarily accepted, and yet authoritatively interpretable definitions of the situation, hence are well adapted to securing rela-

tionships of major and complex importance in large-scale social systems.

The foregoing sketches should indicate that the sociological studies in transformational theory comprise, perhaps, a fascinating mosaic of shrewd and insightful observations and arguments, but not yet a logically integrated, self-consistent body of knowledge. However, despite differences and perhaps inconsistencies in key concepts, they do seem to establish the empirical importance of transformational operations at a plurality of levels in the organization of processes of social action. If the weight of demonstration appears to be heaviest in the domain of micro-sociology, it is also true that significant considerations point toward the importance of transformational analysis for macro-sociology as well. I suggest, therefore, that transformational concepts be taken as elements in general sociological theory concerning the nature of structure and process. One purpose of the following discussion is to lend additional support to this suggestion.

The categories of structure and process have long been complemented in many sociological theories – most systematically in Parsonian theory of action – by the category of function. In recent years, the category of function has been under attack, including the subtle form of attack that manifests itself as simple neglect, from a number of sources in sociology. It has been alleged by conflict theorists that functionalism cannot bring processes of social conflict, change, and system transformation objectively under analysis. Empiricists have doubted that functional theory is scientific because its hypotheses often require consideration of relatively intangible macro-social data, e.g. data about qualities of value orientations underlying many particular institutions, that are difficult to ascertain with clarity and finality. Most radically, ethnomethodology has been sceptical about the entire theoretical superstructure in which functional concepts have emerged, from the idea that facts are synthesized in the conceptual scheme of the observer, to the stance of analytical realism, to concern for the problem of order, to the notions of system and functional requisites of systems.[11] Because transformational theory has entered sociology most prominently through ethnomethodology, and because transformational linguistics itself lacks functional concepts, it has generally been viewed as a kind of theory thoroughly, perhaps essentially, independent of functionalism. The discussion below will challenge any idea that this view of the relation between transformationalism and functionalism is imposed by theoretical necessity. I will not proceed by critical examination of the formal compatibilities of transformational and functional theories, which would require a much longer essay. Rather, I will proceed more substantively by examining the functional significance of the transformational properties of language for systems of social action.

Because the argument I will be developing places great weight on concepts taken from Chomsky's transformational linguistics, it may be helpful to the reader if I present some preliminary comments on my own usage of such terms as transformation, base rules, deep structure, surface structure, and so forth. My intention is to transfer the formal power of transformational analysis from the discipline of linguistics to the intellectual disciplines long associated with the study of social action, especially sociology. I will therefore not be using the concepts of transformational theory to analyse phenomena directly in the domain synthesized by linguistic concepts. My uses of technical terms of transformational analysis will generally not be in reference to the linguistic realities. Rather, I will be attempting to use the transformational terms as means of conceptualizing facts of the cultural, social, and psychological domains. Although I will be attending to the articulations at work between language and other elements of systems of social action, especially to continuities between grammatical rules and other elements of normative order, my principal aim is to work out modes of cognizing cultural, social, and psychological processes that are autonomous from, if interdependent with, linguistic mechanisms. Because the present essay concentrates on developing a rationale and analytical strategy for a general application of transformational concepts to the materials of action theory, but does not present detailed evidence or illustrations beyond what has already been cited, it may appear that I intend my invokings of transformational terms to be merely metaphorical. That is not my intent. I mean to argue that processes of transformation operating in many sectors of action systems have the same order of 'reality' that is now commonly ascribed to linguistic transformations. I recognize, to be sure, that we cannot presently – and may never – show the workings of action-level transformations with the detail, precision, and generality that can readily be demonstrated for a great many linguistic transformations. Recognition of this limitation, which can be ascribed to a variety of differences both in subject-matters and in methods of research between linguistics and the social sciences, need not vitiate the value of transformational concepts for advancing descriptive as well as analytical theory in sociology. The strategy animating the present study is that greater awareness of the diversity of transformational processes at work in action systems and firmer conceptual discrimination among the many kinds of them should provide one (hardly the only) basis for increasing the precision with which their operations can be sought out.

Only in a rather indirect sense may the present argument be regarded as an overview of a Chomskian sociology. Chomsky has himself expressed very little interest in sociological applications or implications of transformational theory. He apparently finds sociolinguistic studies banal, even to the point of encouraging doubt about whether any interesting contributions can in principle result from them. Chomsky has given a great deal of attention to questions of whether or not transformational understandings of the workings of language amount to knowledge of basic psychological capacities of human beings. He has even suggested that his fundamental frame of reference has been designed to bring transformational linguistics to focus upon problems of this order. Transformational theory is thus presented as having its foundations in an idealization of the domain of linguistics that emphasizes the operations of 'one faculty of the mind, the language faculty'.[12] It is apparently this idealization that has structured so firmly Chomsky's lack of interest in sociolinguistic studies and his failure to recognize the near ubiquity of uses of language in social life as suggestive of possibilities for sociological investigations possibly as fundamental as the psychological questions to which he often addresses himself. Obviously, it is an idealization thoroughly unsuitable for guiding the present study. I wish to propose that the implications of transformational linguistics for the study of truly fundamental human capacities can be framed in another way that articulates very suitably with theories of social action. Language, specifically the rules of grammar, may be regarded as a system of normative order embedded deeply in central realities of human social life, such as the extremely diffuse need for precise and creative communication of ideas, feelings, expectations, beliefs, and so forth. If language may be taken as a prototypal normative order, the demonstration that transformational concepts open up a new kind of understanding of the workings of grammar suggests a great deal to the sociologist. We will take guidance from the hypothesis that transformational theory, abstracted as a formal entity from its applications in linguistics, may illuminate the operations of all kinds of normative orders. If we proceed to identify a great many transformational mechanisms located in many sectors of action systems, it is because independent normative structures are so readily found.

2   Language and the internal environment of action systems

Sociological functionalism has arisen largely as an effort to work out fruitful analogues of theories of homeostasis developed in biology. A landmark attempt to embody the biological analogy in technical but non-reductive concepts of the objects of social scientific study was Durkheim's idea of the social milieu, developed under the influence of Claude Bernard's notion of the interior milieu of organisms.[13] When American functionalists first began to develop ideas of system, function, and equilibrium after the models set forth in experimental physiology by such figures as L. J. Henderson and W. B. Cannon, they failed, as Parsons later acknowledged,[14] to include an explicit concept of the internal environment of action systems. The scheme of *Toward A General Theory of Action*,[15] for example, sets forth concepts of the external environment of an action system and of the immediate situation of social interaction, but not a concept, like Durkheim's, of the special interior setting for operative relations among parts of the system. However, a careful reading of the works of Henderson and Cannon[16] reveals that their idea of homeostatic processes gained its precision from being methodically matched to a concept of the internal environment of the organism. A brief review of the physiological concept of internal environment should establish a touchstone for a basic idea in sociological theory.

In evolutionary terms, life is believed to have begun in water. Water provided the environment for very complex sets of chemical reactions to come together in life-creating sequences and balances. Ever since, all living beings, from the simplest proto-viruses to the most complex organisms, have required water-based fluid media to carry out their life-preserving biochemical processes. Cellular organization incorporates a relatively stable fluid environment within the living body, making possible greater continuity and balance in the life processes. Complex organisms of many differentiated cells contain not only intra-cellular fluids, but also fluids that circulate outside the cells and serve, with osmosis, to keep the contents of the cells in specific biochemical balances appropriate to their specialized functions. The circulating fluids have been called the fluid matrix. They comprise the general internal environment of the complex organism through which its various organs, tissues, and cells can act upon one another despite physical and functional separations.

All cells of all organisms must receive nutriments from, and discharge metabolic wastes to, the external environment if they are to live. The living cells of complex organisms typically have no direct relations with the environment, however. The fluid matrix surrounding them mediates their relationships with specialized organs, e.g. lungs, intestines, kidneys, through which nutriments are gained and wastes discharged for the entire organism. Through the specialized operations of functionally differentiated organs, the fluid matrices of complex organisms, especially warm-blooded animals, tend to become highly stable in physical properties and physiologically active chemical components. Compared with the fluctuations typical of external environments, e.g. in availability of nutriments, the immediate surroundings of the cells and tissues tend to be extraordinarily stable. The exigencies of staying alive are immensely alleviated for the protoplasm, which can then sustain far more exacting biochemical balances. The emergence of a constant fluid matrix has strongly favoured the evolution of further complexity. First, the maintenance of protoplasm in more precise conditions of homeostasis has facilitated the emergence of more specialized modes of functioning and more intricate patterns of interdependence among organs. Second, the availability of the fluid matrix as a medium for circulating various types of nutriments has enhanced the capacity of organisms to adjust to new specializations in physiological structure. The functioning of specialized digestive organs, for example, depends on the capacity of the fluid matrix to circulate sugars, proteins, digested carbohydrates and fats, vitamins, and so forth to the cells that metabolize them. Third, the fluid matrix also becomes involved in the regulative processes directly sustaining and adjusting the overall homeostasis of the organism. Thus, the circulating fluids comprise a medium for taking up a large number of hormones from the glands that produce them and for depositing them in the tissues for which they provide catalytic regulation of specific biochemical processes. The circulation of the hormones thereby serves to adjust the rates of functioning of various tissues, organs, and organ systems to one another and to general needs of the organism.

The blood is the rapidly and widely circulating, more intricately composed, and more precisely balanced part of the fluid matrix. It mediates the concentrated biochemical interchanges with such critical organs as the lungs, stomach, intestines, liver, kidneys, and endocrine glands. Its refined composition preserves the life-protecting qualities of a vast variety of molecules as they are circulated to cells in which they can be further metabolized. Along with its pattern of circulation, its composition also protects molecules essential for life from the harmful effects of metabolic wastes that must be transported to specialized organs for excretion. While the more slowly circulating lymph mediates interchanges between the blood and the peripheral protoplasm, the swiftly flowing blood unifies the biochemical environment interior to the organism. The speed, pressure, and pervasiveness of the circulation of the blood enable many specialized tissues to respond quickly and precisely to changes in one another's metabolic needs. The intricacy of the composition of circulating blood, which carries along water, oxygen, sugars, salts, minerals, proteins, enzymes, hormones, immunologic agents, etc., makes the blood content itself closely interdependent with many elements in the general physiological status of the organism. Study of perturbations in the content and circulation of the blood has been perhaps the most incisive method of gaining knowledge about basic physiological operations in animals.

Henderson emphasized that understanding the blood and its circulation required a multi-disciplinary venture, with contributions from fields as diverse as fluid mechanics, biophysics, biochemistry, and evolutionary biology. He demonstrated the multiplicity of levels of organization involved in the functioning of blood by showing that blood sustains its own homeostasis with regard to water content, osmotic pressure, temperature, acid-base balance, oxygen-carbon dioxide levels, sugar levels, serum protein levels, red cells to plasma balance, the composition of haemoglobin, and quantities of various hormones.[17] He also showed that imbalances in these characteristics of blood can precipitate profound, often dramatic, consequences within the homeostatic operations of the organism as a whole. Understanding of how the blood fulfils its circulatory functions, then, appeared to be a strategic path to knowledge of the patterns of functional differentiation and interdependence unifying complex organisms. The basis of integrating multi-level, multi-discipline studies of fundamental metabolic processes would be a conception of the biochemistry of fluid mediation, with blood being viewed as the most important mediating fluid.

I wish to suggest that the internal environment of a system of social action may be conceptualized similarly to the Henderson–Cannon treatment of the fluid matrix. I will use the term *symbolic matrix* to refer to the complex set of symbolic media which together enable the diverse parts of action systems to sustain many kinds of communication with one another. In speaking of the symbolic matrix, I want to emphasize the sense in which all parts or units of action systems are surrounded by or immersed in symbolic media, much as the cells and tissues of organisms live within fluid matrices. The symbolic matrix provides parts of action systems with information about processes in various other parts that may be necessary for their continued operations. The capacity of any given component of an action system to co-ordinate its operations with various other components depends critically on the information it receives through the symbolic matrix. The capacity of the symbolic matrix to circulate information that often requires subtle and precise mediation must extend practically throughout the entire action system. The symbolic matrix must bring together in a unified domain of communicative relations all the varieties of parts of the action subsystems of culture, social system, personality, and mind.[18] Quite a variety of symbolic media, drawing upon somewhat different forms of symbolization and different modes of articulation into the overall patterns of specialization within action systems, are needed to meet the requirements of complex action systems for continuous communication. Modern civilizations, for example, require extraordinarily intricate symbolic matrices, drawing upon very diverse repertoires of symbolic genres that respond quite differentially to needs that are cultural (religious, moral, artistic and expressive, cognitive and intellectual), social (economic, political, communal, socializing), personal (as in dreams, fantasies, or need-representations), and mental (as in representations of events, plans, expectations, and even abstract forms of thought). In bringing the symbolic matrix under analysis, we take up the question of how such diverse genres of symbolic communication can be brought, through many kinds of interrelation, to constitute a fairly unitary internal environment for an action system.

Language appears to be the analogue in the symbolic matrix of the blood in the fluid matrix. The meanings that can be formulated in human languages rest upon 'arbitrary' conventions fixing the significance of expressions with objectivity.[19] By following the conventional constraints for formulating or interpreting sentences embodied in rules of grammar, actors routinely seek to convey to one another with precision and objectivity symbolizations that are formally original and often even creative, intricate, and subtle in meaning. In so far as a variety of conditions of adherence to conventions of grammar can be mastered, language enables actors to mediate symbolic meanings across wide differences in 'location' within action systems. The speaker or writer may be remote from the hearer or reader not only in space and time, but in the mental schemas, personal motives, normatively defined social situations, and specific cultural beliefs that orient their respective courses of action. The mundane fact that, albeit with scholarly assistance in clarifying presuppositions of thought in distant epochs, we still have access to, and can invoke to amplify the senses of our intentions, the meanings of the Old Testament prophets, the philosophers of Graeco-Roman antiquity, the Renaissance humanists, etc., indicates the communicative potential of human language. We routinely use language to extend the internal environment of the action systems in which we are engaged vastly beyond the immediate settings of our interaction. We take for granted as a routine capacity to co-ordinate action that we may communicate with one another in linguistic form to express or clarify ideas, motives, expectations, and beliefs, even across important subjective and objective differences. Indeed, it may be suggested that the differentiatedness of the internal environment of the action system and the diversity of specialized resources available for mobilization into processes of action through linguistic mediation comprise major indices of the 'level' attained by a civilization. In these respects, language appears to be like blood in making possible the rapid, adjustable, and precise circulation of extremely diverse materials to practically all locations within highly complex systems.

The centrality of linguistic signification in the overall communicative capacities of action systems may be analysed in terms of four principal considerations.[20] First, the *a priori* structure of categories embedded, apparently universally, in linguistic form may be regarded as a reflection of the formal essence of human sociation generally. The basic categories of universal elements of grammar – subject, verb, object, and modifiers – correspond to the irreducible elements of social action – actor, orientation, alter, and modalities.[21] Language thus has a built-in structure of essential references to fundamental elements of social action. As we will see in discussion below, various kinds of operation on grammatical constituents of particular sentences generated within sequences of interaction readily take on pragmatic significance in the sense of acting index-ically upon relations among the participants in the situation. Second, language has the property of imposing transformational and hier-archical relations upon expressions or invocations of elements of action that are presented in linguistic terms. The processes of com-position for any particular sequences of action, in so far as they are mediated through uses of language, are necessarily transformational, i.e. generated through a series, short or long, of reorderings or recom-binations of elements under rules and procedures of transformation. Any concrete presentation of significant action therefore has 'depth', a history of a series of transformations through which it has been composed and adapted to the circumstances of its production. Only through a process of using transformations to move interpretations from the surface presentation to recover the underlying, deep com-position can significant action be comprehended at all fully and precisely. Given the categorial correspondences between linguistic and other elements of social action, the interpretive process must recover many pragmatic operations as well as linguistic transfor-mations in order to grasp the underlying meanings of socially situated signification. Third, any 'grammar' setting forth the rule-abiding possibilities for transforming relationships among parts of a signifi-cant action must be complemented by a 'rhetoric' setting forth stan-dards for evaluating the pragmatic efficacy of each possibility.[22] Every completed course of action may be judged in terms of its relative efficaciousness. However, rhetorical standards, and hence the rhetorical judgment that rationalizes choices among transforma-tional alternatives, cannot be confined to strictly linguistic consider-ations. Rhetorical design in uses of language is continuous with calculation about many features of situations, other actors, contingent resources, etc., that also play into the efficaciousness of conduct. The rational use of a variety of media other than language, for example, money or political power, may represent ways of securing the efficacy of a course of action in specialized respects. Fourth, as already suggested, uses of language may be said to carry along many kinds of substances within action systems. Whatever the formal, convention-determined significance of a use of language, its practical meaning will depend largely upon the import of the ideas, feelings, expectations, beliefs, and so forth, that it brings together in a situated composition. Analysis of language uses must attend to the respects in which formal mediation is being given to the circulation of basic resources of action systems.

The perplexing, much debated question of the functions of language appears in a new light once language is viewed as a lifeblood for systems of action. Behind the extraordinarily diverse qualities, forms, and functions which appear in the descriptive treatment of language, we can discern in more integral terms the service performed by language in unifying the internal environment of action systems. Most basically, language appears as the rapidly circulating medium that enables a very wide range of resources for action to flow fairly continuously throughout action systems. The transformational qualities of language seem, then, to be the analogue in action systems of the biochemical properties of blood in organisms. It is the transformational qualities that enable language to mediate the circulation of so many resources and enter into the regulation of their formally creative (generative) use in so many different processes of action. The importance of transformational theories is that, like the biochemistry of blood composition for physiology, they provide an incisive point of entry for the multi-level, multi-disciplinary study of wide-ranging, intricately organized phenomena.

3   Language, transformations, and the pragmatic media

For roughly 20 years, Talcott Parsons and a number of co-workers have explored the functioning of an entire 'family' of circulating media that operate in social life.[23] The original concern of the research on media was to develop a mode of dynamic analysis at the level of macro-sociology. Parsons had the insight that money, regarded as a circulating medium of economic process, might not be an utterly singular phenomenon in social life. In a classic paper, he argued that power, suitably defined, may be treated as an analogous medium facilitating and in part regulating the interactive processes of the polity, treated analytically as a subsystem of society comparable to the economy.[24] He later identified influence, in a sense developed out of its usage in reference group theory, as the circulating medium of the integrative or solidarizing subsystem of society.[25] Finally, Parsons suggested that value-commitments may be taken as the circulating medium that regulates processes within the fiduciary or, broadly, the socializing subsystem of society.[26] With these analytical proposals, Parsons established a framework, rather different from any other in sociology, for studying the general conditions of equilibria in the overall society and in a methodically derived set of its primary subsystems. Terms and concepts were set forth in a highly differentiated scheme for examining such matters as: the institutional regulation of 'expenditures', on the part of the salient kinds of role-incumbents, of each of the several media; the strategies that can be pursued in using or investing quantities of the various media in order to assure an interested party of continued 'incomes' with which to meet ongoing responsibilities; the patterns of aggregate flows or interchanges of the media among the subsystems of society; and, hardly least, processes of inflation and deflation in the values of the various media. A chief accomplishment of the theoretical work on the social media was to lay out a general procedure for investigating the dynamic involvements of particular actions, or aggregations of actions, with equilibrium conditions extending to major subsystems of societies or even whole societies.

The relative success of the original studies of social media encouraged an extension of the investigative strategy. A second series of media, usually termed the general action media, was identified in the operations of the primary subsystems of the entire action system.[27] Intelligence in a sense derived from Piaget came to be treated as the circulating medium anchored in the workings of the behavioural system or mind. Affect was designated as the medium involved with the cathectic structures and motivational predispositions of the personality. Durkheim's term, collective sentiment, was appropriated for the medium circulating most widely in social systems and representing the attachments of members of society to normative standards that may be invoked to define and order situated interaction. Collective representation, another Durkheimian term, was used to identify the circulating medium of cultural systems, standing for the capacity of seriously regarded beliefs to provide constancy of orientation across the many practical contingencies of processes of action. The operations of the set of general action media, which can be examined in terms of problems of expenditure, continued or renewed income, flows among the various subsystems, inflation and deflation, etc., analogous to the problems noted for the media of the societal subsystems, amount in the aggregate view to the processes of mutual adjustment among the primary constituents of action systems. The theory of the general action media thus brings dynamic analysis to the task first undertaken in *Toward A General Theory of Action* of working out the relations of mutual dependence obtaining among the primary subsystems of action.

Both the societal and the general action media are ordinarily bound up with language on the occasions of their practical use. When we expend money to acquire rights in goods or services, we commonly engage in some discussion to clarify the terms of exchange. In complex exchanges, the discussion generally takes the form of deliberation about terms of contracts. Similarly, exercises of power ordinarily involve the giving of directives, orders, or commands. The use of influence may be said to be intimately interdependent with a specialized rhetoric for arousing senses of common solidarity. The invoking of collective sentiment in order to clarify normative obligations taking effect in a situation typically occurs within processes of verbal negotiation among participants. The allocation of affect to specific activities on the part of the individual personality generally involves deliberation, and often discussion with others, about the significant – i.e. objectively or intersubjectively formulizable – meanings embedded in the project of action. These several examples perhaps suffice to show that the specialized media typically enter into processes of action in close mutual dependence with language, spoken or written. Despite the old saying that 'money talks', money is not able to talk by itself. It requires a great deal of linguistic clarification for its message to take determinate effect in most sequences of interaction, and the same principle holds for each of the other media as well. In general, the uses of the specialized media must themselves be mediated through language. Yet, the linguistic messages are also dependent upon invocations of the specialized media if they are to result in definite kinds of pragmatic effects upon the situation of action. It is the handing over of cash, the writing of a cheque, or the giving of a formal commitment to make payment that brings the concluding terms of a negotiation into pragmatic effect. It is the general's capacity to expend power that converts his wish into a command, while the verbal directives of the relatively powerless private can be construed only as a joke. In Habermas's sense of the term, an illocutionary force is exerted upon linguistically given meanings by an expenditure of one of the specialized or pragmatic media. In the case of each medium, the type of illocutionary force that may be exerted to give effect to linguistic action is specialized in nature. The media may be said to comprise a set of mechanisms for regulating the capacities of actors to provide illocutionary force for their activities. As such mechanisms, they are specialized in various ways to serve the functional 'needs' of the specific subsystems and sub-subsystems of action in which their circulation is anchored.[28]

Being closely connected to language, and generally taking effect as specialized modes of giving validity (in the sense of the German term *Geltung*) to uses of language, the pragmatic media seem also to assume the four primary qualities of language discussed above. The societal and general action media may, if not too much is made of the claim, even be considered specialized languages. First, the media impart their effects on action by altering relations among instances of the categories of actor, orientation, alter, and modality.[29] Second, the media enter action by underlying linguistic expressions in the hierarchies of transformational processes through which specific activities are generated. Viewed from the standpoint of the problems of interpreting surface manifestations of action, the media appear as presuppositions that underlie the linguistic deep structures and clarify their pragmatic import. The societal media may be regarded as entities arising from the differentiation of societal institutions at a level of organization that underlies the circulation of the general action media. They represent scarce capacities to give illocutionary force to actions that are determined through macro-social processes, yet take effect by entering into the processes of defining situations as specialized means for regulating the terms on which collective sentiment can be circulated. All of the pragmatic media have their own generative mechanisms characterized by hierarchical depth and by the ability to transform deep-lying elements of pragmatic judgment into composite guidelines for reacting to certain kinds of situational difficulties at their surfaces. The essential qualities of power, for example, cannot be grasped if it is regarded merely as a means for imparting bindingness to directives or commands that are pre-ordained and invariant across situations in their content. Power can be confined to that form only in limiting cases, and then become extremely rigid. More typically, power represents a capacity to validate, as binding, commands that are generated creatively as authoritative responses to fresh difficulties of sustaining effective co-ordination of collective action that arise uniquely within particular situations. Third, given the creativity of the generative processes associated with the media, standards must exist for selecting among the most efficacious courses of action from the many possibilities. Each of the media has consequently given rise to a body of thought, more or less systematized, about how actors may rationalize its use. Formal techniques of accounting, setting quite precise standards for the rational control of economic action through the monetary medium, are an elaborate development. But all of the media have provided foci for systematic reflection about how processes of action may be rationalized. Fourth, the pragmatic media comprise modes of symbolic representation of various kinds of 'real' resources consumed in the operations of action systems. Money, for example, represents, and stands as a generalized claim upon, economic resources. Intelligence represents a claim upon the capacities of human minds to resolve problems of understanding and of the behavioural co-ordination of action. Each medium symbolizes the general category of resources most pervasively involved in the functioning of the action subsystem in which its circulation is anchored. By making it possible to circulate representations of 'real' resources and even prefigure potential courses of action through transformational operations before actual movement of the resources becomes necessary, the media impart crucial freedoms and flexibilities to human social life.[30]

Despite the concentration of most transformational sociology upon micro-level problems, we now see that systematic thought about macro-social dynamics can be articulated in important ways with transformational theory. The mutual involvements between language and the pragmatic media within the symbolic matrix seem to spread transformational properties to many aspects and levels of the organization of action. Although the details of the articulations among the many transformational mechanisms I am positing may seem dismayingly complex, it should be noted that they may all represent the workings of a very simple evolutionary process. Action systems have been able to refine their controls over the central communicative process, the use of language within interactive setting, by establishing additional levels of underlying presuppositions and additional specializations of transformative procedures. The hierarchical depth through which specialized controls over uses of language may 'be elaborated and the complexity of the set of specialized transformational mechanisms for raising generated meanings to the surface of social action may be taken as rough measures of the evolutionary level of a civilization. Some of the major problems of macro-sociology and comparative institutional analysis can be addressed from a new vantage-point if transformational processes are sought out in depths of the generation of social action that underlie the operations on which most sociological transformationalism has concentrated.

4   Micro-sociology, macro-sociology, and the media

The reception of transformational theory appears to have brought sociology to a point of fresh potential for conceptual codification. Transformational theory has been evolving into a scheme of microsociological categories having a new level of capacity for passing out sequences of interaction into their meaningful details, and for highlighting the practical significance of such details in terms that, being transformational, are intrinsically comparative. With certain elaborations and supplementations, transformational theory may also take on the central, integrative status within general sociology that microeconomic theory has long held within the discipline of economics. A transformational view of the sociological actor may provide the general study of social action with the elementary, irreducible universals of conceptualization, description, and analysis that economists have commonly derived for their field from a notion of an economic man striving to maximize want-satisfaction through market exchanges under constraints of supply and demand. A view of the sociological actor as engaged in the interactive transformation of normative materials in order to generate definitions of the situation and thereby co-ordinate creative sequences of social conduct may thus emerge as a ground of schemes and insights central to all technically disciplined sociological knowledge. The centrality of a transformational scheme within sociological theory does not rest simply on its capacity to penetrate into essential characteristics of the normative ordering of social life, however. The hierarchical nature of such a scheme gives it important flexibility in assimilating both underlying presuppositions and pragmatic considerations arising from situational exigencies to its terms for representing normative transformations.

Transformational theory has brought indubitable new strengths to sociology. Its treatment of the formal differences between the deep or base generated underlying elements of normative order, on the one hand, and surface rules, sense of social structure, definitions of the situation, or practical appearances of the facticity of social life, on the other hand, resolves the long-standing controversies over the status of social order as either negotiated or structural.[31] Its grasp of the many levels of generativity in social action enables the sociologist to understand in the terms of particular settings the practical importance of stability in rules and procedures of interaction as well as the necessity for creative judgment in efforts to apply rules and follow procedures. It lays bare, in greater detail and in more orderly fashion than any previous modes of analysis, the intricacies involved in the essential operations of normative complexes. Indeed, the flexibility and adjustability it recognizes within normative operations should enable sociologists to overcome old tendencies to treat the categories of self-interest and of situational conditions as divorced from and even antithetical to values and norms.[32] For example, analysis of various transformations of legitimate expression or implementation of a practical interest can highlight the respects in which the grounds of self-interested action arise not beyond normative order but within its manifolds of potential modes of conduct. Self-interest appears, then, not in opposition to the normative or as the effective factor relative to which the normative is epiphenomenal, but as a grade within the normative through which all projects for social action may be transformed. Thus, in bringing about a large refinement in the understanding of normative operations, transformational analysis has also amplified the sense in which the category of the normative stands at the centre of sociological inquiry.

However significant the advances that transformational theory has brought to sociology, there remain serious ambiguities concerning the extent to which the general categorial schemes of the discipline need be revolutionized. Transformational micro-sociology has continued certain basic notions of earlier voluntaristic and phenomenological theories, such as actor, action, meaning, orientation, social situation, and interaction, while modifying and elaborating certain others, such as order, norm, and perhaps end. It has also tended to reject or at least express wariness about such categories as system and function, while substantially restricting concern with the categories of object and causal relation.[33] The consequent changes in categorial schemes, as compared with the prior voluntaristic functionalism or Parsonian Action Theory for example, have arisen in part from the phenomenological background of most transformational sociology and in part from the micro-sociological focus of most transformational studies. It should be appreciated that an initial focus on micro-level problems concerning the social aspects of the use of language has been a natural concern of initial efforts to bring transformational theory into sociology. A certain freedom from categories such as causal relation, object, function, and system may have helped distance the new transformational research from the positivism of earlier psycholinguistic and sociolinguistic research, thereby contributing importantly to the intellectual advance. Yet, it does not follow that transformational micro-sociology ought permanently to be wedded to a generalized scepticism about or rejection of categories concerned with system, function, and causal relations. I have argued above that transformational analysis can be exploited thoroughly within sociology only if it is closely integrated with functional analysis. Indeed, I have suggested that the consequences of the transformational properties of language for processes of social action can be grasped comprehensively only through functional treatment of the operative importance of language as the central member of the 'family' of communicative media circulating in the internal environments of action systems. By attending to the continuities in form and operation between language and the other generative media of social action, transformational theory can extend essential insights of its micro-sociological schema to analysis of the patterns of differentiation among the principal institutional domains of society, perhaps the primary concern of macro-sociology.

Indeed, the ends of micro-sociology – intensive analysis of particular social relationships or sequences of interaction with respect to observed or imputed meanings and intentions, techniques and stratagems, interpersonal governance, and practical consequences – cannot be realized richly without use of macro-sociological knowledge. However importantly a given relationship or sequence of interaction may be voluntary and autonomous, it is also embedded within complexly extending interconnections with many other processes of action. Unless human activities are explored not simply as entities unto themselves but also in terms of their extensions into an indefinite range of other projects of action, understanding and analysis remain limited. The general schemes of the theory of action can be used to analyse the interconnectedness (or mutual dependence) with other processes of social action that is involved in practically every interactive operation. It is widely appreciated that the problem of mutual dependence entails questions of how particular activities are affected by the outcomes or consequences of other activities. But questions of how quite various projects of action may draw meaning from common groundings, orderings, or presuppositions, even if differently transformed, are perhaps no less important. I have suggested above that the theory of the communicative media may be used to identify the principal dimensions along which efforts to define situations can derive extended significance by drawing upon more constant underlying presuppositions and various potential transformations of them.

We can distinguish the following dimensions for ordering extensions or generalizations of the significance of definitions of the situation. (1) Through the medium of collective representation, actors can invoke beliefs, ideas, and cumulating meanings having significance deep within the continuous traditions of their civilization and operate creatively upon them in order to highlight cultural implications of features of the situation. The cultural resources of intellectual disciplines, the arts, moral thought and speculation, and religion may thus be brought into the interactive processes of clarifying definitions of the situation. (2) The medium of affect serves to mobilize the motivational energies of the individual participants and work symbolically appropriate transformations on them in order to generate personal attachments to the intentionalities embedded within the definition of the situation. The various motives implicated in the situated interaction are thus given significance in relation to the underlying motivational complexes and predispositional patterns of the personalities involved. (3) The medium of intelligence enables actors to assess the capacities having mandate under the definition of the situation, not least the capacities needed to understand and take direction from normative expectations of the various participants. The knowledge and abilities that particular actors contribute to co-operative activities, and that other actors may presuppose as grounds of co-operation, are connected through judgments about their intelligence with potential contributions of the same or alternative participants. (4) The medium of collective sentiment works to assure that particular definitions of the situation generated within specific social settings receive the confidence of the parties to be involved in the prospectively regulated interaction. The collective sentiment aroused in support of specific definitions of the situation has its major source in participants' moral attachments to the institutionalized normative principles and standards that serve as base rules for devising regulations appropriate to the planned interaction. As deep structures are composed through the selective application of base rules and then subjected to transformation so that the resulting surface structures or definitions of the situation can accommodate to the detailed features of the projected interaction and thereby protect the interests of the various parties, collective sentiment operates to test alternative generated formulations against one another with respect to participants' feelings about their propriety, fairness, workability, and so forth. Thus, the collective sentiment developed in the sequence of negotiating exchanges through which a situation gains a surface structure serves to connect the terms of the generated definition of the situation with stable and enduring institutional orders regulating social interaction extensively, i.e. in relation to an indefinitely large set of other situations.

Macro-social constraints receive firmer and more direct representation in the processes of defining situations through the workings of the communicative media associated with the functioning of the primary subsystems of society. Holdings of money, power, influence, and commitments give actors who possess them specialized capacities to perform valid transformations on deep structures in order to assure that certain pragmatic interests will be firmly secured in the definitions of the situation that are eventually derived. Specialized sectors of law and other normative orders have evolved to provide grounds for constraining the uses of money, power, influence, and commitments because these media represent strongly concentrated capacities to transform the terms of situated interaction, hence great potential for exploitation. The potential for exploitation arises in part from actors' needs to rationalize their expenditures of these media impersonally in terms of the macro-social conditions they confront, for example, market constraints and opportunities in the economy, structural arrangements of authority in the polity, the organization of reference groups in the societal community, and institutionally defined duties carrying high priorities within the fiduciary system. Actors make decisions about how to make expenditures from their holdings of money, power, influence, and commitments within specific situations against a background of their understandings about opportunities presented by other situations as well. Expenditures within a situation are typically made with expectations of thereby securing practical advantages that take on importance within longer run, trans-situational courses of action. Yet, the processes of defining situations are conditioned in all but limiting cases by the circumstance that participants have holdings of money, power, influence, and commitments that they may choose to expend in order to gain added control over terms generated in the developing definition of the situation. Tactical competition among actors seeking to transform the deep structures in ways favourable to themselves while also minimizing their expenditures of scarce media must be regarded as typical of the processes of generating definitions of the situation.

In the generation of creative definitions of the situation, each of the media just discussed, collective representations, affect, intelligence, collective sentiments, and, secondarily, money, power, influence, and commitments, may become problematic. By attending to their operations, the transformational micro-sociologist can amplify his understanding of the import, both formal and practical, of the specific definitions of the situation he holds under examination. His analysis is thereby extended into the domains of culture, personality, and mind as well as of social interaction, and the connections of situated activities with enduring systems and structures should become apparent. Moreover, micro-sociological investigation is, in this way also pointed towards the constellations of macro-social structures that provide the environments, sometimes more immediately and sometimes more distantly, of all situated interaction. The notion of a multiply branched hierarchy of transformational operations may thus serve to articulate the micro- and macro-levels of sociological analysis.

5 Conclusion

Viewed in terms of their functional importance for systems of social action, the transformational properties of language may be no less significant for sociology than are the fluid properties of blood for physiology. Like blood in a complex organism, language in a system of social action is a medium in which an extraordinary array of resources, including more specialized media, may circulate among a very large number of structural components. Materials that circulate in language appear to take on its properties as a symbolic and transformational medium, much as materials that circulate in blood must be compatible biochemically with its fluid properties. In this perspective, transformational operations may reasonably be sought in a great variety of the processes of action systems. Research stimulated by the successes of transformational grammars in linguistics, but searching out analogous transformational mechanisms in the domains of psychological systems, cultural systems, and systems of social interaction now suggests that transformations comprise a key characteristic in the ordering of action systems overall. The present essay has been simply a concentrated theoretical meditation on this possibility.

The reception of transformational theory in sociology has flourished mainly in the field of micro-sociology, although it has suggestive applications in macro-sociology as well. Recent work indicates that an incisive transformational codification of basic concepts in micro-sociological analysis may be near at hand. If so, I have argued, care should be taken to articulate the micro-sociological categories with available analytic schemes embodying macro-social concerns. I have sketched programmatically an outline view of how a transformational micro-sociology might be articulated with the theory of communicative media, as developed by Parsons and his collaborators. In developing this outline, I have tried to explicate two complementary concerns. First, micro-sociological theory ought not to be reductive in the sense of abstracting beyond the ways in which continuous cultural traditions, deeply felt personal emotions, basic capacities of human mind, and the hard social realities of major vested interests and established institutional constraints manifest themselves in situated interaction. Rather, micro-sociology ought to have procedures for taking such factors, irreducible not least for detailed empirical description, systematically into account. Second, the transformational qualities of ongoing genesis and creativity should not be sought only in processes of primary interaction, but also in operations of the media upon which the order and equilibria of the whole society, relative as they may be,[34] depend more directly. In expending money, power, influence, or commitments, actors are able to work transformations upon the normative ordering by specific social relationships, often very extensive and impersonal ones, with a generative creativity that is formally analogous to their uses of language. Transformational theory now calls the sociologist to examine such properties of macro-social operations, as s/he now routinely does for micro-social processes.

Notes

1 I am indebted to Rainer Baum, Harold Bershady, Andrew Effrat, Roger Masters, Talcott Parsons, and William Wimsatt for helpful comments on a working paper, 'Blood and Language: Analogous Media of Homeostasis', prepared for the Daedalus Conference on the Relations between Biological and Social Theory, March 1974.
2 The following discussion presumes some familiarity with transformational theory. Competent introductory accounts for sociology are presented in brief compass in other chapters of this volume. For fundamentals of transformational linguistics, see Noam Chomsky, *Syntactic Structure* (The Hague: Mouton, 1957); *Cartesian Linguistics* (New York: Harper & Row, 1966); *Language and Mind*, enlarged edition (New York: Harcourt, Brace & Jovanovich, 1972); and Janet Dean Fodor, *Semantics: Theories of Meaning in Generative Grammar* (New York: Cromwell, 1977).
3 For a recent discussion, see Kenneth Leiter, *A Primer on Ethnomethodology* (Oxford University Press, 1980).
4 William Labov, *Language in the Inner City: Studies in Black English Vernacular* (University of Pennsylvania Press, 1972), especially chapters 7–9.
5 Harvey Sacks, Emmanuel Schegloff, and Gail Jefferson, 'A Simplest Systematics for the Analysis of Turn-Taking in Conversations', *Language* 50 (1974), pp. 696–735.

6 Jürgen Habermas, 'What is Universal Pragmatics?', *Communication and the Evolution of Society* (Boston: Beacon Press, 1979).

7 Aaron V. Cicourel, *Cognitive Sociology* (New York: Free Press, 1974), especially chapters 3 and 4.

8 Erving Goffman, *Frame Analysis* (New York: Harper & Row, 1974).

9 Victor Lidz, 'The Law as Index, Phenomenon, and Element – Conceptual Steps Toward A General Sociology of Law', *Sociological Inquiry* 49 (1979), pp. 5–25.

10 See Victor Lidz, 'Introduction to General Action Analysis', in J. Loubser, R. Baum, A. Effrat, and V. Lidz (eds), *Explorations in General Theory in Social Science* (New York: Free Press, 1976).

11 Interesting background to these differences of opinion in sociological theory appears in Richard Grathoff (ed.), *The Theory of Social Action; The Correspondence of Alfred Schutz and Talcott Parsons* (Indiana University Press, 1978).

12 See Noam Chomsky, *Rules and Representations* (New York: Columbia University Press, 1980), p. 4. This framing of linguistics is developed throughout the book. See also Noam Chomsky, *Language and Responsibility* (New York: Pantheon Books, 1979), especially pp. 54–7 for comments on sociolinguistics. On the reduction of sociological problems to psychology, see Noam Chomsky, *Reflections on Language* (New York: Pantheon Books, 1975), especially, p. 35.

13 Emile Durkheim, *The Rules of Sociological Method* (New York: Free Press, 1950); and *Sociology and Philosophy* (New York: Free Press, 1953), especially chapter 1.

14 See Talcott Parsons, 'Durkheim on Religion Revisited: Another Look at *The Elementary Forms of the Religious Life*', in Charles Y. Glock and Phillip E. Hammond (eds), *Beyond the Classics? Essays in the Scientific Study of Religion* (New York, Harper & Row, 1973).

15 Talcott Parsons and Edward A. Shils, 'Values, Motives, and Systems of Action', in Parsons and Shils (eds), *Toward A General Theory of Action* (Harvard University Press, 1951).

16 Lawrence J. Henderson, *Blood: A Study in General Physiology*, (Yale University Press, 1928). W. B. Cannon, *The Wisdom of the Body* (New York: Norton, 1963; reprint of revised edn of 1939). The following account of the fluid matrix relies upon the classic discussions of Henderson and Cannon. The many refinements that a contemporary text in haematology would add are not essential to the broad analogy I will make to the internal environment of action systems.

17 Henderson, ibid., chapter II.

18 For this conception of the analysis of action into subsystems, see Talcott Parsons, 'Some Problems of General Theory in Sociology', in J. C. McKinney and E. A. Tiryakian (eds), *Theoretical Sociology* (New York: Appleton-Century-Crofts, 1970); also, Talcott Parsons and Gerald M. Platt, *The American University* (Harvard University Press, 1973); Lidz, 'Introduction to General Action Analysis'; and Charles Lidz and Victor Lidz, 'Piaget's Psychology of Intelligence and the Theory of Action', in

Loubser, *et al.* (eds), *Explorations in General Theory in Social Science.* The system called the 'behavioural system' in Lidz and Lidz is here, for the sake of simplicity and clarity, termed the 'mind', following the usage of George Herbert Mead.

19 I here use 'arbitrary' in the classic sense of Ferdinand de Saussure, *A Course in General Linguistics* (London: Peter Owen, 1959).

20 More technically, this set of considerations comprises a four-function paradigm. The elements are listed in the order: pattern maintenance, integration, goal-attainment, adaptation.

21 I have previously called attention to this correspondence between the irreducible elements of social action and universal categories of grammar in Lidz, 'Introduction to General Action Analysis'.

22 Compare Kenneth Burke's treatment of the complementarities between grammar and rhetoric in his analysis of linguistically formulated motives or intentions, in *A Grammar of Motives and A Rhetoric of Motives* (Cleveland: World Publishing, 1962).

23 See especially, Talcott Parsons, *Politics and Social Structure* (New York: Free Press, 1969), chapters 14, 15, 16; Talcott Parsons and Gerald M. Platt, *The American University*; 'Introduction to General Action Analysis'; Lidz and Lidz, 'Piaget's Psychology of Intelligence and the Theory of Action', especially the 'Technical Appendix' by V. Lidz; Marshall Edelson, 'Toward A Study of Interpretation in Psychoanalysis', in Loubser, *et al.* (eds), *Explorations in General Theory in Social Science*; Rainer C. Baum, 'Communication and Media' and 'On Societal Media Dynamics' in Loubser, *et al.*; Mark Gould, 'Systems Analysis, Macrosociology, and the Generalized Media of Social Action', in Loubser, *et al.*; Niklas Luhmann, 'Generalized Media and the Problem of Contingency', in Loubser, *et al.*

24 Talcott Parsons, *Politics and Social Structure*, chapter 14.

25 Ibid., chapter 15.

26 Ibid., chapter 16.

27 I present here the version of the paradigm developed in a seminar on the media that Talcott Parsons and I taught jointly in the Department of Sociology, University of Pennsylvania, Spring, 1975. We had each elaborated somewhat different formulations before agreeing upon the paradigm presented here. See Talcott Parsons, 'Some Problems of General Theory in Sociology', Talcott Parsons and Gerald M. Platt, *The American University*, and Lidz, 'Introduction to General Action Analysis'.

28 It should be noted that the media identified so far, and noted in the present discussion, do not comprise a closed list. Theoretical considerations suggest that it should be possible to identify a number of other media as well.

29 On the theoretical status of these categories, see Parsons and Shils 'Values, Motives, and Systems of Action', and Lidz, 'Introduction to General Action Analysis'.

30 Compare Parsons's treatment of the degrees of freedom imparted to action by the symbolic properties of the media in *Politics and Social Structure*,

chapter 14. See also the essays by R. C. Baum, 'Communication and Media' and 'On Societal Media Dynamics'.

31 Compare Lidz, 'Introduction to General Action Analysis', and 'Law as an Index'.

32 There is no reason that transformational theory need deny the importance of material or ecological factors in social life. From the present perspective, however, it appears clearly that their causal importance cannot be assessed with precision unless the analysis of their effects is carefully articulated with the transformational schemes of general sociology, as outlined here.

33 Some of the underlying issues become evident in Grathoff, *The Theory of Social Action*. In the background was the selectivity with which Schutz came to grips with Weber's methodology, leaving largely aside many problems of causal theory and analytical generalization. Compare, for example, the discussions of Weber's methodology in Alfred Schutz, *The Phenomenology of the Social World* (Northwestern University Press, 1967), and, more comprehensively in Talcott Parsons, *The Structure of Social Action* (New York: McGraw-Hill, 1937), chapters XVI and XVII. However, I refer more directly to the critique of Parsonian action theory that has been central to the emergence and development of ethnomethodology, but which has never been explicated very fully in print. The brief discussion in Leiter, *A Primer on Ethnomethodology*, or that in Cicourel, *Cognitive Sociology*, does not engage the fundamental issues at all comprehensively.

34 As a 'functionalist' response to criticism of the concept of equilibrium, see Victor Lidz, 'On the Construction of Objective Theory', *Sociological Inquiry* 42 (1972), pp. 51–64.

8 Communication about law in interaction systems[1]

Niklas Luhmann

[*Like the chapter by Lidz, the chapter by Luhmann promotes a systems perspective originally informed by Parsons. According to this perspective, it is the increasing complexity of society, or the increasing diversity of interaction systems which pulls apart and separates macro- and micro-levels of system formation. Social integration is no longer achieved through the actual presence of those interacting together, but through mechanisms of functional interdependence or independence and of structural compatibility or incompatibility.*

However, this form of integration can be neglected and subverted through the consensus of those who are present together, which means through the micronegotiations which take place in interaction systems. Thus decisions about the location of an ongoing communication within the total societal system are made in interaction systems, in which the boundaries and the classification of actions as belonging to a particular subsystem are routinely thematized. For example, through a particular thematization of norms in interaction systems the discourse can be moved into another system of higher order, such as law.

Systems theory promotes the conception that (social) systems operate on different levels, and it includes the notion of micro-level interaction systems and macro-level societal systems as special cases. Luhmann points out a specific form of 'micro-macro integration' through the specific allocations of interactions to a particular system-level as accomplished in interaction systems themselves. The locus (or the level) and the boundaries of particular segments of social reality, and their incorporation across levels, are a problem not only of theoretical sociology, but also of the participants of social action.]

1 Interaction systems and societal systems

Distinguishing between macro- and micro-research suggests that there exist different levels of reality – appearing, from the human point of view, as large or small. For the investigation of social reality this is a perfectly realistic assumption; the distinction becomes problematic, however, when it leads to theory disputes in which it is claimed that the one level, or the other, is the better, or even the only correct, starting-point for the investigation of the whole. Theories of interaction and theories of society are often opposed to one another in just such a fashion. This does offer us a choice, but work in sociological theory is thereby confronted prematurely with an option. Whatever one chooses, the theory remains one-sided. As interaction theory, it has difficulty with aggregate phenomena and does not offer an adequate understanding of emergent structures. As theory of society, it has difficulties with all attempts at tracing downward causation. The problem does not lie in distinguishing different levels of reality; it lies in the fact that as soon as this distinction is introduced it is relinquished in an attempt to grasp the whole from one of these levels.

The theory of social systems will allow us to make this distinction between micro-area and macro-area somewhat more precise. What we have here are different levels and processes of system formation being realized at the same time and with reference to each other. On the interaction level, social systems arise because communication entails selection and the presence of other persons makes communication unavoidable. On the societal level, social systems arise through the fact that in all interaction it must be assumed that the participants act within other social relationships as well. Society – as the totality of all communicatively available (however indirectly achievable) action and experience – is itself a social system; it too is based on selectively constituted structures – on 'self implication' – and on boundaries excluding an alien environment.

The distinction between *interaction systems*, on the one hand, and societies or *societal systems*, on the other, presupposes a still higher level of theoretical reasoning or abstraction, i.e. a general theory of *social systems* including both interaction systems and societal systems as special cases. Propositions applying to the whole of social reality can and must be formulated within the framework of such a general theory of social systems, so, for example, statements dealing with general problems of system formation. It is only for such a theory that claims of universal applicability – to the entire subject-matter of sociology – make any sense. But this theory then absorbs *all* universality claims, i.e. neither theories of society nor theories of interaction can claim to furnish a complete picture of social reality. The theory of the inclusive system is certainly not all-inclusive theory; and in a similar sense, the theory of interaction is not, simply because it affords the best methodological opportunities, a sufficient basis for the analysis of the whole of social reality.

Not only must we relinquish as inadequate the nineteenth-century idea of sociology as the science of society, but we must also regard the reaction to this conception, in the form of an interactionally conceived theory of social forms or social relations (Simmel, Von Wiese), as having proved unable to achieve its goal.[2] The micro-area and the macro-area are of equal status; neither can prevail over the other. All statements claiming universal validity or applicability must, instead, be brought within the framework of a general theory of social systems dealing with the emergence of a specifically social order as such. This theory, it should be noted, has no exact correlate in reality, for there do not exist, alongside interaction systems and societal systems, such things as social systems *per se*.[3] The general theory of social systems is, rather, so conceived that in every analysis one is forced to specify the system referents' which one is going to use in carrying out the analysis. What this means is that one must choose (and this choice means giving up claims to universality) what, for a particular analysis, will be the system and what the environment. Only in this way can the analysis be guided by the difference between system and environment; only in this way can functional analyses be made concrete; and only in this way can we give substance to such general statements as, 'systems reduce the complexity of their environments'.

Proceeding to research using interaction theory or a theory of society thus means specifying the concrete system that one wishes to investigate. In either case, the general propositions of the theory of social systems will guide the analysis, which itself proceeds from the difference between system and environment as realized in a particular system or type of system. In this sense we can distinguish macro- from micro-research according to whether it is the system of modern industrial society or that of waiting in line for theatre tickets that we investigate with respect to system/environment problems. Being thus restricted by the necessity of choosing system referents does not, however, mean that concrete research projects must be committed to one single system referent; it is possible to consider several at the same time (although this, of course, means rapidly increasing complexity of both analytical orientation and verbal presentation).[4] To this extent, micro-perspectives and macro-perspectives, interactional analyses and societal analyses, can be combined, if one constantly keeps in mind the differences in level of system formation and tries to make clear, just on the basis of this, how what is possible as an interaction system in its particular environment limits what is possible as a societal system – and vice versa. Fruitful sociological analyses will require that such complicatedly conceived research programmes be accepted. Otherwise, we will be left with theories of inadequate complexity. In the case we want to consider here, a theory of communication about law in interaction systems should be complex enough to allow a combination of perspectives and offer some clarification of the relationship between the relevant micro- and macro-levels of system formation.

2 The thematization of norms

All human communication takes place under normative premises. It assumes structures that are contrafactually stabilized, i.e. structures which continue to maintain their validity in the face of individual violations. Language itself is possible only under the assumption of certain rules governing correct speech, rules which do not have to be revised every time someone transgresses against them, but, instead, themselves mark transgressions as such. Further, such normative premises deal with the unquestioned recognition and acceptance of the evident reality of the *here and now*, with the immediate history of the ongoing interaction, which is created together and held in memory, with prevailing institutionalized basic values, and finally, with fundamental legal principles, in particular the exclusion of a direct or immediate use of force. It is in this sense that we hear: *ubi societas ibi ius*.

Although they are structure-dependent, communication problems do have a certain independence. They are not identical with structural problems, nor with the question of the degree to which structures have been realized. The general recognition, therefore, that law stabilizes expectations in interaction[5] yields little for the question of whether, and under what circumstances, law is made an explicit topic of communication. Decisions about whether one should say something and what it is that one should say are not fully determined by system structures or communication codes. Neither can this be reduced to a mere process of interpretation. (Hermeneutics represents a very late and secondary phenomenon, issuing from the existence of structure in excess of that which can actually be realized within the communication process.) In all communication, one responds to the fact that one's partners are also communicating (have communicated, will communicate), that they choose what they will say, and that they are capable not only of affirmation but also of negation. As a participant in a communication process, one is, therefore, disposed to take the others' selections into account in a way that can subvert all structures, consciously boycott rules, subject them to ironical use or, presupposing agreement, purposely circumvent them. That is, norms are and remain, dependent on being cited; they must be activated on appropriate occasions in actual, ongoing communication processes: they must be made into the theme or topic – 'thematized' – in concrete situations.[6] Where and when this actually occurs is not determined solely by the meaning of the norm or directed by its interpretation.

The fact that all communication presupposes a normative structure therefore says little about whether, and how, participants in a communication process actually thematize or make topics of these norms themselves. Now such *thematization* both directs and limits the negation potential that is diffusely given with the meaningful character and linguistic form of human experience and its processing. It serves to reduce the indefinite complexity of such negation possibilities. Each thematization not only makes it possible to adopt a position with respect to the theme, but also introduces the possibility of different positions being taken and, with this, the possibility of disagreement and dissent. Negations, on the other hand, must be applied to some theme or topic, i.e. they have to refer to something – even if it be to 'existence' – and for this the theme must first be created and introduced into the social process. Themes or topics are possible crystallization points for negations and one knows, or is at least aware of this, when they are introduced. Thematization thus involves taking a risk. It calls for tactical considerations, and sometimes even requires social-structural support in the form of the legitimation of particular topics.

For example – as Garfinkel[7] has shown – thematizations that could push the taken-for-granted elements of everyday life and language into the zone of negatability are generally doomed to failure from the very start. They are simply not taken seriously or, if stubbornly insisted upon, lead to the termination of communication. This apparently occurs in defence of a necessary latency of the premises of ongoing communication, of a kind of validity that cannot be qualified with 'yes' or 'no'. There exists then in the communication process *thematization thresholds*, tied to the function of themes or topics in controlling negation potential. And one may safely assume that such thematization thresholds are adjusted to other functional requirements of social systems as well.

Thematization thresholds cannot be as high in the case of law as in the case of those taken-for-granted elements of everyday life investigated by Garfinkel. It must, after all, be possible in social systems to discuss legal issues – although, of course, not continually and not on every occasion. But there are still significant thematization thresholds for legal questions, for here too there is a considerable risk of negation to be controlled. In the following, we will consider the nature of these thematization thresholds and the question of how they harmonize with the specific functions of law. We assume hereby that it is about their own legal rights and obligations that those participating in a communication process wish (or do not wish) to talk. Purely theoretical discussions of legal questions (e.g. for teaching purposes), talk about others' legal disputes, or communication problems within the workings of the legislative or judicial systems[8] will be of only marginal interest.

3 Conflict and thematization thresholds

The occasion to communicate about legal issues is given by conflicts.[9] To develop a communications-theoretical concept of conflict on the micro-level, we must first realize that communication is essentially a selection of information being offered for selective acceptance; it serves the sequential reproduction of meaningful selections. Its success, however, depends on a double selection, for this initial offer of selections – even (or especially) where it is correctly understood – may be rejected. This very often occurs factually and overtly, but it may take place on the side, as it were, unnoticed, or accompanied by a tactical silence.[10] A conflict always arises in those cases where the refusal to accept the selections being offered is – for whatever reasons – made the topic of further communication.[11] Someone does not believe that the information offered is truthful, that a piece of advice is helpful, that a demand is justified – *and says so*! Since interaction systems can normally handle only one topic at a time,[12] the conflict theme soon comes to monopolize the attention of the participants and becomes the focus of further communication. The interaction system is restructured in accordance with the new topic. It becomes a new type of system: a conflict.

At the same time, this thematic concentration so typical of simple interaction systems results in these having a very low conflict potential; the very prospect of an active dispute leads to such conflicts being avoided wherever possible (or in some cases of course, actively sought – just because this leads to a dispute). Primitive societies limited mainly to such simple interaction systems use this mechanism to suppress or avoid conflict. For complex societies, on the other hand, it can (must?) become very important that the conflict potential be increased – in order to open up a wide range of communication possibilities that are more varied and richer in selection. It then becomes important that conflicts be given a form that can be used by the participants to the interaction, one that is suited for interaction and at the same time stabilized from the outside, supported by the environment. Such possibilities are afforded by law. It renders conflicts of a more general interest, understandable even for those external to the interaction, and removes the odium of merely local unpleasantness. It also takes the criteria for resolving the dispute out of the hands of the interaction partners. They are allowed to quarrel – as long as they don't try to rely on their own power in settling the matter.

After a long evolutionary development, a clearly binary structure has been institutionalized in law, i.e. in certain respects one can be either in the right or in the wrong, but not both at the same time. This entails, further, that one may determine right through negation of wrong and wrong through negation of right, and that chances for deviating from this hard alternative into something less determinate –

like love or belief or art – are blocked wherever possible. A discussion of the special social-structural prerequisites of such binary schemata is beyond the scope of this paper; what interests us here is that, and how, these function in establishing thematization thresholds in communication processes.

Important here is, further, that, in case of law, such binary schemata deal with normative questions, i.e. with topics that involve the contrafactual stabilization of expectations.[13] In making legal claims, one defines oneself – with respect to one's own expectations – as being unwilling to learn and pretty much commits oneself to the position that if these expectations are not met they will not be changed but, instead, appropriate action taken. A person is much more closely identified with a legal claim than with a factual claim, which can always be regarded as mistaken and changed if necessary. Starting a legal discussion usually means going beyond a point of no return: one defines oneself for the future as prepared to stand up and actively defend one's rights. It thus entails much more of a commitment to a particular course of action, a much clearer acceptance of the possibility of a fight than do, say, ordinary conversations, exchanges of information or opinions, or scientific discussions – and is therefore not something to be entered into lightly. One is entering what Erving Goffman describes as a 'character contest' from which one may emerge in the wrong or, perhaps, in the right, but in any case not unscathed.[14]

In the face of all this, it takes a certain amount of courage to openly confront the other with the question of whether he is actually in the right. The comfortable consensus that can normally be assumed in living and acting together will be shattered. The question requires of the other that he actually confront the possibility of being in the wrong – and this not merely in theoretical reflection, but in an open and public accounting. He is confronted with an alternative that he – simply as an alternative – may find unpleasant. The binary character of right/wrong leaves him without other possibilities. The very prospect of such a closed set of alternatives may endanger the 'in-common' character of unreflected living-in-the-world, the intersubjective constitution of this world. What may be an alternative for one person is not necessarily – especially in the here and now of the concrete situation – an alternative for another.[15]

Whoever is confronted with such a question will assume that there are reasons for its being put, that the person posing it indeed suspects him of being in the wrong, that he perhaps even has a certain interest in this being demonstrated. This is especially true in those cases where there is an obvious conflict of interests, where it appears that one being in the right will probably require that the other be in the wrong, and vice versa. If the person posing the question anticipates all of this, if he can – in the sense of 'role-taking' – put himself in the other's position,[16] he will find it necessary to cross a certain inhibition threshold if he still wishes to introduce the question of law.

The problems become even more acute when such legal claims are actually brought forward. Doing so has the effect of thematizing the controversy, while at the same time claiming to be able to decide how it should be resolved. Such legal claims, so to speak bypass the impending conflict by anticipating its outcome. That can, in turn, provoke objections and opposition even from those who are not entirely sure about their legal position, and thus force them into a confrontation. And this must be known or at least sensed by anyone who is preparing to defend his interests through recourse to law.

These considerations should make it clear that the inhibition surrounding thematization is dependent on the type of premises guiding the communication process. Although the thematization threshold is extremely high for premises so taken-for-granted that their negation would seem too absurd for explicit communication, this is no longer the case for questions of law. 'Legal-izing' the premises of interaction by expressing the hitherto taken-for-granted in terms of explicit legal norms – with a binary scheme forcing all topics under the dichotomy of right or wrong – has the initial effect of lowering the thematization threshold, and leads to a reformulation of the conditions under which this threshold will be crossed. Crossing this threshold does not in itself totally disqualify someone as a communication partner, but he will have to activate some special source of motivation, e.g. anger or a sense of injustice, or call upon some special sources of security, such as legal texts that can be cited, expert advice, or social support. Simply wishing to provoke or irritate someone, or to enjoy a joke, is not sufficient to propel a communication process into the legal sphere. Thematization thresholds thus work as a kind of filter for the conditions and circumstances that make raising legal questions probable. And in this sense they are relevant not only for communication theory but for the theory of society as well. They help to determine whether it is worth while to develop a special legal system.

4 Thematization of law and social support

Whether or not someone will venture to raise questions of law is determined to a considerable extent, though not exclusively, by the prospects for social support in case conflict should arise. Thematizing legal issues initiates a chain of events that develops a certain autonomy and unpredictability. More social support is needed here than for a single act, above all *certain* support for as yet *uncertain* situations. The more uncertain the future the more it must be met together.

This situation is presented pretty much in its original form in investigations of primitive societies that have not developed a special judicial system with decision-making capabilities. In such cases, not only the raising of legal issues, but even the very making of legal rules, depends on whether conflicts can be socially generalized, 'politicized', and carried out beyond the confines of one's personal group, and also on the availability of support from larger groups with a greater capacity for conflict.[17] Important here is that uncertainty is absorbed because of a segmental social structure which allows a person to rely on a general willingness of those close to him to extend support, relatively independently of the theme in question. Conflicts within the household are thus not to be dealt with by law; even in early advanced civilizations, they remained outside the sphere of law – which itself was developed as the law of the political community (*ius civile*).

The *filter* for both thematization and development of law is thus to be found in the *reference group* that – even (or especially) in times of duress – can be turned to for *social support*, agreement and a common orientation for future action. This is true today as well, although under radically different circumstances.[18] Only 'the strongest is strongest alone'; everyone else has to seek support. The choice of the relevant reference group is not free, but determined or restricted on the macro-level by the social structure of the macro-system – and it is this aspect that has become more complex in modern societies.

Once it has been established that legal issues will be resolved by the binding decision of a neutral third party, the orientation of those involved becomes divided and dependent on strongly divergent conditions. Whoever considers formulating his interests, complaints, expectations, or disappointments as legal issues must be able to predict with some degree of certainty how the legal system will dispose of the matter; he must also anticipate what attitude the social environment directly relevant for him will take towards this decision. He is thus dealing with two thematization thresholds, either of which might be sufficient to dissuade him from formulating his concern in terms of law. Is the thematization of legal issues made more difficult by such a double barrier? Is there a cumulative effect? Or does just this double orientation make it possible to keep both thematization thresholds low, with each holding the other down? And under what conditions would this be the case?

Before looking at all of this, we should consider one important evolutionary achievement on which all legal culture is based. It is, in short, the *separation* at the primary interactional level of questions of power from those of law, and the reformulation of their relationship on the macro-level of the total society.[19] Decisions about legal issues become the province of a *distant* authority, one that has no direct connection with the interactionally present, immediately available power of the participating actors.[20] Social support becomes less important; legal claims can be presented in an apparently objective fashion, by quoting legal texts and referring to decision-making premises and probabilities. Law itself is no longer that dispute-laden, 'agonal' mass of actual and verbal weapons, allies, and arguments which even pre-classical Roman law must be seen as;[21] it can be called upon as something with a fixed and definite existence and cited with an appearance of objectivity – a pretension that is difficult to counter, or even to question, within the communication process itself. That makes thematization a lot easier: one lets the rules speak for themselves.

But it also makes thematization more difficult: when someone turns something into a legal issue, he thereby indicates that he is not dependent on the motive structure of the concrete interaction of which he is a part. Whoever is, or claims to be, in the right in this fashion no longer needs to communicate, no longer needs to rely on a local suspension of doubt, no longer needs to present himself as being prepared to take up and respond to the other's communication; he is not even willing to argue.[22] Not all interaction systems can handle this kind of alienation. Recourse to law – just as such a demonstration of independence or of concern with a foreign reference group – is something that must be very carefully considered.

5 The separation and interdependence of systems

There does not appear to be much sense in trying to answer the question of whether or not, as society has evolved, the development and formalization of a legal system with decision-making capacities has made the thematization of legal issues any easier. This development changes so much that it becomes difficult to adequately compare different situations. Moreover, a detailed investigation of the willingness to 'legal-ize' issues in various regions of contemporary society – say, Japan, Mexico, the USA, and Germany – would certainly yield widely divergent results.[23] Especially under conditions of industrialization, the critical variable of 'social support' in conflict situations can take on very different values. It will perhaps be more profitable to take a closer look at the systems-theoretical frame of reference used here, and then to use the results of this to formulate further questions.

We start with the assumption that increasing complexity in society opens the way for an increasing *diversity* of interaction systems, and that this diversification *pulls apart* or separates the macro- and micro-levels of system formation. The societal system itself comprises all (however indirectly) communicatively attainable experience and action. Interaction systems, on the other hand, are constituted by concrete communication among participants who are actually present together. Society can exist only on the basis of such interaction but, with increased complexity and diversity, its *integration* can no longer be achieved in terms of actual presence.[24] What becomes relevant instead are questions of functional interdependence/independence and structural compatibility/incompatibility. However, for the very reason that these are no longer mediated solely by possible presence, they can – within the structures of the interaction system – be neglected or subverted by the consensus or common orientation of those present together. This allows the functional differentiation of society with the formation of, for example, special systems for politics, religion, law, education, economic production, scientific research, etc. – without these societal subsystems having to be integrated on the basis of interaction. Interaction organized around, say, production must no longer be concerned with educating, with observing the sacred or the profane, with seeing that the law is observed, with achieving a political consensus, and so on. Such systems-theoretical considerations should help make clear the real significance of the thematization of legal issues in the interaction systems. When a legal system has been developed as a subsystem within the total societal system and is recognizable as such, starting to thematize legal issues unavoidably signals the *attempt to move the interaction into the legal system*, to treat it as part of the legal system – and not as falling within family life, the economic system, and so on.[25] Thematization of legal issues thus entails a decision about the status or *location of the ongoing interaction within the total societal system* – and although such ascriptions are not necessarily strictly mutually exclusive, they are to a considerable extent incompatible.

When we first considered thematization thresholds, we restricted our attention to interaction and communication among actors actually present together, but it is now clear that these thresholds are also of importance for the system of society as a whole. They prevent the unhindered, thoroughgoing 'legal-izing' of all interaction systems and thus, so to speak, defend the interests of other functional areas or subsystems within the society. This was what one government minister had in mind when he said that he couldn't always go around with a copy of the constitution in his pocket. Politics, especially in a functionally viable constitutional state, must be guaranteed an independent existence, and – although not at the level of ideology or quotable ministerial wisdom – it must be protected from being treated exclusively under the dichotomy of right or wrong. This is even truer for family life, research, and education. Now this is not to deny the interdependence that doubtlessly and obviously exists between all of these functional subsystems and the legal system; this *interdependence*, however, can be formulated in premises for behaviour that exist independently of the frequency with which legal issues are actually thematized in interaction belonging to other functional subsystems.

The legal system for its part, though, is probably more dependent than any other subsystem on receiving impulses or input from interaction systems with *other* functional orientations. It is necessary to grasp the complex nature of this dependence. It can arise, namely, only on the basis of independence. As a system in which decisions are based on rules, the legal system is actually indifferent to the question of when and why a process of legally significant communication is initiated. This is one important function of such a rule-orientation: the system becomes compatible with arbitrary beginnings (whereas in normal disputes, the question of 'who started' tends to be important).[26] This independence, however, results in a generalized (and thus not easily controllable) dependence on the aggregate effect of many interactions. As a conflict-regulating system that is always belatedly set in motion,[27] i.e. only when called upon, the legal system very seldom takes the initiative. With the exception of criminal law, it has no organization independently initiating the search for cases or topics.[28] Even legislation follows and depends on the political process. Excessive inhibition of the thematization of law may, therefore, lead to a kind of drying up of the legal system, and so leave the regulation of conflict to other mechanisms – e.g. morality, ignorance,[29] class structure,[30] or the use of force[31] outside the law – whose social structural compatibility may be problematic.

A systems-theoretical approach thus reveals the following situation: although, as a *subsystem of society*, the legal system is organized for dealing with random beginnings and, in a broader sense, for taking up contingent conflict within the society, these cannot be strictly the result of chance on the level of *interaction systems* as well. Only for a given system is this randomness actually random, not in and of itself. In interaction systems, it must be controllable through the *thematization thresholds* in the communication process – and this not only has important functions within the individual interaction systems, but also has a part to play in maintaining differentiation within the overall society. As elsewhere in evolution, it is a *finely regulated* randomness that produces the variation necessary for the formation and continued existence of complex systems.

6 Conflict resolution by contract

It will now be clear why we consider the beginning of a process of communication about legal issues to be of such importance. Once it has begun, the participants are no longer entirely free. What cannot be made to disappear at this point is at least the possibility of seeing their mutual relationship from the point of view of making and sustaining legal claims, and thus also of attributing blame or declaring someone in the wrong. This does not fully determine the further communication process, but it certainly does '*modalize*' it, i.e. its selection style is determined by a possibility now both recognized and kept available, a possibility that can always be turned to, and that, at the same time, is seen as existing for the other participants as well. Even where legal issues are not explicitly discussed, communication remains latently within the legal sphere, inasmuch as one, for example, keeps in mind questions of responsibility or of proof, stalls for time, or purposely chooses topics that avoid the disputed issue.

Such general considerations do not allow an adequate explanatory or prognostic treatment of the course taken by communication processes; this would require more concrete data about the parameters of the particular system being considered and more information about the matter being contested. However, we can still, on the very broad level of our discussion here, point to certain general relational or functional problems confronting interaction systems openly moving towards a legal contest or accepting this as a real and permanent possibility. These problems lie in increased interdependence and increased uncertainty.[32] The recognized possibility of conflict increases interdependence by artificially linking up a large number of topics, thereby organizing them, so to speak, into a 'front'.[33] These interdependencies soon come to surpass the ability of the participants to weigh things objectively and deal with them smoothly and step by step within the communication process. They come then almost inevitably to be simplified under the heading of enmity or hostility; that, at least, is something certain. All that much more uncertain, though, is the extent to which this front is legally secure or what proportion of the many arguments, precautions, searches, etc., will be successful in court. The behaviourally relevant uncertainties come to be shifted away from the interaction system itself and onto its relationship to the legal system.

If we keep the nature of such difficulties in mind, we shall understand more clearly the significance of two very different communication processes that seek to avoid them, namely, communication leading to a settlement which is conceived from the very beginning as a legally binding (typically written) *contract*, and then a complex that we will treat in the following section under the heading of the '*de-thematization*' of law.

Even for agreements that are understood as binding, insistence on a written, legally unassailable form is probably more the exception than the rule.[34] It does happen fairly often that one party requests the signing of a standardized form, but then the person making such a request has obviously not produced this form himself or just for this particular occasion; he is acting no more freely or on his own than the person being presented with such a form. In this way, thematization difficulties within an interaction system are mitigated by reference to an organization and its requirements. In this important area then, *interaction* problems relevant for the larger society are, in the end, resolved through *organization*. With the exception of the possibility just mentioned, and of those situations (e.g. real-estate transactions) where the law itself makes validity dependent on legal form – which also 'excuses' thematization – it is probably quite rare that with agreement on a contract interaction is thereafter explicitly understood as belonging to the legal system, and its topics fixed accordingly. If this does not happen, the participants will have given up the chance of a 'friendly legal-izing' of their relationship in favour of the possibility that everything can be concluded without any communication about law. Should this become necessary after all, the thematization threshold will be higher than before, having been raised by signs of impending conflict and uncertainty about the legal situation.

The principle of contract has a long tradition and, as a principle uniting both freedom and obligation, has been used to characterize society itself. Durkheim, however, raised doubts when he pointed to the non-contractual bases of contract. If carried out on a large enough scale, empirical communications-theoretical investigations would probably reinforce such scepsis.

In discussions of the principle of contract, the result, i.e. consensus, has received too much emphasis, and the process of communication surrounding the closing of a contract, too little. The problem of the binding effect, of obligation, has been adequately duplicated in the *social* dimension, namely brought into the form of a normative postulate, but has not been adequately analysed in the *temporal* dimension. It is only as existing at the same time, not one after the other, that freedom and obligation constitute a contradiction. And just this is the function of the system of interaction directed towards reaching a contract: to bring about a solution to a *social* problem by transforming it into a *sequence* of communication.

It is thus important that when the participants commit themselves they do so *one after the other*, so that each can base his actions on those of the other, and they do not constantly have to deal with the situation as completely open at both ends. It is not only acceptance of the basic norm of the binding nature of contracts, and the solidarity this presupposes, that make contracts possible. These alone cannot overcome the 'double contingency' involved in all social situations. Rather, what happens in contract-generating situations is that every single communication is understood as establishing or defining a commitment and used accordingly, being made even more binding by subsequent behaviour. For both sides, preceding commitments concerning interests, positions, intentions, etc., are a prerequisite for the rational management of one's own behaviour, right up to the point where the participants recognize that they are in agreement or that an agreement cannot be reached. Each may feel free as long as he looks primarily at the commitments made by the other; no side, however, is free to completely avoid committing itself, as long as the process is directed towards agreement on a contract. Until such time as the contract is closed the participants can, of course, always opt out, using the remaining open points to dissolve the ever-tightening net of commitments and obligations. After this, however, reinstating freedom is not without its price: the contract is abandoned, as are hopes of achieving the goals associated with it.

The process aimed at reaching a contract does not require communication about law. It can be included to prevent certain demands and can help in establishing that an agreement has been reached, but whether turning to law is helpful, or troublesome, or destructive, is something the participants must decide for themselves. It is not necessary for the functioning of this process, nor is it a prerequisite for the validity of the contract. It is not coming to a contract but the question of its fulfilment that requires appropriate provisions within the legal system; and here, too, the reasons why such provisions are necessary lie not in the concrete interaction but in the legal system, which views questions of agreement or of fulfilment from its own perspective, having to perform a regulative function in case difficulties or disagreements should arise during the course of a contract – something experience has shown to occur very frequently.

7 The de-thematization of law

Once begun, legal communication is carried by a certain internal logic to a decision that rigorously separates right and wrong and apportions them to the participants. Seen from a strictly legal point of view, the decision is a necessary correlate of the conflict; the legal system is bound to come to a – particular – decision. That is not true of the interaction system formed by those communicating about legal issues. In the course of such communication the immediate past or the future prospects for their interaction system may give the participants the impression that it would be better to end their hostilities and to come to terms with each other out of court. How does this happen?

We are not posing this question with reference to any conflict whatsoever,[35] but, rather, with reference to conflict-charged inter-action systems in which controversial legal positions have been thematized. Ending the conflict in such systems requires and aims at the *de-thematization* of law. This, of course, does not mean that law somehow vanishes from the minds of the participants, but with the help of third parties it may be possible to substitute other topics and push legal questions out of the sphere of common attention. Ample illustrations of this are afforded by the practice of mediation and arbitration.[36]

De-thematization can occur in a number of ways and, accordingly, can be consciously pursued using a number of different strategies. One obvious possibility is to consider the results for the participants within an expanded framework that goes beyond questions of strictly legal relevance. What was perhaps silently considered is now thematized and made into a question demanding an explicit answer: what are the consequences? Once they have been thematized, it can be seen that such consequences are really not legal criteria: they strengthen no assertion, offer no proof; they are simply the pleasant or unpleasant results of the final legal decision. A further possibility is to relax the criteria with which one argues in this interaction system, broadening these to include points that may still have an appeal decision. Lutz Gussek[37] has investigated the idea of 'reasonable demands' (*Zumutbarkeit*) from this perspective. The thematic use of such 'reasonable' criteria also has the effect of unthematically assuming or implying a willingness to continue the relationship, or at least of once again making claims on the moral continuum of a common way of life. Such indirect, suggestive effects can also emanate from secondary topics that interrupt the more specifically legal communication, e.g. from eating or drinking or smoking together, from the necessity of moving together from place to place, and so on. In all of this, there enter into the communication process elements of meaning that cannot be brought under the binary scheme of right or wrong, and that should – just for this reason – gradually come to determine the thematic development and, as far as possible, the development of opinion as well.

If this is successful, the participants will perhaps venture one last time into the legal sphere and agree to agree on a contract, with the hope of being done once and for all with communication about law.

Notes

1 The major part of this essay is an English-language version of my 'Kommunikation über Recht in Interaktions-systemen', in Erhard Blankenbourg *et al.* (eds), *Alternative Rechtsformen und Alternativen zum Recht* (Wiesbaden: Westdeutscher Verlag, 1980), pp. 99–112.

2 On the level of micro-theory, the sense of being truly scientific is typically reinforced by the belief that there is only one micro-sociology but several macro-sociologies (disputed as ideologies). Cf., for example, David Koigen, *Der Aufbau der sozialen Welt im Zeitalter der Wissenschaft: Umrisse einer soziologischen Strukturlehre* (Berlin: Carl Heymann, 1929), pp. 32f.

3 Doubts about the possibility of such a general theory have often been expressed, especially with reference to the different kinds of objects dealt with in micro- and macro-analyses. Cf., for example, Helmut R. Wagner, 'Displacement of Scope: A Problem of the Relationship between Small-Scale and Large-Scale Sociological Theory', *American Journal of Sociology*, 69 (1964), pp. 571–84. This difference, however, does not imply impossibility; it merely necessitates a higher level of abstraction.

4 The terminological difficulties and apparent laboriousness and formality that characterize Parsons's theory of the general action system offer an instructive example. They result from the necessity of distinguishing the system of reference in a double fashion – according to level and to functional focus of system differentiation. These problems exist here on the level of general theory, i.e. prior to any further specification in terms of theory of interaction or of society.

5 Cf., for example, Lon L. Fuller, 'Human Interaction and the Law', in Robert P. Wolff (ed.), *The Rule of Law* (New York: Simon & Schuster, 1971), pp. 171–217.

6 Cf. Shalom H. Schwartz, 'Words, Deeds, and the Perception of

Consequences and Responsibility in Action Situations', *Journal of Personality and Social Psychology*, 10 (1968), pp. 232–42; and 'Awareness of Consequences and the Influence of Moral Norms and Interpersonal Behavior', *Sociometry*, 31 (1968), pp. 355–69; and B. C. Cartwright and R. D. Schwartz, 'The Invocation of Legal Norms: An Empirical Investigation of Durkheim and Weber', *American Sociological Review*, 38 (1973), pp. 340–54.

7 Cf. Harold Garfinkel, *Studies in Ethnomethodology* (Englewood Cliffs: Prentice Hall, 1967).

8 For a discussion of this, cf. Niklas Luhmann, *Legitimation durch Verfahren* (Darmstadt-Neuwied: Luchterhand, 1975).

9 For the following, cf. the overview of relevant research prepared by Klaus F. Röhl: 'Gegenstandsströmungen der Rechtssoziologie', *Informationsbrief für Rechtssoziologie, Sonderheft*, 1 (Berlin: 1977), pp. 67ff.

10 A conflict-avoidance theory that recommends just such behaviour (and thus no legal action!) is outlined in the various *Essais de moral* of Pierre Nicole (1671ff.) – a little noticed but none the less interesting alternative to the frequently cited legal and political theory of Thomas Hobbes. Cf. in particular 'Des Moyens de conserver la paix avec les hommes', 'De la Civilité chrétienne', 'Des Jugements téméraires', 'De la Guérison des soupçons', 'Dangers à craindre dans les contestations', 'Danger des entretiens des hommes', in Pierre Nicole, *Oeuvres philosophiques et morales* (Paris: Hachette, 1845; reprinted Hildesheim: Olms, 1970).

11 Thus there are also thoroughly 'chance' conflicts that can be explained only through the history of the interaction itself or out of the changing moods of the participants. In no way are *all* conflicts to be explained with reference to structural contradictions within the larger social system. And for this reason, not every absorption of conflict can be seen as helping to stabilize existing conditions.

12 Cf. the concept of 'focused interaction' in Erving Goffman, *Encounters: Two Studies in the Sociology of Interaction* (Indianapolis: Bobbs-Merrill, 1961), pp. 7f. Cf. also Niklas Luhmann, 'Einfache Sozialsysteme', in Luhmann, *Soziologische Aufklärung*, vol. 2 (Opladen: Westdeutscher Verlag, 1975), pp. 21–38.

13 Cf. Niklas Luhmann, 'Normen in soziologischer Perspektive', *Soziale Welt*, 20 (1969), pp. 28–48; and *Rechtssoziologie*, vol. 1 (Reinbek: Rowohlt, 1972), pp. 40ff.

14 Erving Goffman, 'Where the Action Is' in Erving Goffman, *Interaction Ritual: Essays in Face-to-Face Behavior* (Chicago: Aldine, 1967), pp. 149–270. If we look closely at Goffman's analyses here, we also become aware of the extent to which a thoroughly civilized legal framework for carrying out character contests is missing even in modern societies. The need for action remains, and other avenues are turned to – above all those of illegality, provocation, or personal risk. This can be seen in cases where young intellectuals on trial show less concern with obtaining their legal rights then with challenging the judge or the society. Apparently, the law itself offers them no adequate opportunities for the presentation of self.

15 Cf. George A. Kelly, 'Man's Construction of His Alternatives', in Gardner Lindzey (ed.), *Assessment of Human Motives* (New York: Holt, Rinehart & Winston 1958), pp. 33–64 (37).

16 As in George H. Mead, *Mind, Self and Society: From the Standpoint of a Social Behaviorist* (University of Chicago Press, 1972).

17 For a discussion of the critical question of the 'expandability of certain disputes and the containment of others', cf. Sally F. Moore, 'Legal Liability and Evolutionary Interpretation: Some Aspects of Strict Liability, Self-Help and Collective Responsibility', in Max Gluckman (ed.), *The Allocation of Responsibility* (Manchester University Press, 1972), pp. 51–107 (especially 68, 96). See also Lloyd Fallers, 'Political Sociology and the Anthropological Study of African Politics', *Europäisches Archiv für Soziologie*, 4 (1963), pp. 311–29.

18 Comments on the significance of the concept of reference groups for a sociological theory of law may be found in Adam Podgórecki, *Law and Society* (London: Routledge & Kegan Paul, 1974), pp. 262ff.

19 Cf. in this context the comments of Edward Shils, 'Center and Periphery', in *The Logic of Personal Knowledge: Essays Presented to Michael Polanyi* (London: Routledge & Kegan Paul, 1961), pp. 117–30, and Samuel N. Eisenstadt, *Social Differentiation and Stratification* (London: Scott, Foresman & Co., 1971), on the development of urban centres containing functionally specialized institutions, and their importance for the rise of advanced civilizations and of stratification systems with the consequent problems of admission and participation.

20 One interesting aspect of this phenomenon will not be discussed at length here but should be mentioned. There are interaction systems having topics and decision-making functions that inhibit an adequate 'legal-izing' of the substance of the participants' interests. Typical examples are seen in organizations among colleagues, committees, councils, boards, etc., within larger organizations. In such cases, a majority voting principle may offer a functional equivalent to the device of citing the law. Demanding a vote terminates the process of consensus-seeking by invoking an apparently neutral binary formalism. Among other things, the institutionalization of 'opposition' has the effect of making a *quick* demand for a vote easier, or, more generally put, of making it easier to thematize questions of procedure. There are structural reasons – and thus also different probabilities – that this will or will not occur. And, just as in the case of law, the chances of profiting from this are unevenly distributed. Cf. F. G. Bailey, 'Decisions by Consensus in Councils and Committees', in *Political Systems and the Distribution of Power*, ASA Monographs, 2 (London: 1965), pp. 1–20; Rue Bucher, 'Social Process and Power in a Medical School', in Mayer N. Zald (ed.), *Power in Organizations* (Vanderbilt University Press, 1970), pp. 3–48 (44ff.); J. David Edelstein and Malcolm Warner, 'Voting and Allied Systems in Group Decision-Making', *Human Relations*, 24 (1971), pp. 179–88; Johan P. Olsen, 'Voting, "Sounding Out", and the Governance of Modern Organizations', *Acta Sociologica*, 15 (1972), pp. 267–83.

21 Cf. Dieter Nörr, 'Zur Entstehung der gewohnheitsrechtlichen Theorie', in *Festschrift für Wilhelm Felgentraeger zum 70. Geburtstag* (Göttingen: 1969), pp. 353–66.

22 This problem exists not only with normative questions but with cognitive ones as well. I once met a newly married couple at a social gathering and was told that on the occasion of their marriage they had bought an encyclopedia. The husband was a lawyer.

23 Cf. Kahei Rokumoto, 'Problems and Methodology of Civil Law Disputes', *Law in Japan*, 5 (1972), pp. 97–114, and 6 (1973), pp. 111–27; Volkmar Gessner, *Recht und Konflikt: Eine soziologische Untersuchung privatrechtlicher Konflikte in Mexiko* (Tübingen: Mohr, 1976); William L. F. Felstiner, Influences of Social Organization on Dispute Processing', *Law and Society Review*, 9 (1) (1974), pp. 63–94, and the following discussion in ibid., 9 (4) (1975), pp. 675–706.

24 This, by the way, was the premiss under which Pierre Nicole recommended keeping the peace on the interaction level.

25 It is for this reason that legal norms and decisions are quoted with increasing frequency as the interaction moves closer to formalized legal proceedings. See the findings in Cartwright and Schwartz, 'The Invocation of Legal Norms'.

26 This is also one prerequisite for fairness or justice in the sense of equality before the law. It is practically impossible to eliminate the uneven distribution of both the opportunity and the necessity of beginning legal communication; all that can be done is to eliminate its relevance for the process of decision making. In the same way, the different chances existing for those in different legal positions of being the plaintiff or the defendant must be accepted, and can be neutralized only in their influence on the outcome. Cf., for example, Hartmut Koch and Gisela Zanz, 'Erfahrungen und Einstellungen von Klägern in Mietsprozessen', *Jahrbuch für Rechtssoziologie und Rechtstheorie*, 3 (1972), pp. 509–28 (518f.), on tenants and landlords.

27 Cf. Ottmar Ballweg, *Rechtswissenschaft und Jurisprudenz* (Basel: Helbig & Lichtenhahn, 1970).

28 In the ancient world there was a widespread opinion that lawyers did just that, and should therefore receive no fees.

29 Cf., for example, Folke Schmidt, Leif Gräntze, and Alex Roos, 'Legal Working Hours in Swedish Agriculture', *Theoria*, 12 (1946), pp. 181–96; Vilhelm Aubert, 'Some Social Functions of Legislation', *Acta Sociologica*, 10 (1966), pp. 98–120.

30 Cf., for example, Bernard S. Cohn, 'Anthropological Notes on Disputes and Law in India', *American Anthropologist*, 67 (1965), Part III, pp. 81–122.

31 Cf., for example, Germán Guzmán, Orlando Fals Borda and Edvardo Umana Luna, *La violencia en Columbia: Estudio de un Proceso Social* (Bogotá: Ed. tercer mundo, 1964).

32 This is true for distrust in general. Cf. Niklas Luhmann, *Trust and Power* (Chichester: John Wiley 1979), pp. 71ff.

33 In this way, conflict actually aids system formation, not only in the sense

that it strengthens solidarity within rival groups, but also in the more
fundamental sense that it joins the conflicting parties into a system –
similar to what happens in exchange situations.

34 Cf. Stewart Macaulay, 'Non-Contractual Relations in Business: A
Preliminary Study', *American Sociological Review*, 28 (1963), pp. 55–67,
abridged in Vilhelm Aubert (ed.), *Sociology of Law: Selected Readings*
(Harmondsworth: Penguin, 1969), pp. 194–209; cf. also Macaulay, *Law
and the Balance of Power: The Automobile Manufacturers and Their Dealers* (New
York: Russel Sage, 1966). Especially in the legal cultures of the Far East
there is reportedly a widespread reluctance to fix the terms of contract in a
legal form; this, it is felt, would show a feeling of distrust and assume from
the outset a situation of conflict:

> Parties to a contractual agreement are not expected to become involved
> in any serious differences in the future. Whenever they enter such a
> relationship they are supposed to be friendly enough not to consider
> eventual disputes, much less preparation for a lawsuit. Parties do not, or
> at least pretend that they do not, care about an instrument or other
> kinds of written evidence and rather hesitate to ask for any kind of
> written document, fearing that such a request might impair the
> amicable inclination of the other party' [Takeyoshi Kawashima,
> 'Dispute Resolution in Contemporary Japan', in Arthur T. von Mehren
> (ed.), *Law in Japan: The Legal Order of a Changing Society* (Harvard
> University Press, 1964), pp. 41–52 (46), abridged in Aubert, *Sociology of
> Law: Selected Readings*, pp. 182–93 (188)].

Cf. also Kawashima, 'The Notion of Law, Right and Social Order in
Japan', in Charles A. Moore (ed.), *The Status of the Individual in East and West*
(University of Hawaii Press, 1968), pp. 429–47. Eiichi Hoshino, 'The
Contemporary Contract', *Law in Japan*, 5 (1972), pp. 1–46 (41ff.).

35 Cf. Lewis A. Coser, *Continuities in the Study of Conflict* (New York: Free Press,
1967), pp. 37ff.

36 A systematic evaluation of the written records of such practice (e.g. in the
form of reports about personal experience or tips for practitioners, such as
those found in the organ for professional mediation and arbitration in
Germany, the *Schiedsmannzeitung* (Berlin: Heymann, beginning 1926))
would be a worthwhile undertaking for the sociology of law or
communications theory. An overview, along with some relevant details, is
to be found in Lutz Gussek, *Die Zumutbarkeit – ein Beurteilungs-maßstab? Die
Stellung der Zumutbarkeit in gütlichen, schlichtenden und gerichtlichen Verfahren*
(Berlin: Duncker & Humblot, 1972), pp. 83ff.

37 Ibid.

Part 4

The production of societal macro-structures: aspects of a political economy of practice

9 Toward a reconstruction of historical materialism*

Jürgen Habermas

[*Habermas conceives of the micro-macro problem in evolutionary terms. He holds that the specific macro-structures of a society, which he takes to be mechanism of social integration such as the kinship system or the political institutions, are a function of the stage of an* evolutionary learning process. *The process develops in response to system problems which overstrain the steering capacity of an existing form of order.*

It is this evolutionary learning process in which we can see the main contribution of Habermas's reconstructed historical materialism to the question of the relationship between the micro- and the macro-order. Since learning is done by individuals or groups, the evolutionary learning of a society depends crucially on the learning capacities of its members. According to Habermas, learning capacities first acquired by individuals in marginal groups enter the system of interpretations of a society by providing exemplars for non-marginal members. Collectively shared structures of consciousness and knowledge constitute a potential of moral–practical and empirical insight which can be utilized for reorganizing action systems. Introducing new principles of organization means establishing new levels of social integration.

In sum we can say that a specific macro-order is the institutional embodiment of a specific moral–practical consciousness which first develops and operates on the micro-level of practical action. Changes of the macro-order are made necessary by system (i.e. macro-) problems, but these changes depend on new moral–practical competences which the members of the system must acquire.]

* This chapter is an expanded and revised version of a preliminary draft that appeared first in *Theory and Society*, 2 (1975), pp. 287–300. For a more comprehensive and detailed treatment of the issues raised in this chapter, see Jürgen Habermas, *Zur Rekonstruktion des Historischen Materialismus* (Frankfurt-Main: Suhrkamp, 1976), especially pp. 144–99.

1   Introductory remarks

In order to give a preliminary indication of the thrust of this chapter, I want to mention three perspectives or vantage-points from which I do not wish to view historical materialism. Occasionally Marx and Engels described historical materialism as a method or an approach. This description might give the impression that historical materialism has the status of a purely *heuristic* guide supplying a systematic outline to narrative historiography; or else that its status is that of a commentary supplementing historiography with metatheoretical reflections. By contrast, I intend to take seriously the cognitive claims of historical materialism and shall treat it as an outline for a *theory of social evolution* awaiting empirical validation. In adopting this view, I take a stand against interpretations that I consider too weak or limited.

At the same time, however, I do not wish to treat historical materialism as a blueprint for an *objectivistic doctrine of historical development*. In rejecting this alternative, I take a stand against those exaggerated or excessively strong claims which have been advanced by spokesmen of the Second International and by adepts of Stalinism. Together with Marx I find in the human anatomy the key to the anatomy of the ape; in other words, the most highly developed social systems display a pattern of structures whose developmental logic can be traced through past stages of social evolution. To be sure, this (still sufficiently ambitious) claim requires careful checks and safeguards. Above all, theorizing must remain aware of its hermeneutical premises and underpinnings. Objectivism may result both from a naive endorsement of the cultural preconditions of research and from a presumed immunity of research from social and cultural contexts.

Yet, methodological constraints of this type do not entail the necessity to view historical materialism purely in a *retrospective* manner, that is, from the vantage-point of a supposedly 'finished' theory of capitalist evolution as contained in Marx's *Grundrisse* and *Kapital*. What I am opposing at this point is a perspective that assigns absolute primacy to political economy and its critique. Perhaps, an application of the basic principles of historical materialism is going to reveal that political economy today is no longer the crucial problem area for analytical purposes; we certainly cannot exclude this possibility.

Thus, my initial thesis can be formulated as follows: historical materialism should be equated neither with a heuristic design, nor with an objectivistic doctrine, nor with a retrospective construct restricted to the categories of nineteenth-century political economy. Rather, it should be treated as an alternative and a challenge to prevailing theoretical approaches to social evolution. Here I intend to assess the merits and limitations of historical materialism to the extent that it is viewed in this manner. I would like to begin by introducing and critically scrutinizing the fundamental concepts and central hypotheses of historical materialism. After indicating some of the problems or shortcomings, I shall propose and illustrate possible solutions. I shall start out by examining the concepts of 'social labour' and 'history of the species'.

2 Social labour

With the concept of 'social labour' or 'socially organized labour' Marx designates the specific way through which humans as distinguished from animals reproduce their life. As he writes in *German Ideology*:

One can make the distinction between man and animal by virtue of consciousness, religion or whatever else one may choose. Man himself begins to differentiate himself from the animals as soon as he starts to produce his own means of subsistence. By producing his own means of subsistence he indirectly produces his material life.

The concept of social labour can be analysed in terms of three different types of rules: rules of instrumental, strategic, and communicative action. We commonly illustrate the meaning of labour by referring to the activity of artisans or craftsmen; decisive in this case is the aspect of the purposive or goal-directed transformation of material in accordance with *rules of instrumental action*. Marx understands by labour not only the instrumental actions of a single individual but also the co-operation of several individuals. The instrumental actions of individuals are socially co-ordinated with a view toward a certain production goal; thus, the *rules of strategic action* that guide this co-operation are an essential element of the labour process. It goes without saying, moreover, that the means of subsistence are produced only in order to be used. Just like labour itself, the distribution of its products is socially organized. The rules of distribution have a distinct structure, for what is at issue here is not the transformation of material nor the goal-directed organization of means, but rather the reciprocal linkage of behavioural expectations or interests. The distribution of products requires intersubjectively recognized norms, that is, *rules of communicative action*.

We call a system that socially organizes labour and distribution an economy; thus Marx is convinced that the 'economic' mode of the reproduction of life is specific for the human stage of development. Here, a significant question is whether this Marxist concept of social labour sufficiently captures the form of reproduction of human life. If we consider this question in the light of recent anthropological findings, it appears that the concept of social labour extends too deeply into the scale of evolution: Not only *Homo sapiens*, but even the hominids are distinguished from other primates in that they reproduce themselves through social labour and develop an economy. This is the period of hominization: it begins with a common ancestor for both chimpanzee and man, and reaches over *Homo erectus* to *Homo sapiens*. Here, among the hominids, the adult men form hunting groups that (1) employ weapons and tools (technology); (2) co-operate through a division of labour (co-operative organization); and (3) collectively distribute the prey (rules of distribution).

The Marxist concept of social labour is thus suitable for distinguishing the mode of life of the hominids from that of the primates; however, it does not grasp the specifically *human* mode of reproduction of life. What is specific for human beings is that they are the first to break up the social structure that had emerged from the vertebrates; only they overcome that one-dimensional status order in which each animal has a single status in the hierarchy. As far as we know, the hominid societies based on social labour had not yet been organized in kinship relationships. Only a family system allows status, in the adult males' system of the hunting group, to be linked (via the father role) to status in the system of the female and young, thus integrating functions of social labour with functions of nurture of the young. Furthermore, this arrangement co-ordinates male hunting functions with female gathering activity (sexual division of labour).

It seems, then, that we can refer to the reproduction of human life in

Homo sapiens only when the economy of the hunt is supplemented by kinship structures. This process lasted several million years; it represents an important replacement of the animal status system. Among the primates, this status system already relies on a certain kind of symbolic interaction; but the role system of kinship implies behavioural norms and thus presupposes language. For the fundamental anthropological assumptions of historical materialism this would seem to imply the following: (1) the concept of social labour is fundamental because the social organization of labour and distribution obviously precede the development of explicit linguistic communication, which, in turn, precedes the formation of social role systems; (2) the specifically human mode of life, however, can be adequately described only if we unite the concept of social labour with that of the kinship structure; (3) the structures of role behaviour mark a new evolutionary threshold compared to the structures of social labour; the rules of communicative action, that is, intersubjectively valid norms of action, cannot be reduced to rules of instrumental or strategic action; (4) production and socialization, the life processes in the spheres of social labour and child rearing, are of *equal* importance for the reproduction of the species. The kinship structure, which controls the integration of both the external as well as the internal nature, is therefore basic for *Homo sapiens*.

3   History of the species

Marx links the concept of social labour with that of the 'history of the species'. This term signals above all the materialist message that natural evolution is now continued within the range of one single species by different means, namely through the productive activity of the socialized individuals themselves. The key to a reconstruction of the history of mankind is offered by the idea of the *mode of production*.

History is conceived as a succession of different modes of production, which in their pattern of development reveal the direction of social evolution. As is well known, for Marx a mode of production is characterized by a particular stage in the development of the productive forces and by particular forms of social exchange, that is, relations of production. The *productive forces* consist: (1) of the labour force of the producers; (2) of technical knowledge, in so far as it is converted into production techniques; (3) of organizational knowledge, in so far as it is efficiently employed to set labour power in motion, to produce skilled labour, and to co-ordinate specialized labour (mobilization, qualification, and organization of labour power). The productive forces determine the extent to which we can control natural processes and exploit natural resources. The *relations of production*, on the other hand, are those institutions and social mechanisms that specify in what way labour can be combined with the available means of production. The regulation of access to the means of production or the channels of control of socially utilized labour also indirectly determines the distribution of the social wealth. Hence the relations of production express the distribution of power; they determine the distributional pattern of opportunities and thereby the interest structure that exists in society. Historical materialism proceeds from the assumption that productive forces and relations of production do not vary independently of each other, but rather form structures that: (1) are mutually related; and (2) produce a finite number of developmental stages homologous in their structure, so that (3) the succession of the modes of production reveals a developmental logic. ('The hand-mill produces a society of feudal lords, the steam-mill a society of industrial capitalists.')

The orthodox version of historical materialism differentiates between five modes of production: the primitive, communal mode of production of the band and tribe; the ancient mode of production based on slaveholding; the feudal; the capitalist; and finally the socialist mode of production. A discussion centred on the classification of the ancient Orient and the ancient Americas led to the insertion of an Asiatic mode of production, with which the development of civilization begins. These six modes of production should define universal stages of social evolution. This means that, from an evolutionary standpoint, the economic structure of every distinctive society can be analysed in terms of the various modes of production that have entered into a hierarchical association in that society.

In primitive societies, labour and distribution are organized through kinship; there is no private access to nature and to the means of production, which are primitive and communal. Administered by the priesthood, the military, and the bureaucracy, there exists in the early civilizations of Mesopotamia, Egypt, ancient China, ancient India and ancient America landed property belonging to the state that is superimposed upon the residue of village community property (the so-called Asiatic mode of production). In Greece, Rome, and other Mediterranean societies, the private landholder combines the status of slaveholder in the context of the domestic economy with the status of citizen in the political community of town or state (ancient mode of production). In medieval Europe, feudalism is based on large, private, landed estates allotted to many individual holders. The landholders enter into various political and economic relations of dependency (even serfdom) with the feudal lord (feudal mode of production). Finally, in capitalism the labour force becomes a commodity, so that the dependence of the direct producers upon those who own the means of production becomes legally institutionalized through the labour contract and economically through the labour market.

The dogmatic formulation of the concept of the history of the species shares a set of weaknesses with the models of a philosophy of history rooted in the eighteenth century. However, historical materialism does not need to presuppose a macro-subject to which the evolutionary process is assigned. The bearers of evolution are society and its members. Evolution can be read from those structures that, following a rational pattern, are replaced by ever more comprehensive structures. In the course of this structure-creating process the social entities involved also change. In addition there is the question of the sense in which one can interpret the emergence of new structures as movement; certainly only the empirical substrata are in motion, that is, the societies and their individuals.

The most disputed issue is teleology, which historical materialism sees as inherent in history. By evolution we mean, in fact, cumulative processes that allow a direction to be perceived. Neo-evolutionist theories consider increasing complexity as a reasonable criterion. The more states a system can choose, the more complex the environment with which it will be able to cope. Marx also ascribed great importance to the 'social division of labour'. This refers to the processes that enhance the adaptive capacity of a society. However, historical materialism does not judge progress by this criterion of complexity, but according to the development of productive forces and to the maturation of forms of social integration that permit increased participation in politically relevant decision-making processes. These two dimensions are not selected arbitrarily. Because further productive forces and new forms of social integration are a result of the social implementation of technical and moral–practical knowledge, the selection of both these dimensions in the last analysis is determined by two related claims to validity: namely, by the truth of propositions and the justifiability of norms. I would therefore defend the position that the criteria of historical progress that historical materialism identifies with the development of the productive forces and the emancipation from social constraint are capable of a systematic justification.

In any case, I assume that the idea of the history of the species can be reformulated so as to meet the objections against the idea of one-dimensional, necessary, and irreversible social evolution of a reified species subject. Having elucidated the concepts of 'social labour' and of 'history of the species', I shall now turn briefly to two basic assumptions of historical materialism: first, to the theory of base and superstructure and, second, to the dialectic of production forces and relations of production.

4   Basic assumptions

In every society productive forces and the relations of production form an *economic structure* by which the other subsystems are determined. For a considerable length of time an economistic version of this thesis has prevailed. The context in which Marx propounds his theory makes it clear that the dependence of superstructure on base is valid only for the critical phase during which a social system is passing onto a new developmental level. What is meant is not some *ontological constitution* of society, but rather the *guiding role that the economic structure assumes in social evolution.* Thus the thesis purports that evolutionary innovations solve such problems as may arise at the substructural level of a society and that demand a change within the base.

The identification of substructure with economic structure could lead to the assumption that the substructural level is always equivalent to the economic system. That is, however, valid only for modern societies. Relations of production are defined by their function of regulating access to the means of production and indirectly the distribution of social wealth. This function is assumed in primitive societies by kinship systems and in traditional societies by political institutions. It is not until the market, in addition to its cybernetic function, also takes over the function of stabilizing class relations through the institution of wage labour that the relations of production assume a purely economic form. Theories of 'postindustrial society' (Bell, Touraine) envisage a situation in which evolutionary primacy shifts from the economy (and complementary institutions of the 'state') to the educational and scientific system.

In any case, the particular institutional core that takes over the functions of the relations of production determines the dominant form of *social integration*. I use this term in the Durkheimian sense of integration through norms and values. If system problems – for example ecological, demographic, economic problems – can no longer be solved in accord with an existing form of social integration, if this form itself must be revolutionized in order to create latitude for the solution of problems, then the identity of the society is challenged and society itself is thrown into a crisis. Marx sees the mechanism of this crisis in the *dialectic of productive forces and relations of production.*

This theory can be interpreted in the following way: an endogenous learning mechanism exists that provides for spontaneous growth of technical knowledge and for the development of the productive forces. In this context, a mode of production is only in a state of equilibrium when structural homologies exist between the developmental stages of the productive forces and the relations of production. Correspondingly, this means that the endogenous development of productive forces generates structural incompatibilities that in turn evoke imbalances in the existing mode of production and thereby lead to a revolution in the existing relations of production. In this structuralist sense, Godelier, for example, has adopted the theory.

However, in such a formulation we still cannot precisely locate the developmental mechanism. The postulated *learning mechanism* explains the growth of a cognitive potential (and also perhaps its conversion into increasing labour productivity). It can explain the *emergence* of system problems that, if the structural homologies between productive forces and relations of production break down, threaten the stability of the mode of production. However, this learning mechanism does not explain how these problems can be solved; for the introduction of new forms of social integration, as for instance the replacement of the kinship system with the state, demands knowledge of a practical–moral kind. What is required is not technical knowledge that can be implemented through rules of instrumental and strategic action nor an expansion of our control over external nature, but rather a knowledge that can find its embodiment in structures of interaction. We can understand the development of productive forces as a problem-generating mechanism that *releases* but does not *create* the evolutionary renewal of the mode of production.

Even in this form, however, the theory cannot be maintained as a universal proposition on empirical grounds. In the case of the great endogenous thrusts of evolution that led to the birth of ancient civilizations or to the rise of capitalism in Europe, we find a significant development of the productive forces, not as a prior condition, but rather as a consequence. Only when a new institutional framework had emerged could the unresolved problems be treated with the aid of the accumulated cognitive potential. This in turn resulted in an increase in the productive forces.

The question which still remains unanswered at this point is *how* such evolutionary thrusts occur. The *descriptive* response of historical materialism is: through social movements and political struggles, that is, through class conflict. But only a *causal-analytical* response can explain why a given society undergoes evolutionary thrusts and in which manner social struggles under certain conditions lead to *new forms of social integration* and thus to new levels of social evolution. The solution that I would like to propose is as follows: the species is able to *learn* not only in the domain of technical knowledge – a domain decisive for the growth of productive forces – but also in the domain of moral–practical awareness that governs the development of structures of interaction. Instead of simply reflecting changes in the areas of instrumental and strategic action, the rules of communicative action unfold in accordance with their *own internal logic*.

The short discussion of the two main assumptions of historical materialism leads to the following tentative conclusions: (1) that all system problems that cannot be solved without evolutionary innovations arise in the substructure of a society; (2) that higher modes of production signify new forms of social integration, which in each case crystallize around a new institutional core; (3) that an endogenous learning mechanism provides for the accumulation of a cognitive potential that can be employed to solve an evolutionary crisis; (4) that this knowledge, however, can only be effectively utilized for the development of the productive forces, once a new institutional framework and a new form of social integration have been established. At this point I would like to add a few comments on the internal developmental logic of moral–practical consciousness.

5   Moral–practical development

Evolutionary learning processes cannot be ascribed exclusively either to society or individuals. Certainly the personality system bears the learning process of ontogenesis, and, to a certain extent, only individuals are capable of learning. However, social systems can form new structures by utilizing the learning capacities of their members in order to cope with problems that threaten system maintenance. In this respect the evolutionary learning process of societies is dependent on the competence of their individual members. These in turn acquire their competence, not as isolated monads, but by growing into the symbolic structure of their social world.

If we follow this process from the perspective of the socialized child, social reality gains a new depth dimension. At first actions, motives and actors are still combined on one single level of reality. At the next stage, actions and norms begin to separate; norms, together with actors and their motives, move onto a level that lies behind the level of observable actions. At the final stage, principles on the basis of which norms of action can be derived and criticized are distinguished from the norms themselves. The principles together with the actors and their motives recede behind the level of norms, that is, behind the established interaction systems. In this manner we acquire basic concepts for a genetic theory of action that can be used in two ways: either as concepts for the individual acquisition of the capacity for speech and action in a symbolic universe; or as concepts for the development of this social-symbolic universe itself.

In so far as conflicts of action are not resolved by force or strategic means but on a consensual basis, structures come into play that shape the moral consciousness of individuals and the moral and legal codes of societies. The concepts of 'good' and 'evil' crystallize around the idea of reciprocity, which lies at the base of all interactions. In the research tradition of Piaget, it is customary to differentiate between three developmental stages of moral consciousness that correspond to levels of interactive or communicative competence. At the *preconventional level*, where actions, motives, and actors are still merged on a single plane of reality, only the manifest consequences of action are assessed in case of behavioural conflicts. At the *conventional level*, motives can be assessed independently of the concrete consequences of action; decisive is the intentional conformity with social expectations and existing norms. At the *postconventional level*, these norms lose their traditional authority and require justification through recourse to universal criteria.

I would suggest that such individual competences can also be used for the solution of system problems and for the innovation of legal institutions. This is what is meant by socio-evolutionary learning processes in the domain of moral–practical consciousness. Incidentally, in the case of both individual and social development, it is advisable to distinguish structures designed for normal performance from structures that become operative in conflict or crisis situations. Frequently, normal structures operate on a higher developmental level than structures applicable to situations of conflict. As a first step in the analysis of social learning processes, I shall attempt to indicate different levels of social integration. In doing so, I shall differentiate between (1) the infrastructure of institutions and prevailing world-views, on the one hand, and (2) moral beliefs and legal norms, on the other.

Neolithic societies: (1) *conventional* differentiation between actions and norms, with mythical world-views still enmeshed in the system of action; (2) resolution of conflicts according to *preconventional* criteria: assessment of the consequences of action, restitution of the former *status quo*, that is, compensation for damages caused (feuding law, court of arbitration).

Archaic civilizations: (1) *conventional* interaction systems, but formation of a differentiated mythical world-view that can assume functions of legitimation for political authorities; (2) resolution of conflicts from the standpoint of a *conventional* morality dependent on the ruler: assessment of the intentions of the actor; punishment in relation to culpability.

Developed premodern civilizations: (1) *conventional* interaction systems; formation of a rationalized world-view (ethical system founded on cosmologies or monotheism); legitimation of the political system independent of the person of the ruler; (2) resolution of conflicts from the standpoint of a *developed conventional* morality: system of jurisdiction to which the ruler is subject on principle; punishment for deviance from traditionally justified norms.

6 Origin of class societies

I would like to illustrate with one example how this approach works. I shall select the problem of the origin of class societies as I can rely here on a study by Klaus Eder.[1]

Class societies arise within the framework of a political system; social integration here no longer needs to proceed through the kinship system, but can be taken over by the *state*. There have been a number of theories on the origin of the state that I would first like to mention and criticize.

(1) The *subjugation theory* explains the emergence of political rulers and the establishment of a state apparatus through nomadic pastoral tribes conquering settled agricultural peasants. This theory today has been refuted: because nomadism occurs later than the first civilizations, the emergence of the state must have had endogenous causes.

(2) The *division of labour* theory is usually stated in a complex way. Agricultural production achieves a surplus and permits (in combination with demographic growth) the release of workers for other purposes. This leads to a social division of labour. The various social groups that thereby emerge appropriate social wealth differentially and form social classes, at least one of which assumes political functions. Despite its apparent plausibility, this theory is not consistent. An argument is missing that could show why political functions originate from differentiated interests rooted in professional specialization. Actually, the social division of labour occurs as much within the politically dominant classes (between priesthood, military, and bureaucracy) as within the working population (for example, between farmers and artisans).

(3) The *theory of social inequality* traces the emergence of the state to distribution problems. A surplus arises from the productivity of labour, and the increasing wealth differentials result in social inequalities with which the basically egalitarian kinship system cannot cope. The distribution problems demand a different, that is, political organization of social exchange. This thesis could, if true, explain at least the origin of system problems that were solved by state organization. Nevertheless, it would not be sufficient to explain this new form of social integration itself. Furthermore, the assumption of automatic growth in the productive forces is not true for agricultural production.

(4) The *irrigation hypothesis* explains the integration of several village communities into a political unity by reason of their need to master drought through large-scale irrigation systems. These huge construction projects require an administration that becomes the institutional core of the state. This assumption has been refuted empirically, because in Mesopotamia, China, and Mexico, the formation of states preceded irrigation projects. Furthermore, this theory again would explain only the origin of system problems, not the manner of their solution.

(5) The *theory of population density* explains the origin of the state primarily by ecological and demographic factors. An endogenous population growth is assumed that normally leads to a spatial expansion of segmentary societies (that is, to emigration into new areas). When, however, the ecological situation – neighbouring mountains, the sea or the desert, barren tracts of land, and so forth – hampered emigration or flight, conflicts arose due to population density and land scarcity. They allowed no other alternative than for large sections of the population to submit to the political rule of the victorious tribe. The complexity of the densely populated settlements could be controlled only by state organization. Even if population problems of this kind could be proved to have existed in all former civilizations, this theory does not explain why and how such problems have been resolved.

None of the theories mentioned differentiates between system problems that overstrain the steering capacity of the kinship system and the evolutionary learning process that might explain the change to a new form of social integration. Only with the help of learning mechanisms can we explain why some societies find solutions to their problems at all, and why the particular solution to a state organization was chosen. I shall therefore proceed from the following main hypotheses: (1) normally the interactive and the cognitive development of a child proceeds in stages, so that the child reaches a new learning level at each stage. In ontogenesis, not learning processes, but learning interruptions and retardation are the phenomena that must be explained; (2) a society can learn evolutionally by solving the problems that overstrain its present steering capacity through converting and incorporating the surplus of individual learning capacities into new institutional arrangements; (3) the first step in the social evolutionary learning process is the establishment of a new form of social integration that permits an increase in the productive forces and an expansion of the system's complexity.

These hypotheses lend support to the following explanatory sketch for the origin of class societies:

(1) The *phenomenon to be explained* is the origin of a political order that organizes a society so that its members can belong to different lineages. The function of social integration moves from kinship to the political system. The collective identity is no longer embodied in the figure of a common ancestor, but rather in the figure of a common ruler.

(2) *Theoretical description* of the phenomenon: a ruling position is characterized by the fact that the position *per se* confers legitimacy on the occupant. Legitimacy no longer depends on a former *status quo* that must be restored as soon as it is upset. On the contrary, it is attached to a position that empowers the holder to administer justice without having to limit himself to the evaluation of concrete actions and consequences of actions. Thus the ruler is not directly circumscribed by actual constellations of power. At the same time, mythical belief systems that justify genealogically the ruler's privileges assume for the first time, in addition to their explanatory functions, functions of legitimation as well.

(3) The *goal of the explanation*: the differentiation of a ruling position means that the ruler practises jurisdiction at the level of conventional morality. Consequently, the origin of the state should be explained by the structural transformation of legal institutions moving from the preconventional to the conventional level of consensual settlement of conflicts.

The following is the explanatory sketch in greater detail:

(4) *The initial state*: I take the neolithic societies where the complexity of the kinship system has greatly increased to be promising from an evolutionary point of view. As Eder writes:

> They in a way institutionalize political roles already. But the chieftains, kings or leaders are still judged by their concerted actions; their actions are not legitimate *per se*. Such roles are only temporarily institutionalized (e.g., for warfare) or limited to special tasks (e.g., to provide a good harvest or rain). These roles have not yet advanced into the centre of social organization.

(5) *Particular system problems*: in the evolutionally promising neo-

lithic societies, system problems sometimes arise that cannot be controlled by the steering capacity of the kinship system. They may involve problems of land scarcity and population density or of unequal distribution of social wealth. These problems are perceived once they lead to conflicts that overburden the archaic legal institutions (court of arbitration, feuding law).

(6) *The testing of new structures*: in societies that are under pressure from such problems, the conventional structures available at the level of individual moral consciousness are used to test the administration of justice on a new, that is, conventional level. So, for example, the war chief may be empowered to adjudicate in cases of conflict, not merely according to the contingent constellations of power, but rather according to socially recognized traditional norms. At this point, law is no longer restricted to arrangements agreed upon by the parties in concrete cases.

(7) *Stabilizing the innovations*: these roles can become the pacemakers of social evolution. However, not all promising experiments lead via such judicial functions to a permanent authority, that is, to an evolutionary success. This is shown in the example of the Barotse Kingdom. Only if other conditions are present – for example, the military victory of a dominant tribe or a huge construction project – can such roles stabilize and become the core of a political system. Such a development marks off the successful societies in evolutionary terms from those that are merely promising.

(8) *Emergence of class structures*: 'On the basis of political authority,' Eder writes, 'the material process of production can then be uncoupled from the limiting conditions of the kinship system and be reorganized in terms of political relations.' The ruler secures the loyalty of his officials, priests, and warrior families by providing them privileged access to the means of production (temple and palace economy).

(9) *Development of the forces of production*: to quote Eder again:

> The forces of production, which had already been uncovered by the neolithic revolution, can only now be used on a large scale: the intensification of agriculture and stock-farming and the expansion of crafts are the result of the extended steering capacity of the class society. This leads to new forms of cooperation (e.g., in irrigational farming) or of exchange (e.g., in the market exchange between town and country).

The preceding explanatory sketch may cause surprise in view of the topic of this chapter, for at no point does the sketch refer to a particular mode of production. Instead, the two forms of social integration are described in a relatively abstract manner in terms of interactional and moral structures. Actually, the advantage of the sketch lies precisely in this abstraction; for the application of the orthodox scheme of six modes of production has led to numerous difficulties. During the past century, discussions have concentrated mainly on the demarcation of paleolithic from neolithic society; on the identification of the Asiatic mode of production; on the differentiation between archaic and developed civilizations; and on the interpretation of feudalism. These discussions in no way suggest the barrenness of the research programme of historical materialism; but they clearly demonstrate one point: the concept of the mode of production is not sufficiently abstract to encompass the universals of developmental levels.

I therefore propose the search for abstract principles of organization. These principles should comprehend those innovations that institutionalize a new level of learning in a given case. The organizational principle of a society specifies the range of options; in particular, it determines the limits within which institutional changes can occur. The principle further defines to what degree the available capacities of productive forces can be socially employed, or to what degree the development of new forces of production can be stimulated; in the same manner it determines how far the complexity of a system's steering capacities can be increased.

If empirically validated, the sketch could also explain why two aspects seem to be linked in the course of social evolution: on the one hand, the cumulative learning process without which history could not be viewed as evolution or as a linear process; and on the other hand, the practice of domination and social exploitation that first emerged with the rise of class societies. Historical materialism has always tended to identify linear progress with the expansion of productive forces and to apply dialectical modes of analysis to the development of the relations of production. On the basis of the reconstruction proposed in this chapter, it is possible to ascertain learning processes not only in the domain of technical knowledge, but also in the dimension of moral-practical awareness. The structural types of social integration can be arranged in a developmental sequence. However, the development of social integration is by no means synonymous with a sequential decrease in social exploitation.

From an evolutionary perspective, the type of social integration that is tied to the kinship system and that, in conflict situations, is maintained through preconventional legal sanctions belongs to a lower stage of development than the type that involves political rule and that, in conflict situations, is maintained through conventional legal practices. Yet, from the vantage-point of moral standards applicable to both primitive and civilized societies, the form of exploitation necessarily practised in class societies must be judged as a regression in comparison with the moderate social inequalities possible in kinship systems. This explains why class societies are structurally unable to satisfy the need for legitimation that they produce. This is the key to the recurring class struggles in postkinship societies.

Note

1 Compare Klaus Eder, *Zur Entstehung staatlich organisierter Gesellschaften* (Frankfurt-Main: Suhrkamp, 1976).

10 Unscrewing the big Leviathan: how actors macro-structure reality and how sociologists help them to do so

Michel Callon and Bruno Latour*

Canst thou fill his skin with barbed irons? . . . Lay thine hand upon him remember the battle, do no more . . . . None is so fierce that dare stir him up: who then is able to stand before me?

Job 41:7,8,10

[*Like Habermas, Callon and Latour conceive of micro-macro relations in dynamic terms, but they do not conceive of them in evolutionary terms. The process they have in mind is not a process in which forms of social integration become replaced by new forms on the basis of social learning, but rather a process* by which micro-actors successfully grow to macro-size.

Callon and Latour consider the macro-order to consist of macro-actors who have successfully 'translated' other actors' wills into a single will for which they speak. This enrolment of other actors allows them to act like a single will which is, however, extremely powerful because of the forces on which it can rely. How do micro-actors grow to such formidable sizes like that of big multinational corporations? Callon and Latour say that unlike baboons, human actors are able to rely not only on symbolic relations, but also on more 'durable' materials, for which they provide examples. It is this difference which allows the human society to produce macro-actors and which forces the baboon society to enact all its relations on a micro-level of symbolic practice.

The present chapter is the contribution to the book which most forcefully reminds us of a possible correlation between power and the macro-level. It is also the chapter whose conception of macro-actors is perhaps most similar to Harré's notion of structured collectivities to which he attributes causal powers (see chapter

* Authors in alphabetical order. We especially thank John Law, Shirley Strum, Karin Knorr, Lucien Karpik and Luc Boltanski for their sharp criticism which we failed, most of the time, to answer.

4), and which has some overlap with Cicourel's focus on the summarizing procedures through which the macro is generated within micro-social action (see chapter 1 and section 5 of the Introduction). In a sense it can be seen as the macro-counterpart of the last mentioned micro-conceptions.]

1   Hobbes's paradox

Given: a multitude of equal, egoistic men living without any law in a merciless state of nature that has been described as, 'the war of every one against every one'.[1] How can this state be brought to an end? Everyone knows Hobbes's reply: through a contract that every man makes with every other and which gives one man, or a group of men bound to none other, the right to speak on behalf of all. They become: the 'actor' of which the multitude linked by contracts are the 'authors'.[2] Thus 'authorized',[3] the sovereign becomes the *person* who says what the others are, what they want and what they are worth, accountant of all debts, guarantor of all laws, recorder of property registers, supreme measurer of ranks, opinions, judgments and currency. In short the sovereign becomes the Leviathan: 'that Mortal God, to which we owe under the Immortal God, our peace and defense'.[4]

The solution proposed by Hobbes is of interest to political philosophy and of major importance to sociology, formulating clearly as it does for the first time the relationship between micro-actors and macro-actors. Hobbes sees no difference of level or size between the micro-actors and the Leviathan *which is not the result of a transaction.* The multitude, says Hobbes, is at the same time the Form and the Matter of the body politic. The construction of this artificial body is calculated in such a way that the absolute sovereign is nothing other than the sum of the multitude's wishes. Though the expression 'Leviathan' is usually considered synonymous with 'totalitarian monster', in Hobbes the sovereign says nothing on his own authority. He says nothing without having been authorized by the multitude, whose spokesman, mask-bearer and amplifier he is.[5] The sovereign is not *above* the people, either by nature or by function, nor is he higher, or greater, or of different substance. He is the people itself in another state – as we speak of a gaseous or a solid state.

This point seems to us of capital importance, and in this paper we should like to examine all its consequences. Hobbes states that there is no difference between the actors which is *inherent in their nature*. All differences in level, size and scope are the result of a battle or a negotiation. We cannot distinguish between macro-actors (institutions, organizations, social classes, parties, states) and micro-actors (individuals, groups, families) on the basis of their dimensions, since they are all, we might say, the 'same size', or rather since size is what is primarily at stake in their struggles it is also, therefore, their most important result. For Hobbes – and for us too – it is not a question of classifying macro- and micro-actors, or reconciling what we know of the former and what we know of the latter, but posing anew the old question: how does a micro-actor become a macro-actor? How can men act 'like one man'?

The originality of the problem posed by Hobbes is partly concealed by his solution – the social contract – which history, anthropology and now ethology have proved impossible. The contract, however, is merely a specific instance of a more general phenomenon, that of translation.[6] By translation we understand all the negotiations, intrigues, calculations, acts of persuasion and violence,[7] thanks to which an actor or force takes, or causes to be conferred on itself, authority to speak or act on behalf of another actor or force:[8] 'Our interests are the same', 'do what I want', 'you cannot succeed without going through me'. Whenever an actor speaks of 'us', s/he is translating other actors into a single will, of which s/he becomes spirit and spokesman. S/he begins to act for several, no longer for one alone. S/he becomes stronger. S/he grows. The social contract displays in legal terms, at society's very beginnings, in a once-and-for-all, all-or-nothing ceremony, what processes of translation display in an empirical and a reversible way, in multiple, detailed, everyday negotiations. The contract need only be replaced by processes of translation and the Leviathan will begin to grow, thus restoring to Hobbes's solution all its originality.

The aim of this article is to show what sociology becomes if we maintain Hobbes's central hypothesis – provided we replace the contract by a general law of translation. How can we describe society, if our aim is the analysis of the construction of differences in size between micro- and macro-actors?

The methodological constraints we impose for describing the Leviathan should not be misunderstood. We should miss the point completely, if we distinguish between 'individuals' and 'institutions'; if we supposed that the first fell within the sphere of psychology, and the second of economic history.[9] *There are* of course macro-actors and micro-actors, but the difference between them is brought about by power relations and the constructions of networks that will *elude analysis* if we presume *a priori* that macro-actors are bigger than or superior to micro-actors. These power relations and translation processes reappear more clearly if we follow Hobbes in his strange assumption that all actors are isomorphic.[10] Isomorphic does not mean that all actors have the *same* size but that *a priori* there is no way to decide the size since it is the consequence of a long struggle. The best way to understand this is to consider actors as networks. Two networks may have the same shape although one is almost limited to a point and the other extends all over the country, exactly like the sovereign can be one among the others and the personification of all the others. The financier's office is no larger than the cobbler's shop; neither is his brain, his culture, his network of friends nor his world. The latter is 'merely' a man; the former is, as we say, a 'great man'.

Too often sociologists – just like politicians or the man in the street – *change their framework of analysis* depending on whether they are tackling a macro-actor or a micro-actor, the Leviathan or a social interaction, the culture or individual roles. By changing the framework of analysis while this is under way they confirm the power relations, giving aid to the winner and giving the losers the 'vae victis'.

This problem has become urgent – as the contributors to this volume suggest – because no sociologists at present examine macro-actors and micro-actors using the same tools and the same arguments. They take it for granted that there are differences in level between micro-sociological analysis and macro-sociological analysis, though they may still want to reconcile them in a broad synthesis.[11]

It seems to us that sociologists are too often on the wrong foot. Either, believing that macro-actors really do exist, they anticipate the actors' strength by helping them to grow more vigorous.[12] Or else they deny their existence, once they really do exist, and will not even allow us the right to study them.[13] These two alternate but symmetrical errors stem from the same presupposition: the acceptance as a given fact that actors can be of different or of equal size. As soon as we reject this presupposition, we are once again faced with Hobbes's paradox: no actor is bigger than another except by means of a transaction (a translation) which must be examined. We show in this article that if one remains faithful to Hobbes's paradox, one avoids the symmetrical errors and understands how the Leviathan grows.

In section 2 we attempt to resolve the following paradox: if all actors are isomorphic and none is by nature bigger or smaller than any other, how is it that they eventually end up as macro-actors or individuals? In section 3 we shall examine how actors wax and wane, and how the methods we propose enable us to follow them through their variations in size, without having to alter the framework for analysis. Lastly, in the conclusion, we consider in more detail the role of sociologists in such variations in relative size.

2 Baboons, or the impossible Leviathan

Let us leave Hobbes's myth of the Leviathan and take another myth: the impossible Monkey-Leviathan or the difficulty of building up macro-actors in a herd of baboons living in the wild.[14] Hobbes believed that society only emerged with man.[15] This was believed for a long time, until gatherings of animals were observed closely enough for it to become clear that theories about the emergence of societies were pertinent for primates, ants, the Canidae, as well as for men.

This 'disordered' herd of brute beasts – eating, mating, howling, playing and fighting one another in a chaos of hair and fangs – surely tallies closely with the 'state of nature' postulated by Hobbes. Without any doubt at all the life of a baboon is 'poor, nasty, brutish and short'.[16] This image of total disorder enabled a contrast to be made, right from the beginning, between human society and bestiality, between social order and chaos. At least this is how animals were imagined before people actually went and studied them.

When, before the Second World War, but more intensively since the 1950s, people began to study baboons, each observer reconstructed Hobbes's Leviathan on his own account.[17] The baboons no longer live in disordered bands. They started living in rigid cohorts where the females and their young are surrounded by dominant males organized according to a strict hierarchy. In the 1970s, the image of a pyramid-shaped society of monkeys has gradually come to be used as a foil for human societies which have been said to be more flexible, freer and more complex. Over 30 years, the study of primates has thus been used as a projective test: first, bestial chaos was observed, then a rigid, almost totalitarian system. Baboons have been obliged to re-structure the Leviathan and to move from the war of all against all to absolute obedience.

Despite this, observers closer to the monkeys have gradually worked out a different Leviathan. The baboons do indeed have organization: not everything is equally possible in it. One animal does not go close to just any other; an animal does not cover or groom another by chance; nor does it move aside just at random; animals cannot go just where they wish. However, this organization is never rigid enough to constitute an integrated system. As the observers have come to know their baboons better, the hierarchies of dominance have become more flexible, finally dissolving – at least in the case of the males.[18] Primary aggressiveness has become rarer: it has been seen to be consistently channelled and socialized until finally the groups of baboons have become surprisingly 'civil'. The famous elementary impulses which fuel the war of all against all – eating, copulating, domination, reproduction – have been observed to be constantly suspended, halted and diffracted by the play of social interactions. There is no chaos, but no rigid system either. Now the baboons live in units, none of which is rigid, but none of which is flexible. In addition to differences of size, sex and age, social links, are the family, clan and friendship networks, or even habits due to traditions and customs. None of these categories is clearly defined since they all come into play together, and can break apart again. Observers now construct the baboon society as one whose texture is much stronger than was imagined by those who thought it a chaos of brute beasts, but infinitely more flexible than postwar observers thought.

For a society of baboons to be at the same time so flexible and yet so close-knit, an amazing hypothesis had to be advanced: more and more extensive social skills had to be bestowed on the monkeys in order to make them competent to repair, accomplish and ceaselessly consolidate the fabric of such a complex society.[19]

A baboon's life is not easy in the new society that has been forged for it and is no less difficult than our life as revealed by ethnomethod-ological works. He must constantly determine who is who, who is superior and who inferior, who leads the group and who follows, and who must stand back to let him pass. And all he has to help him are fuzzy sets whose logic is fashioned to evaluate hundreds of elements. Each time it is necessary, as the ethnomethodologists say, to repair indexicality. Who is calling? What is it intending to say? No marks, no costumes, no discreet signs. Of course, many signs, growls and hints exist, but none of them is unambiguous enough. Only the context will tell, but simplifying and evaluating the context is a constant headache. Hence the strange impression these animals give today. Living as they do in the heart of the bush, all they should be thinking about is eating and mating. But all they care about is to stabilize their relations, or, as Hobbes would say, durably to attach bodies with bodies. As much as we do they build up a society which is their surroundings, shelter, task, luxury, game and destiny.

To simplify we might say that baboons are 'social animals'. The word 'social' derives, we know, from 'socius', which is akin to 'sequi', to follow. First of all to follow, then to form an alliance or to enlist, then to have something in common, to share. Several act like a single entity, the social link is there. Baboons are social like all social animals in the sense that they follow each other, enrol each other, form alliances, share certain links and territories. But they are social, too, in that they can maintain and fortify their alliances, links and partitions only with the tools and procedures that ethnomethodologists grant us to repair indexicality. They are constantly stabilizing the links between bodies by acting on other bodies.[20]

Only among the baboons are the living bodies alone, as Hobbes requires, at the same time the Form and the Matter of the Leviathan. But what happens when this is the case? There is no Leviathan. We must now formulate the central question: if the baboons realize Hobbes's conditions and offer us the spectacle of a society made with no solid Leviathan or durable macro-actor, how are the solid, durable macro-actors which we see forming everywhere in human societies, actually constructed?

Hobbes thought the Leviathan could be built with bodies, but then he was only talking about baboons. His Leviathan could never have been built if bodies had been the Form *and* Matter of the social body. Although in order to stabilize society everyone – monkeys as well as men – need to bring into play associations *that last longer than the interactions that formed them*, the strategies and resources may vary between societies of baboons or of men. For instance, instead of acting straight upon the bodies of colleagues, parents and friends, like baboons, one might turn to more solid and less variable materials in order to act in a more durable way upon the bodies of our colleagues, parents and friends. In the state of nature, no one is strong enough to hold out against every coalition.[21] But if you transform the state of nature, replacing unsettled alliances as much as you can with walls and written contracts, the ranks with uniforms and tattoos and reversible friendships with names and signs, then you will obtain a Leviathan: 'His scales are his pride, shut up together as with a close seal. One is so near to another that no air can come between them. They are joined one to another; they stick together that they cannot be sundered' (Job 41:15–17).

A difference in relative size is obtained when a micro-actor can, in addition to enlisting bodies, also enlist the greatest number of durable materials. He or she thus creates greatness and longevity making the others small and provisional in comparison. The secret of the difference between micro-actors and macro-actors lies precisely in what analysis often neglects to consider. The primatologists omit to say that, to stabilize their world, the baboons do not have at their disposal any of the human instruments manipulated by the observer. Hobbes omits to say that no promise, however solemn, could frighten the contracting parties enough to force them to obey. He omits to say that what makes the sovereign formidable and the contract solemn are the palace from which he speaks, the well-equipped armies that surround him, the scribes and the recording equipment that serve him.[22] The ethnomethodologists forget to include in their analyses the fact that ambiguity of context in human societies is partially removed by a whole gamut of tools, regulations, walls and objects of which they analyse only a part. We must now gather up what their analysis leaves out and examine with the same method the strategies which enlist bodies, materials, discourses, techniques, feelings, laws, organizations. Instead of dividing the subject with the social/technical, or with the human/animal, or with the micro/macro dichotomies, we will only retain for the analysis *gradients of resistivity* and consider only the *variations in relative solidity and durability of different sorts of materials*.

By associating materials of different durability, a set of practices is placed in a hierarchy in such a way that some become stable and need no longer be considered. Only thus can one 'grow'. In order to build the Leviathan it is necessary to enrol a *little more* than relationships, alliances and friendships. An actor grows with the number of relations he or she can put, as we say, in black boxes. A black box contains that which no longer needs to be reconsidered, those things whose contents have become a matter of indifference. The more elements one can place in black boxes – modes of thoughts, habits, forces and objects – the broader the construction one can raise. Of course, black boxes never remain fully closed or properly fastened – as it is particularly the case among the baboons – but macro-actors can do *as if* they were closed and dark. Although, as ethnomethodologists have shown, we are all constantly struggling for closing leaky black boxes, macro-actors, to say the least, do not have to negotiate with *equal intensity* everything. They can go on and count on a force while negotiating for another. If they were not successful at that, they could not simplify the social world. In mechanical terms, they could not make a machine, that is hide the continued exercise of a will to give the impression of forces that move by themselves. In logical terms, they could not make chains of arguments, that is stabilize discussion of certain premises to allow deductions or establish order between different elements.

If the expression 'black box' is too rigid to describe the forces which shut off the stacks of boxes, and keep them hermetically sealed and obscure, another metaphor is possible, one Hobbes might have used had he read Waddington.[23] In the first moments of fertilization, all cells are alike. But soon an epigenetic landscape takes form where courses are cut out which tend to be irreversible; these are called 'chreods'. Then cellular differentiation begins. Whether we speak of black boxes or chreods, we are dealing with the creation of asymmetries. Let us then imagine a body where differentiation is never fully irreversible, where each cell attempts to compel the others to become irreversibly specialized, and where many organs are permanently claiming to be the head of the programme. If we imagine such a *monster* we shall have a fairly clear idea of the Leviathan's body, which we can at any moment see growing before our very eyes.

The paradox with which we ended the introduction has now been resolved. We end up with actors of different size even though they are all isomorphic, because some have been able to put into black boxes more elements durably to alter their relative size. The question of method is also resolved. How can we examine macro-actors and micro-actors, we were wondering, without confirming differences in size? Reply: by directing our attention not to the social but towards the processes by which an actor creates lasting asymmetries. That among these processes some lead to associations which are sometimes called 'social' (associations of bodies), and that some of the others are sometimes called 'technical' (associations of materials), need *not* concern us further. Only the differences between what can be put in black boxes and what remain open for future negotiations are now relevant for us.

To summarize, macro-actors are micro-actors seated on top of many (leaky) black boxes. They are neither larger, nor more complex than micro-actors; on the contrary, they are of the same size and, as we shall see, they are in fact simpler than micro–actors. We are able, now, to consider how the Leviathan is structured, since we know that we do not need to be impressed by the relative size of the masters, or to be frightened by the darkness of the black boxes.

3   Essay in teratology

In this section, we leave Hobbes's barbarous, juridical Leviathan, as well as the 'bush and savannah' Leviathan we saw in action among the baboons. We shall follow up one detail of the huge, mythical monster in a modern context: the way in which two actors – Electricity of France (EDF) and Renault – varied their relative dimensions in the course of a struggle that took place between them during the 1970s.[24]

To replace the usual divisions (macro/micro; human/animal; social/technical), which we have shown to be unprofitable, we need terms in keeping with the methodological principles stated above. What is an 'actor'? Any element which bends space around itself, makes other elements dependent upon itself and translates their will into a language of its own. An actor makes changes in the set of elements and concepts habitually used to describe the social and the natural worlds. By stating what belongs to the past, and of what the future consists, by defining what comes before and what comes after, by building up balance sheets, by drawing up chronologies, it imposes its own space and time. It defines space and its organization, sizes and their measures, values and standards, the stakes and rules of the game – the very existence of the game itself. Or else it allows another, more powerful than itself, to lay them down. This struggle for what is essential has often been described but few have tried to find out how an actor can make these asymmetries last, can lay down a temporality and a space that is imposed on the others. And yet the answer to this question is in principle quite simple: by capturing more durable elements which are substituted for the provisional differences in level s/he has managed to establish. Weak, reversible interactions, are replaced by strong interactions. Before, the elements dominated by the actor could escape in any direction, but now this is no longer possible. Instead of swarms of possibilities, we find lines of force, obligatory passing points, directions and deductions.[25]

3.1   Electricity of France and Renault: hybrids and chimera

Let us take the case of the Electricity of France (EDF) which, in the early 1970s, was struggling to launch an electric vehicle. EDF ventures out onto a terrain that is new to it, with the aim of bringing the ideal electric vehicle into existence. It does this by redefining the totality of a world from which it will cut out what is natural and what is technical. EDF places the evolution of industrial societies as a whole in a black box and enrols it for its own advantage. According to the ideologists within this public enterprise, the all-out consumption characteristic of the postwar years is doomed. Henceforth, the direction of future production must take into consideration man's happiness and the quality of life. With this vision of our future societies, the ideologists deduce that the petrol-driven car – which best symbolizes the successes and deadlocks of growth for its own sake – must now be doomed. EDF proposes to draw the conclusions from this 'ineluctable' social and economic evolution, gradually replacing the internal combustion engine with its electric vehicle.

Having defined the evolution of the social world, EDF next determines evolution of techniques, this being carefully distinguished from that of the social world: a new black box that is indisputable and ineluctable. EDF chooses to consider the VEL (Electric Vehicle) as a problem concerned with generators. Once these premises have been laid down, EDF marks out possible choices – which it evocatively calls 'channels'. Associated – always ineluctably – with each channel are a set of procedures, a set of laboratories and industrialists and – most important of all – a chronology. Lead accumulators, providing they are properly developed by this or that firm, could be used until

1982; the years 1982–90 will be the years of zinc-nickel accumulators and the zinc-air circulation generator; from 1990 onwards, fuel cells will be ready for use. These sequences of choices are made up of scattered elements taken from different contexts, gleaned by EDF's engineers, leaders and ideologists wherever they are available. From these scattered parts EDF creates a network of channels and regulated sequences.

Not content with making parallel connections between overall social development and technical channels, EDF begins to translate into simple language the products which industrialists cannot fail to want to produce, and the needs which clients and consumers cannot fail to feel. EDF foresees a huge market for lead accumulators, that of light commercial vehicles. Zinc accumulators cannot fail to be preferred for use in electric taxis, whilst fuel cells are certain to conquer the private car market as a whole.

In the space of a few years, and by dint of organizing channels, branches and developments, EDF begins to translate the deep desires, the technical knowledge and the needs and aptitudes of a large number of actors. EDF thus structures a reality by building up a gigantic organizational chart in which each black box, each carefully demarcated islet, is linked to other boxes by a set of arrows. The islets are shut off, and the arrows are unequivocal. Thus is the Leviathan structured. The actor tells you what you want, what you will be able to do in 5, 10 or 15 years, in which order you will do it, what you will be glad to possess, and of what you will be capable. And *you really believe this*, you identify with the actor and will help him or her with all your strength, irresistibly attracted by the differences in level he or she has created. What Hobbes described as an exchange of words during a period of universal warfare should be described more subtly in the following way: an actor says what I want, what I know, what I can do, marks out what is possible and what impossible, what is social and what technical, their parallel developments and the emergence of a market for zinc taxis and electric mail vans. How could I possibly resist when that is exactly what I want, when that is the correct translation of my unformulated wishes?

An actor like EDF clearly displays how the Leviathan is built up in practice – and not juridically. It insinuates itself into each element, making no distinction between what is from the realm of nature (catalysis, texture of grids in the fuel cell), what is from the realm of the economy (cost of cars with an internal combustion engine, the market for buses) and what comes from the realm of culture (urban life, Homo automobilis, fear of pollution). It ties together all these scattered elements into a chain in which they are all indissociably linked. One is forced to go through them just as if a line of reasoning was being unfolded, a system developed or a law applied. This chain or sequence traces a chreod or a set of chreods which thus define the margin for manoeuvre enjoyed by the other actors, their positions, desires, knowledge and abilities. What they will want and be able to do is channelled. Thus the EDF, like every Leviathan, gradually deposits interactions. There now exists something resembling contents, and something resembling a container, the contents fluid and the container stable. Our wills flow into the EDF's canals and networks. We rush towards the electric engine just as the river water rushes towards the Seine along the stone and concrete pipes designed by the hydraulic engineers. Contrary to what Hobbes states, thanks to this preliminary mineralization, certain actors became the Form of the Leviathan's body and certain others its Matter.

And yet, as we have already stated, an actor is never alone, despite everything it has. In vain does it saturate the social world, totalize history and the state of wills, it can never be alone since all the actors are isomorphic and those it enrols can desert it. One actor, for example, had its role redefined by EDF in the course of this vast connecting-up of necessities. Renault, which then produced petrol-driven cars, seemed to have a brilliant future ahead of it, and symbolized industrial success in France. EDF changed its destiny, taking away its future. Now Renault symbolizes industries doomed because of city congestion, pollution and the future of industrial societies. It must now – like the others – make changes in its intended production. Now Renault would like to make the chassis for the electric vehicles planned by EDF. This modest role suits the company well, and corresponds to what it cannot but want. So Renault goes along with what EDF wants, just like the rest of France, moving towards an all-electric future.

So far we have not said whether for EDF this is a question of something dreamed up by engineers, or a reality. In fact no one can make this distinction *a priori*, for it is the very basis of the struggle between the actors. The electric vehicle is thus 'real'. The actors that EDF has approached and mobilized to play the role of a firm foundation – designed for them by EDF – thus adhere to the differences in level which the public enterprise has laid out. But now something happens which will help us understand what we have been seeking to explain since the beginning of this chapter, that is how relative dimensions are changed.

In a few years' time Renault will disappear as an autonomous actor. Together with the petrol engine, it is doomed, and has no option but to reorientate its activities – unless the landscape which EDF projects before and around itself can be remodelled. But can this be done? During the first few years Renault is unable to fight its way back against the EDF's predictions. Everyone agrees that the private car is doomed.

How can this black box be opened? As all sociologists agree, no one will want a private car any more. How can the situation be reversed? Who can reveal technical ignorance in the scenario of an enterprise which has a monopoly of production and distribution of electricity? In these circumstances the only possible conclusion is that Renault will fail, and one must begin as best one can to adapt to the new landscape, one without the thermal car. And yet Renault has no wish to disappear; Renault wants to remain autonomous and indivisible, itself deciding what will be the social and technical future of the industrial world. What EDF so firmly associates, Renault would dearly like to dissociate. So Renault begins the work of undermining the edifice, probes the walls, makes up lost ground, seeks allies. How can Renault transform into fiction what will – if it is not careful – become the reality of tomorrow? How can it force EDF to remain, as we say, 'on the drawing board'?

EDF stated that no one would want a thermal car any more. And yet, despite increases in petrol prices, demand for cars is growing all the time. These two elements, which EDF links together in a strong interaction, prove dissociable in practice. Oil prices can rise concurrently with demand for cars, concurrently with the fight against pollution and with city congestion. Renault's hopes rise once more, and it begins to translate consumer desires differently: now they want the traditional private car at any price. As a result the future is altered yet again: the electric car has no natural market. The word is out. The natural laws as interpreted by the EDF Leviathan are not the same as for Renault. The consumer, by his or her very nature, demands performances with regard to speed, comfort and acceleration that the electric car will never approach. Already one of EDF's premises has been upset, a difference in level flattened out or filled in and one of the black boxes opened and profaned. Renault becomes bolder. If EDF's interpretation of social evolution can be thrown out of joint, perhaps the same is true of its knowledge of electrochemistry? Perhaps the technical demands could be altered?

Renault sets out on the long task of dissociating the associations made by EDF. Each interaction is tested, every calculation redone, every black box opened. The engineers are requestioned, the laboratories revisited, the records re-examined, the state of electrochemistry called into question. EDF had chosen to simplify certain information and to incorporate masses of figures which Renault now considers contradictory. As a consequence the chronology is disturbed. For EDF the internal combustion engine was a dead-end. Renault discovers that, by using electronics, it can be perfected so as to be unbeatable for several decades. Conversely, EDF had mentioned channels with regard to zinc accumulators. Renault does the sums again, assesses the estimates, gets another expert opinion from the experts, and shelves the zinc accumulator technically so that, at the very best, it would be suitable to equip a few tip-lorries much later than planned by EDF. Similarly, what EDF called the fuel cell 'channel' was for Renault a cul-de-sac. Instead of being the chreod through which flowed the wills of the engineers, it became just a rut. Into it fell only those laboratories which backed the wrong technical revolution and placed all their hopes in the study of catalysis. Like the rivers in China which sometimes suddenly change their course, demands and technical channels are thus diverted. The industrial society was running towards an all-electric future. Now it continues its majestic course towards the private car with an improved thermal engine. As Renault grows larger its future looks more rosy than it ever seemed before this confrontation. EDF shrinks in proportion. Instead of defining transport and reducing Renault to the role of subordinate, EDF has had to retire from the field, withdraw its troops and transform the world which it was building out of an engineer's dream.

3.2 The rules of sociological method

This confrontation clearly displays how the Leviathan is structured, making no *a priori* distinction between the size of actors, between the real and the unreal, between what is necessary and what contingent, between the technical and the social. Everything is involved in these primordial struggles through which Leviathans are structured: the state of techniques, the nature of the social system, the evolution of history, the dimensions of the actors and logics itself. As soon as sociological language avoids the assumption that there is an *a priori* distinction between actors, these combats are revealed as the fundamental principle underlying the Leviathan. Sociological analysis is nevertheless involved, since it follows the associations and dissociations, but it follows them wherever they are produced by the actors. The actors can bond together in a block comprising millions of individuals, they can enter alliances with iron, with grains of sand, neurons, words, opinions and affects. All this is of little importance, providing they can be followed with the same freedom as they themselves practise. We cannot analyse the Leviathan if we give precedence to a certain type of association, for example associations of men with men, iron with iron, neurons with neurons, or a specific size of factors. Sociology is only lively and productive when it examines *all associations with at least the same daring as the actors who make them.*

In the primordial conflicts we have just described, there are indeed winners and losers – at least for a while. The only interest of our method is that it enables these variations to be measured and the winners to be designated. This is why we stress so strongly that they must be looked at in the same way, and dealt with using similar concepts. What concept will enable us to follow the actors in all their associations and dissociations and to explain their victories and defeats, though without our admitting belief in the necessities of every kind which they claim? An actor, as we have seen, becomes stronger to the extent that he or she can firmly associate a large number of elements – and, of course, dissociate as speedily as possible elements enrolled by other actors. Strength thus resides in the power to break off and to bind together.[26] More generally, strength is *inter*vention, *inter*ruption, *inter*pretation and *inter*est, as Serres has so convincingly shown.[27] An actor is strong in so far as he or she is able to intervene. But what is intervention? Let us go back to the Leviathan: You want peace, so do I. Let us make a contract. Let us return to the baboons: Sara is eating a nut. Beth appears, supplants her, takes her place and her nut. Let us return to EDF: a laboratory is studying the fuel cell. The engineers are questioned, their knowledge simplified and summed up: 'we shall have a fuel cell in 15 years'. The Leviathan once more: we have made a contract, but a third party appears who respects nothing and steals from us both. The baboons once more: Sara yelps, this attracts her faithful friend Brian. He is now enrolled, he approaches and supplants Beth. The nut falls to the ground and Brian grabs it. The EDF once more: the Renault engineers read through the literature again and alter their conclusions: 'There will be no fuel cell in 15 years.' All this is still 'the war of all against all'. Who will *win in the end*? The one who is able to stabilize a particular state of power relations by associating the largest number of irreversibly linked elements. What do we mean by 'associate'? We return again to the Leviathan. Two actors can only be made indissociable if they are one. For this their wills must become equivalent. He or she who holds the equivalences holds the secret of power. Through the interplay of equivalences, hitherto scattered elements can be incorporated into a whole, and thus help to stabilize other elements.

3.3   'None is so fierce that dare stir him up: who then is able to stand before me?' (Job: 41,10)

By comparison with the Leviathan revealed by the sociologist, the one Hobbes describes is a pleasant idealization:

> Art goes yet further, imitating that Rational and most excellent work of Nature, *man*. For by Art is created that great LEVIATHAN called a Commonwealth, or a State which is but an artificial Man; though of greater stature and strength than the Natural, for whose protection and defence it was intended; and in which the Sovereignty is an Artificial Soul, as giving life and motion to the whole body; the Magistrates and other officers of Judicature and Execution, artificial joints.[28]

For the Leviathan is a body, itself designed in the image of a machine. There is a single structural principle – an engineer's plan – and a homogeneous metaphor which orders the whole, that of an automaton. The true Leviathan is far more monstrous than this. Is the Leviathan a machine? It is, but what is a machine without an operator? Nothing more than a broken-down heap of iron. So the metaphor of the automaton is not valid. If the machine can move, build and repair itself, it must be a living thing. Let us move on to biology. What is a body? A machine once again, but there are many kinds: thermal, hydraulic, cybernetic, data-processing – from which the operator is again absent. Shall we say finally that it is a set of chemical exchanges and physical interactions? Can we compare it with the interest of a market or an exchange system? In the field of the economy with what is it comparable? Once again with chemical interactions. And these in their turn may be compared with a field of struggling forces. The Leviathan is such a monster that its essential being cannot be stabilized in any of the great metaphors we usually employ. It is at the same time machine, market, code, body, and war. Sometimes, forces are transmitted as in a machine, sometimes operating charts come into place in the same way as cybernetic feedbacks. Sometimes there is a contract, sometimes automatic translation. But one can never describe the whole set of elements using only one of these metaphors. As in the case of Aristotle's categories, we jump from one metaphor to another whenever we try to express the meaning of one of them.

Monstrous is the Leviathan in yet another way. This is because, as we have seen, there is not just *one* Leviathan but many, interlocked one into another like chimera, each one claiming to represent the reality of all, the programme of the whole. Sometimes some of them manage to distort the others so horribly that for a while they seem the only soul in this artificial body. The Leviathan is monstrous too because Hobbes built it using only contracts and the bodies of ideal, supposedly naked, men. But since the actors triumph by associating with themselves other elements than the bodies of men, the result is terrifying. Steel plates, palaces, rituals and hardened habits float on the surface of a viscous-like gelatinous mass which functions at the same time like the mechanism of a machine, the exchanges in a market and the clattering of a teleprinter. Sometimes whole elements from factory or technical systems are redissolved and dismembered by forces never previously seen in action. These forces then in turn produce a rough outline of a chimera that others immediately hasten to dismember. Neither Job on his dunghill, nor the teratologists in their laboratories have observed such dreadful monsters.

Impossible not to be terrified by this primordial combat which concerns everything that political philosophy, history and sociology consider indisputable frameworks for description. Impossible not to be terrified likewise by the flood of speeches Leviathans make about themselves. On some days and with some people they allow themselves to be sounded or dismantled (depending whether they choose that day to be body or machine). Sometimes they sham dead or pretend to be a ruin (metaphor of a building), a corpse (biological metaphor), or a huge heap of iron from some museum of industrial archeology. At other times they are inscrutable and delight in admitting themselves monstrous and unknowable. The next moment they change and, depending on their audience, stretch out on a couch and whisper their most secret thoughts or, crouching in the shadows of the confessional, admit their faults and repent of being so big or so small, so hard or so soft, so old or so new. We cannot even state that they are in a continuous state of metamorphoses, for they only change in patches and vary in size slowly, being encumbered and weighed down with the enormous technical devices they have secreted in order to grow and to restrict precisely this power to metamorphose.

These imbricated Leviathans more resemble a never-ending building-site in some great metropolis. There is no overall architect to guide it, and no design, however unreflected. Each town hall and each promotor, each king and each visionary claim to possess the overall plan and to understand the meaning of the story. Whole districts are laid out and roads opened up on the basis of these overall plans, which other struggles and other wills soon restrict to the egoistic and specific expression of a period or an individual. Constantly – but never everywhere at the same time – streets are opened, houses razed to the ground, watercourses covered over. Districts previously thought out-of-date or dangerous are rehabilitated; other modern buildings become out of fashion, and are destroyed. We fight about what constitutes our heritage, about methods of transport and itineraries to be followed. Consumers die and are replaced by others, circuits by degrees compel their recognition, enabling information to run along the wires. Here and there one retires within oneself, accepting the fate decided by others. Or else one agrees to define oneself as an individual actor who will alter nothing more than the partitions in the apartment or the wallpaper in the bedroom. At other times actors who had always defined themselves and had always been defined as micro-actors ally themselves together around a threatened district, march to the town hall and enrol dissident architects. By their action they manage to have a radial road diverted or a tower that a macro-actor had built pulled down. Or again, as in the case of the famous 'trou des Halles' in central Paris, they put forward 600 alternative projects, in addition to the hundreds the Paris Town Hall had already considered. A tiny actor becomes a macro-actor, just like in the French nursery rhyme: 'The cat knocks over the pot, the pot knocks over the table, the table knocks over the room, the room knocks over the house, the house knocks over the street, the street knocks over Paris: Paris, Paris, Paris has fallen!' We cannot know who is big and who is small, who is hard and who is soft, who is hot and who is cold. The effect of these tongues which suddenly start to wag and these black boxes that suddenly snap shut is a city, uncountable Leviathans with the beauty of the beast or of the circles of hell.

Hobbes's Leviathan was indeed a paradise by comparison with what we have described here. As for the baboons' Leviathan, it is a dream of the unadulterated society amid the beauty of the still-wild savannah. The monster that we are, that we inhabit and that we fashion sings a quite different song. If Weber and his intellectual descendants found that this monster was becoming 'disenchanted', this was because they allowed themselves to be intimidated by techniques and macro-actors. This is what we shall now show.

4   Conclusion: the sociologist Leviathan

In order to grow we must enrol other wills by translating what they want and by reifying this translation in such a way that none of them can desire anything else any longer. Hobbes restricted this process of translation to what we now call 'political representation'. The scattered wills are recapitulated in the person of the sovereign who says what we want, and whose word has force of law and cannot be contradicted. And yet it is a very long time now since 'political representation' was alone sufficient to translate the desires of the multitude. After political science, the science of economics also claims to sound loins and coffers, and to be able to say not only what the goods, services and people making up the Leviathan desire, but also what they are worth. In this article we are not interested in political science or economics. We are interested in the latecomers, the sociologists, who also translate – using polls, quantitative and qualitative surveys – not only what the actors want, not only what they are worth, but also *what they are*. On the basis of scattered information, replies to questionnaires, anecdotes, statistics and feelings, the sociologist interprets, sounds out, incorporates and states what the actors are (classes, categories, groups, cultures, etc.), what they want, what interests them and how they live. Self-designated and self-appointed, spokesmen of the people, they have, for more than a century now, taken over from Hobbes's sovereign: the voice that speaks in the mask is their own.

4.1 The sociologist Leviathan

We have followed through the creation of the political Leviathan on the basis of a contract, the formation of the monkey-Leviathan and, last, the construction of the monster-Leviathan. Now we shall see how the sociologist-Leviathan is built. We can already state as a matter of principle that Leviathans formed like sociologies or sociologies like Leviathans.

So what do sociologists do? Some say that there is a social system. This interpretation of the social credits translation processes with a coherence that they lack. To state that there is a system is to make an actor grow by disarming the forces which he or she 'systematizes' and 'unifies'. Of course, as we have seen, the Leviathan's arithmetic is very special: each system, each totality *is added* to the others without retrenching itself, thereby producing the hybrid monster with a thousand heads and a thousand systems. What else does the sociologist do? He or she interprets the Leviathan, saying for example that it is a cybernetic machine. So all associations between actors are described as circuits of an artificial intelligence, and translations are seen as 'integrations'. Here again the Leviathan is built up by this type of description: it is proud to be a machine and immediately, like any machine, starts to transmit forces and motions in a mechanical way. Of course this interpretation is added to all the others and struggles against them. For the Leviathan is – sometimes and in some places – a traditional and not a cybernetic machine, likewise a body, a market, a text, a game, etc. Since all interpretations act upon it simultaneously, per*forming* and trans*forming* forces according to whether they are machines, codes, bodies or markets, the result is this same monster again, at one and the same time machine, beast, god, word and town. What else can sociologists do? They can say, for

example, that they 'restrict themselves to the study of the social'.
They then divide the Leviathan into 'reality levels' leaving aside, for
example, the economic, political, technical and cultural aspects in
order to restrict themselves to what is 'social'. The black boxes that
contain these factors are thus sealed up and no sociologist can open
them without stepping outside the field. The Leviathans purr with
relief, for their structure disappears from view, whilst they allow their
social parts to be sounded. Of course, as we know (see the EDF), no
actor is so powerful that its decisions and associations as a whole will be
finally and definitely considered as technical reality. The other actors,
helped by sociologists, push back and trace anew the boundaries
between what is technical, economic, cultural and social. The result is
that here again the Leviathans are hacked about by conflicting teams
of sociologists, and are covered with scars like Frankenstein. What
else do sociologists do? Like everyone else, they never stop working to
define who acts and who speaks. They tape the recollections of a
workman, a prostitute or an old Mexican; they interview; they hand
out open and closed questionnaires on every subject under the sun;
they unceasingly sound out the opinions of the masses. Each time they
interpret their surveys they inform the Leviathan, transforming and
performing it. Each time they construct a unity, define a group,
attribute an identity, a will or a project;[29] each time they explain what
is happening, the sociologist, sovereign and author – as Hobbes used
the term – add to the struggling Leviathans new identities, definitions
and wills which enable other authors to grow or shrink, hide away or
reveal themselves, expand or contract.

Like all the others, and for the same reason, sociologists work on the
Leviathan. Their work is to define the nature of the Leviathan
whether it is unique or whether there are more than one, what they
want and how they transform themselves and evolve. This specific
task is in no way unusual. There is no 'metadiscourse' – to speak
archaically – about the Leviathan. Every time they write sociologists
grow or shrink, become macro-actors – or do not – expand, like
Lazarsfeld, to the scale of a multinational,[30] or shrink to a restricted
sector of the market. What makes them grow or shrink? The other
actors whose interests, desires and forces they translate more or less
successfully, and with whom they ally or quarrel. Depending on the
period, the strategies, the institutions and the demands, the sociologist's work can expand until it becomes what everyone is saying

about the Leviathan, or shrink to what three PhD students think about themselves in some British university. The sociologists' language has no privileged relationship with the Leviathan. They act upon it. Suppose they state that the Leviathan is unique and systematic, suppose they create cybernetic, hierarchically integrated subsystems: either this will be accepted, or not, will spread, or not, will be used as resources by others – or will not. The success of this definition of the Leviathan proves nothing about the latter's own nature. An empire is born, that of Parsons, and that is all. Conversely, the fact that ethnomethodologists might manage to convince their colleagues that macro-actors do not exist proves nothing about their non-existence. Sociologists are neither better nor worse than any other actors. Neither are they more external nor more internal, more nor less scientific.[31] Common, too common.

4.2 How to slip between two mistakes

A macro-actor, as we have seen, is a micro-actor seated on black boxes, a force capable of associating so many other forces that it acts like a 'single man'. The result is that a macro-actor is by definition no more difficult to examine than a micro-actor. Growth is only possible if one can associate long lasting forces with oneself and thereby simplify existence. Hence a macro-actor is at least as simple as a micro-actor *since otherwise it could not have become bigger*. We do not draw closer to social reality by descending to micro-negotiations or by rising towards the macro-actors. We must leave behind the preconceptions which lead us to believe that macro-actors are more complicated than micro-actors. The opposite might be true as the example of the baboons showed us. A macro-actor can only grow if it simplifies itself. As it simplifies its existence, it simplifies the work of the sociologist. It is no more difficult to send tanks into Kabul than to dial 999. It is no more difficult to describe Renault than the secretary who takes telephone calls at the Houston police station. If it were much more difficult the tanks would not move and Renault would not exist. There would be no macro-actors. By claiming that macro-actors are more complex than micro-actors sociologists discourage analysis, and hamstring investigators. And they prevent the secret of the macro-actors' growth from being revealed: making operations childishly simple. The king is not only naked, he is a child playing with (leaky) black boxes.

The other preconception, too often shared by sociologists, is that individual micro-negotiations are truer and more real than the abstract, distant structures of the macro-actors. Here again, nothing could be further from the truth for almost every resource is utilized in the huge task of structuring macro-actors. Only a residue is left for the individuals. What the sociologist too hastily studies is the diminished, anaemic being, trying hard to occupy the shrinking skin left to it. In a world already structured by macro-actors, nothing could be poorer and more abstract than individual social interaction. The dreamers who would like to restructure macro-actors on the basis of the individual will arrive at an even more monstrous body for they must leave out all the hard parts which have enabled the macro-actors to simplify their lives and to take over all the space.

4.3   More than a monster, a monster and a half

What then is a sociologist? Someone who studies associations and dissociations, that is all, as the word 'social' itself implies. Associations between men? Not solely, since for a long time now associations between men have been expanded and extended through other allies: words, rituals, iron, wood, seeds and rain. The sociologist studies all associations, but in particular the transformation of weak interactions into strong ones and vice versa. This is of special interest because here the relative dimensions of the actors are altered. When we use the word 'study' we must make clear there is of course no suggestion of knowledge. All information is transformation, an emergency operation on and in the Leviathan's body.

When we slip between two mistakes, we do not intend to withdraw to some distant planet. What is valid for the others is valid for us too. We too work on the Leviathan, we too aim to sell our concepts, we too seek allies and associates and decide who it is we want to please or displease. By taking for granted differences in level and size between actors, the sociologist ratifies past, present and future winners, whoever they may be, finding favour with the powerful because they make them look reasonable. By agreeing to restrict the study of associations to the residual social, the sociologist affixes seals onto the black boxes, and once again guarantees that the strong will be secure and the cemeteries peaceful – filled with lines of hermetically closed black boxes crawling with worms.

For the sociologist then the question of method boils down to knowing where to place oneself. Like Hobbes himself, he or she sits just at the point where the contract is made, just where forces are translated, and the difference between the technical and the social is fought out, just where the irreversible becomes reversible and where the chreods reverse their slopes. There, only a tiny amount of energy is necessary to drag a maximum of information about its growth from the newborn monster.

The sociologists who choose these places are no longer anyone's lackey or ward. They no longer need dissect the corpses of Leviathans already rejected by others. They no longer fear the great black boxes which dominate the whole of the 'social world' where they no more wander like ghosts, cold as vampires, with wooden tongues, seeking the 'social' before it coagulates. The sociologists – teratologists – are in the *warm, light* places, the places where black boxes open up, where the irreversible is reversed and techniques return to life; the places that give birth to uncertainty as to what is large and what is small, what is social and what technical. They inhabit the blessed place where the betrayed and translated voices of authors – Matter of the social body – become the voice of the sovereign actor described by Hobbes – the Form of the social body.

Notes

1   T. Hobbes, *The Leviathan* (1651) (London: Pelican Books, 1978), p. 185. All quotations are from that edition.
2   Ibid., p. 218.
3   Ibid., p. 219.
4   Ibid., p. 227.
5   Ibid., p. 217.
6   Concept developed by Michel Serres, *La Traduction, Hermès III* (Paris: Ed. de Minuit, 1974), and then applied to sociology by M. Callon 'L' Opération de traduction', in M. Roqueplo (ed.), *Incidence des rapports sociaux sur le développement scientifique et technique* (Paris: CNRS, 1975).
7   Even the sacrificial victim of R. Girard, *Des Choses cachées depuis la fondation du monde* (Paris: Grasset, 1978), is nothing but a more solemn and cruel form of contract and a particular case of translation. It cannot be made the foundation of the other forms.
8   By the term 'actor' we mean, from now on, the semiotic definition by A. Greimas in *Dictionnaire de sémiotique* (Paris: Hachette, 1979): 'whatever unit

of discourse is invested of a role', like the notion of force, it is no way limited to 'human'.

9 See the devastating criticism of psychoanalysis made by G. Deleuze and F. Guattari, *L'Anti-Oedipe, capitalisme et schizophrénie* (Paris: Ed. de Minuit, 1972). For them there is no difference of size between a child's dreams and a conqueror's empire or between the family life story and the political story. The unconscious, anyway, is not 'individual', so that in our innermost dreams we still act inside the whole body politic and vice versa.

10 On this point, like on most, C. B. Macpherson, *The Political Theory of Possessive Individualism: Hobbes to Locke* (Oxford: Clarendon Press, 1962), missed Hobbes's originality. It is not Marxism that helps interpret what is beneath Hobbes's theory; it is, on the contrary, the latter that might explain what is beneath the former.

11 See R. Collins (this volume) and P. Bourdieu (this volume).

12 See the conclusion of this chapter.

13 For instance A. Cicourel, *Method and Measurement in Sociology* (New York: Free Press, 1964), as an example of the requirements that tie the observer's hands. Ethnomethodologists have since much increased the constraints on what can be said about society.

14 This part is based on an ongoing study on the sociology of primatology by one of us (B.L.). Most of this chapter is inspired by the work of Shirley Strum. She is in no way responsible for the awkward situation in which we put her baboons, but only for the new and revolutionary way she understands animal sociology. For direct references see S. Strum, 'Life with the Pumphous-Gang', *National Geographic*, May (1975), pp. 672–791; 'Interim Report on the Development of a Tradition in a Troop of Olive Baboons', *Science* 187 (1975), pp. 755–7; 'Agonistic Dominance in Male Baboons – An Alternate View' (forthcoming). For an analysis of the link between primatology and political philosophy, see Donna Haraway, 'Animal Sociology and a Natural Economy of the Body Politic', *Signs*, 4/1 (1978), pp. 21–60.

15 Except insects, of course, Hobbes, *The Leviathan*, p. 225.

16 Ibid., p. 186.

17 For two general presentations, see H. Kummer, *Primate Societies* (New York: Aldine, 1973); and T. Rowell, *Social Behaviour of Monkeys* (London: Penguin, 1972). For a historical background see Donna Haraway, 'Animal Sociology and a Natural Economy of the Body Politic', and 'Signs of Dominance: From a Physiology to a Cybernetics of Primate Societies, C. R. Carpenter 1930–1970' (forthcoming).

18 S. Strum, 'Agonistic Dominance in Male Baboons – An Alternate View'.

19 This was already visible in H. Kummer, 'Social Organization of Hamadryas Baboons' (Chicago: Aldine, 1968), and very clear in H. Kummer, 'On the Value of Social Relationships to Non-Human Primates. A Heuristic Scheme', *Social Science Information*, 17 (1978), pp. 687–707.

20 This is the case either in the sort of Bourdieu sociology that Kummer used to describe his baboons ('On the Value of Social Relationships'), or in the sociobiological myth of defence of investments.

21 Hobbes, *The Leviathan*, p. 183, for human, and Strum, 'Agonistic Dominance in Male Baboons – An Alternate View', for baboons.

22 In his *Myth of the Machine* (New York: Harcourt, 1966), Lewis Mumford tries to integrate different sorts of materials, but he makes two major mistakes: first, he sticks to the metaphor of the machine, instead of dissolving it; second, he takes for granted the size of the megamachine instead of tracing its genealogy. The same thing can be said of A. Leroi-Gourhan, *La Geste et la parole* (Paris: Albin Michel, 1964), although he tries very hard to blur the limits between technics and culture, but favours, nevertheless, one sort of division and one sort of determinism.

23 C. H. Waddington, *Tools for Thought* (London: Paladin, 1977).

24 Michel Callon, *De Problèmes en problèmes: itinéraire d'un laboratoire universitaire saisi par l'aventure technologique* (Paris: CORDES, 1978); and *Rapport sur le véhicule électrique* (Paris: CORDES, 1978).

25 For more complete descriptions, see F. Nietzsche, *The Will to Power* (New York: Garden Press, 1974); G. Deleuze and F. Guattari, *Mille Plateaux* (Paris: Ed. de Minuit, 1979); B. Latour, *Irréductions: précis de Philosophie* (Paris: Chèloteur, 1981).

26 Hobbes, *The Leviathan*, p. 150.

27 Michel Serres, *Le Parasite* (Paris: Grasset, 1980).

28 Hobbes, *The Leviathan*, p. 18.

29 For instance, see Luc Boltanski, 'Taxinomie sociale et lutte de classe', *Actes de la recherche en sciences sociales*, 29 (1979), pp. 75–110.

30 Michael Pollak, 'Paul Lazarsfeld, une Multinationale des Sciences Sociales', *Actes de la recherche en sciences sociales*, 25 (1979), pp. 45–60.

31 The lack of distinction between soft and hard sciences is shown in B. Latour and S. Woolgar, *Laboratory Life: The Social Construction of Scientific Facts* (London: Sage, 1979).

11 Men and machines

Pierre Bourdieu

[*The last chapter of this book is interesting because of what it suggests and entails without spelling out details. I take this to be a conception of (macro) structures as a set of positions held in place by the interplay of various forces that work for or against it, like the stability of a physical body which may be explained by motions rather than by its internal endurance or external persistence.*

Bourdieu, too, emphasizes the notion of power as of key importance to our question. But he does not see this power as a force which stems from or accrues to a prime mover (a macro-actor), but rather as springing from the actions and reactions of agents who have no choice but to struggle to maintain their position of specific capital in a social field. In doing so, each actor helps to subject all the others to often intolerable constraints which in turn force the maintenance of certain structural conditions, and which hold in place the major societal divisions.

Bourdieu's contribution has been placed last in this volume because it is also the one which locates our problem most exclusively on a macro-level. The paper rejects distinctions such as that between action and structure altogether, and argues instead for a conception of the present in terms of two histories: the frozen, objectified past manifest in positions and the embodied history manifest in the habitus (the dispositions) of an individual. Both positions and dispositions are social in nature since dispositions are the history of a group or class acquired in socialization. The individual is either predisposed to enact an objectified history or engaged in investments which make him or her inclined to take interest in the functioning of institutions.]

1 Macro-structures as fields of struggle

There is a common fallacy which social scientists almost invariably commit whenever they fail to make allowance, in the course of their scientific practice itself, for the specificity of a scientist's relationship to the object of his science. It is the fallacy of projecting into the object of study the academic relationship to the object or the constructs which this academic relationship has made possible; in short, the fallacy of taking 'the things of logic for the logic of things', as Marx said of Hegel.[1] Having discovered the regularities or structure in accordance with which the phenomena are organized, and having stated them in the form of more or less formalized models or theories, the social scientist tends to place these models, which belong to the order of logic, in the individual or collective consciousness of the individual agents or groups. The same fundamental error lies behind action theories and philosophies of history that are apparently (and also in reality, though only in secondary ways) as different as the rational actor theory, with its calculating strategists consciously pursuing maximum profit, or functionalism, whether in its 'optimist' form – of which Parsons's writings are still the paradigm – or its 'pessimist', structural-Marxist form. The latter version culminates in the notion of the 'apparatus', a mechanical generator of teleology which enables mechanism to be – verbally – reconciled with final causes.

Historians and sociologists have tended to allow themselves to be trapped in sterile oppositions, such as that between 'events' and 'longue durée', or, at another level, between 'great men' and collective forces, between individual wills and structural determination. These alternatives are all based on the distinction between the *individual* and the *social*, the latter being identified with the collective. To find a way out of these dilemmas, it is sufficient to observe that every historical action brings together two states of history: objectified history, i.e. the history which has accumulated over the passage of time in things, machines, buildings, monuments, books, theories, customs, law, etc.; and embodied history, in the form of *habitus*. A man who raises his hat in greeting is unwittingly reactivating a conventional sign inherited from the Middle Ages, when, as Panofsky reminds us, armed men used to take off their helmets to make clear their peaceful intentions.[2] This re-enactment of history is the work of the habitus, the product of a historical acquisition which makes it possible to appropriate the legacy of history. History in the sense of *res gestae* is a part of objectified history that is carried, enacted, and carries its bearer (through the dialectic of carrying and being-carried which Nicolaï Hartmann so well describes).[3] Just as a text is raised from the state of a dead letter only through the act of reading which presupposes an acquired disposition and aptitude for reading and deciphering the meaning inscribed in it, so objectified, instituted history – the institution – becomes historical action, i.e. enacted, active history, only if it is taken in charge by agents whose own history predisposes them to do so, who, by virtue of their previous invest-ments, are inclined to take an interest in its functioning, and endowed with the appropriate attributes to make it function. The relationship to the social world is not the mechanical causality that is often assumed between a 'milieu' and a consciousness, but rather a sort of ontological complicity. When the same history inhabits both habitus and habitat, both dispositions and position, the king and his court, the employer and his firm, the bishop and his see, history in a sense communicates with itself, is reflected in its own image. History as 'subject' discovers itself in history as 'object'; it recognizes itself in 'antepredicative', 'passive syntheses', structures that are structured before any structuring operation or any linguistic expression. The doxic relation to the native world, a quasi-ontological commitment flowing from practical experience, is a relationship of belonging and owning in which a body, appropriated by history, absolutely and immediately appropriates things inhabited by the same history.[4]

This native relationship to a familiar world is a *possessing* which implies the possession of the owner by his belongings. As Marx puts it, when the estate has appropriated the heir, the heir can appropriate the estate. And the taking over of the inheritor by his heritage, which is the precondition for the appropriation of the heritage (and is by no means mechanical or inevitable), takes place under the combined effect of the conditionings entailed by his position as inheritor and the educative action of his predecessors, the previously appropriated owners. The inherited inheritor, appropriated to his estate, has no need to will, i.e. to deliberate, choose and consciously decide, in order to do what is appropriate for the interests of the estate, its conserva-tion and enlargement. He may, strictly speaking, know neither what he is doing nor what he is saying and yet say and do nothing that is not consistent with the demands of the heritage. Louis XIV was so totally identified with the position he occupied in the gravitational field of which he was the Sun, that it would be futile to try to determine which of all the actions occurring in the field is or is not the product of his volition, just as it would be futile to distinguish in an orchestral performance between what is done by the conductor and what is done by the players. His will to dominate was itself a product of the field he dominated, a field which turned everything to his advantage:

> The holders of privileges, imprisoned by the nets they cast over one another, kept one another in their positions even if they only reluctantly accepted the system. The pressure which their inferiors or the less privileged exerted on them forced them to defend their privileges. And *vice versa*: pressure from above compelled the less privileged to escape from it by imitating those who had risen to a more favourable position; in other words, they entered the vicious circle of status competition. The one who had the right to figure in the first *entrée* and hand the King his shirt despised the one who only had the third *entrée*, and had no intention of giving way to him; the Prince felt superior to the Duke, and the Duke superior to the Marquis; and all of them, as members of the 'nobility', would not and could not give way to commoners who paid taxes. One attitude engendered another; through pressure and counter-pressure, the social mechanism settled into a sort of unstable equilibrium.[5]

Thus, a 'state' which has become the symbol of absolutism and which, in the eyes of the absolute monarch himself ('l'état, c'est moi'), who has most *interest* in this representation, offers the appearance of an apparatus, in fact conceals a field of struggles in which the holder of 'absolute power' must himself participate, at least sufficiently to maintain the divisions and tensions, i.e. the field itself, and to mobilize the energy generated by the balance of tensions. The perpetual motion which runs through the field does not stem from some motionless prime mover – here, the Sun King, but from the struggle itself, which is produced by the structures of the field and in turn reproduces its structures, i.e. its hierarchies. It springs from the actions and reactions of the agents, who, short of opting out of the game and falling into oblivion, have no choice but to struggle to keep up or improve their position in the field, i.e. to conserve or increase the specific capital which is only created within the field. In so doing, each one helps to subject all the others to the often intolerable constraints arising from the competition.[6] In short, no one can take advantage of the game, not even those who dominate it, without being taken up and taken in by it. Thus there would be no game without belief in the game and without the wills, intentions and aspirations which actuate the agents; these impulses, produced by the game, depend on the agents' positions in the game, and, more precisely, on their power over the objectified degrees of the specific capital – which the king controls and manipulates within the room for manoeuvre the game allows him.[7]

A certain type of pessimist functionalism, which imputes the effects of domination to a single, central will, makes it impossible to see the contribution the agents (including the dominated ones) make, willingly and knowingly or not, to the process of domination, through the relationship between their dispositions – linked to the social conditions in which they were produced – and the expectations and interests entailed by their positions within the fields of struggle for which words like state, church or party are shorthand terms.[8] Submission to transcendent goals, meanings or interests, i.e. interests superior and external to individual interests, is practically never the result of forcible imposition and conscious submission. This is because so-called objective goals, which only reveal themselves as such, at best, after the event and from outside, are practically never perceived and posited as such at the time, in practice itself, by any of the agents concerned, not even by the most interested parties, i.e. those who would have most interest in making them their conscious goals, namely the dominant agents. The subordination of the whole set of practices to a single objective intention, a sort of conductorless orchestration, can only take place through the harmony which is established, as it were, outside the agents and over their heads, between what they are and what they do, between their subjective 'vocations' (what they feel 'made' for) and their objective 'missions' (what is expected of them), between what history has made them and what history askes them to do. This harmony may be expressed in their sense of being 'at home' in what they are doing, of doing what they have to do and doing it happily (in the subjective and objective senses), or with a resigned conviction that they cannot do anything else, which is another way, though a less happy one, of feeling 'made' for one's job.

2 Institutions enacted: positions and dispositions

Objectified, institutionalized history only becomes enacted and active if the job, or the tool, or the book, or even the socially designated and recognized 'role' – 'signing a petition', 'going on a demonstration', etc. – or the historically attested 'character' – pioneering intellectual or 'devoted wife and mother', loyal civil servant or 'man of honour' – like a garment or a house, finds someone who finds an interest in it, feels sufficiently at home in it to take it on. This is why so many actions, and not only those of the functionary who merges with his function,[9] present themselves as ceremonies in which the agents – who do not thereby become *actors* performing *roles* – enter into the spirit of the social character which is expected of them and which they expect of themselves (such is a vocation), by virtue of the immediate and total coincidence of habitus and habit which makes the true monk. The café waiter does not play at being a café waiter, as Sartre supposes. When he puts on his white jacket, which evokes a democratized, bureaucratized form of the dutiful dignity of the servant in a great household, and when he performs the ceremonial of eagerness and concern, which may be strategy to cover up a delay or an oversight, or to fob off a second-rate product, he does not make himself a thing (or an 'in-itself'). His body, which contains a history, espouses his function, i.e. a history, a tradition which he has only ever seen incarnated in bodies, or rather, in those habits 'inhabited' by a certain habitus which are called café waiters. This does not mean that he has learnt to be a café waiter by imitating café waiters whom he took as models. He identifies with the job of café waiter, just as a child identifies with his (social) father and, without even having to 'pretend', takes on a way of walking or talking which appears to be part of the social being of the accomplished adult.[10] He cannot even be said to take himself for a café waiter; he is too much taken up in the job which was naturally (i.e. socio-logically) assigned to him (e.g. as the son of a small shopkeeper who needs to earn enough to set up his own business) even to have the idea of such role-distance. By contrast, one only has to put a student in his position (such as can now be seen running some 'avant-garde' restaurants) to see him manifesting in countless ways the aloofness he intends to maintain, precisely by affecting to perform it as a *role*, *vis-à-vis* a job which he does not feel 'made' for and in which, as the Sartrian customer observes, he 'refuses to be imprisoned'. And for proof of the fact that the intellectual's relationship to his own position as an intellectual is no different, and that the intellectual distances himself no more than the waiter from his own position and from what specifically defines it, i.e. the illusion of distance from all positions, one only has to read as an anthropological document the passage in which Sartre analyses and 'universalizes' his famous description of the café waiter:[11]

> In vain do I fulfill the functions of a café waiter. I can be he only in the neutralized mode, as the actor is Hamlet, by mechanically making the *typical gestures* of my state and by aiming at myself as an imaginary café waiter through those gestures taken as an 'analogue'. What I attempt to realize is a being-in-itself of the café waiter, as if it were not just in my power to confer their value and their urgency upon my duties and the rights of my position, as if it were not my free choice to get up each morning at five o'clock or to remain in bed, even though it meant getting fired. As if from the very fact that I sustain this role in existence I did not transcend it on every side, as if I did not constitute myself as one *beyond* my condition. Yet there is no doubt that I *am* in a sense a café waiter – otherwise could I not just as well call myself a diplomat or a reporter.[12]

Every word merits attention in this almost miraculous product of the social unconscious, which, by an exemplary manipulation of the phenomenological *ego*, projects an intellectual's consciousness into a café waiter's practice, or into the imaginary analogue of that practice, producing a sort of social chimera, a monster with a waiter's body and a philosopher's head. One surely has to have the freedom to stay in bed *without* being fired in order to find that someone who gets up at five to sweep the café and start the percolator before the customers arrive is (freely?) freeing himself from the freedom to stay in bed even if it means being fired. This logic of narcissistic identification is the same logic which nowadays enables others to produce a worker entirely committed to 'struggles' or, alternatively, desperately resigned to being only what he is, a 'being-in-itself' devoid of the freedom which others derive from being able to count among their possible positions those of diplomat or journalist.[13]

Thus, when there is a fairly close correspondence between 'vocation' and 'mission', between the 'demand' that is, for the most part, implicitly, tacitly, even secretly inscribed in agents' positions and the 'supply' contained in their dispositions, it would be futile to seek to distinguish those aspects of their practice which derive from their positions and those which derive from the dispositions they bring into those positions. These dispositions tend to govern their perception and appreciation of their position, their behaviour within it, and consequently the 'reality' of the position. This dialectic is, paradoxically, most clearly seen in the case of positions situated in 'grey' areas of social space and in occupations that have not yet been greatly 'professionalized', i.e. which remain ill-defined as regards entry to and performance of the job. These positions, which are there to be made and are what the agents make of them, are made for those who feel made to make their jobs, and who opt (in terms of the classic opposition) for the 'open' rather than the 'closed'.[14] The definition of these ill-defined, unguaranteed positions lies, paradoxically, in the freedom they allow to their holders to define and delimit them by freely bringing into them their own limits and their own definition, all the embodied necessity which constitutes the habitus. These jobs become what their occupants are, or, at least, those occupants who, in the struggles within the 'profession' and in confrontations with neighbouring and rival professions, succeed in imposing the definition of the profession that is most favourable to what they are. This does not depend solely on themselves and their competitors, i.e. on the power relations within that particular field, but also on the state of the power relations between the classes, which, quite apart from any conscious 'recuperating' strategy, will determine the social success conferred on the different goods or services produced in and for the struggle with immediate rivals, and the institutional consecration bestowed on their producers. The institutionalization of 'spontaneous' divisions which occurs little by little, under the pressure of events, through the positive or negative sanctions the social order exerts on organizations (subsidies, commissions, appointments, granting of tenure, etc.), leads to what can eventually be seen as a new division of the work of domination, but one which surpasses the schemes of the most ambitious technocrats. Thus the social world comes to be peopled with institutions which no one designed or wanted; those who are ostensibly 'in charge' cannot say, even with the advantage of hindsight, how 'the formula was found', and are themselves astonished that such institutions can exist as they do, so well adapted to ends which their founders never explicitly formulated.

3   The functioning of institutions

But the dialectic between the propensities contained in habitus and the demands entailed in job descriptions has equally strong, though less visible, effects in the most regulated and rigid sectors of the social structure, such as the oldest, most codified branches of the civil service. Some of the most characteristic features of the conduct of junior officials – a tendency towards formalism, fetishism about punctuality, strict adherence to regulations, etc. – are far from being a mechanical product of bureaucratic organization. They are in fact the manifestation, within the logic of a situation particularly favourable to its implementation, of a set of dispositions that also manifests itself outside the bureaucratic situation and which would be sufficient to predispose the members of the petty bourgeoisie to practise the virtues demanded by the bureaucratic order and exalted by the ideology of 'public service': probity, meticulousness, rigour and a propensity for moral indignation.[15] This hypothesis has received a sort of experimental confirmation from the changes that have occurred in recent years in various public organizations, especially the French post office, linked to the recruitment of young, low-ranking civil servants who are victims of structural deskilling and whose dispositions correspond less well to the expectations of the institution.[16] So it is not possible to understand the functioning of bureaucratic institutions unless one moves beyond the fictitious opposition between, on the one hand, a 'structuralist' view which tends to see structural and morphological characteristics as the basis of the 'iron laws' of bureaucracies, which it regards as mechanisms capable of defining their own teleology and imposing it on their agents; and, on the other hand, an 'interactionist' or psycho-sociological view which tends to see bureaucratic practices as the product of the agents' interactions and strategies, ignoring both the social conditions of production of the agents (both inside and outside the institution) and the institutional conditions in which they perform their functions (e.g. forms of control over recruitment, promotion and remuneration).

It is true that the specificity of bureaucratic fields, relatively auto-nomous spaces structured by institutionalized positions, lies in the capacity, which is constitutive of these positions (since they are defined by their rank and scope), to induce their holders to produce all the practices implied in their job description. They do this through the effect of regulations, directives, circulars, etc. (a direct, visible effect which is commonly associated with the idea of bureaucracy), and especially through the whole set of vocation–co-option mechanisms which tends to adjust agents to their jobs, or, more precisely, their dispositions to their positions. These fields then have the further capacity to confer on these practices, and only these, the recognition of a certain status authority. But even in this case it is a mistake to try to understand the practices in terms of the immanent logic of the structure of positions (defined at a given moment, i.e. after a certain history, as regards number, legal status, etc.), just as it is a mistake to try to account for them solely in terms of the agents' 'psychosocio-logical' dispositions, especially if these are separated from their con-ditions of production. In reality, we find here, once again, a particular case of a more or less 'successful' encounter between positions and dispositions, i.e. between objectified history and internalized history.

The tendency of the bureaucratic field to 'degenerate' into a totali-tarian institution which demands complete, mechanical identifica-tion (*perinde ac cadaver*) of the functionary with his function, the *apparatchik* with the apparatus, is not linked mechanically to the morphological effects which scale and number may have on its struc-tures (e.g. through the constraints on communication) and its functions. It only occurs to the extent that it encounters the conscious collaboration of certain agents or the unconscious complicity of their dispositions (and this leaves room for the liberating effect of raised consciousness). The further one moves from the ordinary functioning of fields as fields of struggle towards limiting-states, which are perhaps never reached, in which all struggle and all resistance to domination have disappeared, so that the field hardens and contracts into a 'totalitarian institution', in Goffman's sense, or – in a rigorous sense, an *apparatus* – which is able to demand everything, without conditions or concessions and which, in its extreme forms – barracks, prisons, concentration camps – has the physical and symbolic means of restructuring earlier habitus, the more the institution tends to consecrate agents who give everything to the institution (e.g. 'the party' or 'the church'). Such agents perform their oblation all the more easily because they have less capital outside the institution and therefore less freedom *vis-à-vis* the institution and the specific capital and profits that it provides. The *apparatchik*, who owes everything to the apparatus, is the apparatus incarnate and he can be trusted with the highest responsibilities because he can do nothing to advance his own interests that does not *ipso facto* help to defend the interests of the apparatus. He is predisposed to defend the institution, with total conviction, against the heretical deviations of those whose externally acquired capital allows and inclines them to take liberties with internal beliefs and hierarchies. In short, in those cases most favourable to a mechanistic description of practices, analysis reveals a sort of unconscious adjustment of positions and dispositions, the true principle of the functioning of the institution, precisely in the aspect which gives it the appearance of an infernal machine.

Thus, the most alienating and irksome working conditions of those closest to forced labour, are still taken up by a worker who perceives, assesses, accommodates and puts up with them in terms of his own history and indeed the history of his whole lineage. The reason why descriptions of the most alienating work conditions and the most alienated workers are so often unconvincing – not least because they do not help to explain why things are as they are and remain as they are – is that, following the logic of the Sartrian chimera, they fail to account for the tacit agreement between the most inhuman working conditions and men who have been prepared to accept them by inhuman living conditions. The dispositions inculcated by a childhood experience of the social world which, in certain historical conditions, can predispose young workers to accept and even wish for entry into a world of manual labour which they identify with the adult world, are reinforced by work experience itself and by all the consequent changes in their dispositions (which can be understood by analogy with the changes Goffman describes as constituting the 'asylum-making' process). A whole process of investment leads workers to contribute to their own exploitation through their effort to appropriate their work and their working conditions, which leads them to bind themselves to their 'trade' by means of the very freedoms (often minimal and almost always 'functional') that are left to them, and as a result of the competition arising from the differences (*vis-à-vis* unskilled workers, immigrants, women, etc.) that structure their occupation as a field. Indeed, setting aside the extreme situations that are closest to forced labour, it can be seen that the objective reality of wage labour, i.e. exploitation, is made possible partly by the fact that the subjective reality of the labour does not coincide with its objective reality. The worker who no longer expects his work (and his work-place) to give him anything more than a wage experiences his situation as unnatural and untenable, and the indignation it arouses confirms this.[17]

Differences in dispositions, like differences in position (to which they are often linked), engender real differences in perception and appreciation. Thus the recent changes in factory work, towards the limit predicted by Marx, with the disappearance of 'job satisfaction', 'responsibility' and 'skill' (and all the corresponding hierarchies), are appreciated and accepted very differently by different groups of workers. Those whose roots are in the industrial working class, who possess skills and relative 'privileges', are inclined to defend past gains, i.e. job satisfaction, skills and hierarchies and therefore a form of established order; those who have nothing to lose because they have no skills, who are in a sense a working-class embodiment of the populist chimera, such as young people who have stayed at school longer than their elders, are more inclined to radicalize their struggles and challenge the whole system; other, equally disadvantaged workers, such as first-generation industrial workers, women, and especially immigrants, have a tolerance of exploitation which seems to belong to another age. In short, in the most oppressive working conditions, those which would seem to be most favourable to the mechanistic interpretation which reduces the worker to his 'position in the relations of production', and even directly *derives* him from that position, his activity is in fact the interaction of two histories and his present is the meeting of two pasts.[18]

Notes

1 On the forms and scientific effects of this fallacy in anthropology, linguistics and sociology, and on the social conditions which make it possible, see P. Bourdieu, *Le Sens pratique* (Paris: Editions de Minuit, 1979). For an English translation of an earlier version, see *Outline of a Theory of Practice* (Cambridge University Press, 1977).

2 E. Panofsky, *Studies in Iconology* (Oxford University Press, 1939), p. 4.

3 N. Hartmann, *Das Problem des geistigen Seins* (Berlin: de Gruyter, 1933), p. 172.

4 This, it seems to me, is what Heidegger, in his later works, and Merleau-Ponty (especially in *Le Visible et l'invisible*), endeavoured to express in the language of ontology, i.e. a 'savage' or 'barbarous' – I would say simply 'practical' – relationship to objects, falling short of intentionality.

5 N. Elias, *Die höfische Gesellschaft* (Neuwied, Luchterhand, 1969), pp. 134–5.

6 The only absolute freedom the game leaves is freedom to withdraw from the game, by a heroic renunciation which – unless one manages to set up another game – secures tranquillity only at the cost of social death, from the point of view of the game and the *illusio*.

7 'The King does not simply preserve the hierarchical order handed on by his predecessors. Etiquette leaves him a certain scope for manoeuvre, even in unimportant matters. He takes advantage of the psychological dispositions which reflect the hierarchical and aristocratic structures of the society; he takes advantage of the rivalry among the courtiers, who are always looking for prestige and favours, to modify the rank and consideration of the members of court society in accordance with the requirements of his own power, by means of a careful distribution of his marks of favour, so as to create internal tensions and to shift the balance as it suits him' (N. Elias, *Die höfische Gesellschaft*, pp. 136–7).

8 The 'apparatus' theory no doubt owes part of its success to the fact that it can lead to an abstract denunciation of the state or the education system which acquits the agents of personal responsibility, so that their occupational practice and their political choices can be treated as separate issues.

9 The official who points out that 'rules are rules' demands (in accordance with the rules) that the 'person' is to be identified with the rules, in opposition to those who appeal to the 'person', his feelings, his 'understanding', his 'indulgence', etc.

10 As Carl Schorske shows apropos of Freud (*Fin-de-Siècle Vienna: Politics and Culture* (New York: A. Knopf, and London: Weidenfeld & Nicolson, 1980), pp. 181–213), the 'psychological' obstacles to identification and the social obstacles are inextricably linked and need to be considered together in any analysis which endeavours to account for deviations from the path implied by an individual's social heritage ('failures' who can clearly be successes from a different point of view, such as a banker's artist son).

11 It is somewhat unfair to analyse in this way a text which has the merit of making completely explicit (hence its interest) the most hidden and even secret aspects of a lived experience of the social world of which partial or impoverished manifestations can be observed every day.

12 J.-P. Sartre, *Being and Nothingness*, trans. H. E. Barnes (London: Methuen, 1969), p. 60.

13 As I have tried to show elsewhere, this tendency to present the intellectual's relation to working-class conditions as if it were the working-class relation to those conditions does not necessarily disappear when, as observer or actor, the intellectual briefly occupies the worker's position in

the relations of production. (The exception, which makes it a remarkable document on, for example, the mythifying and demythifying of the working class, is for me Nicolas Dubost's book, *Flins sans fin* (Paris: Maspero, 1979).)

14 One always has a spontaneous philosophy of history, and also a philosophy of one's own history, i.e. of one's position and trajectory in social space. This 'central intuition', which makes it possible to take up a position on the great 'theoretical' or 'political' alternatives of the day (determinism/freedom, 'structuralism'/spontaneism, Communist Party/ultra-leftism, etc.) and which very directly expresses one's relation to the social world, is the basis not only of one's view of the social world and political positions but also of the seemingly most elementary and innocent choices in scientific practice. (The scientificity of social science can be measured by its capacity to constitute these alternatives as a scientific object and to grasp the social determinants of the choices made in relation to them. One of the difficulties of writing is due, in the case of the social sciences, to the fact that it must endeavour to disappoint and refute in advance those readings that will perceive the analysis in terms of the grids it is endeavouring to objectify.)

15 Cf. P. Bourdieu and J.-C. Passeron, *Reproduction in Education, Society and Culture* (London and Beverly Hills: Sage Publications, 1977), pp. 191–2.

16 Cf. P. Bourdieu and L. Boltanski, 'Formal Qualifications and Occupational Hierarchies', in *Reorganizing Education*, Sage Annual Review, Social and Educational Change, Vol. 1. (London and Beverly Hills, Sage Publications, 1977).

17 P. Bourdieu *et al.*, *Travail et travailleurs en Algérie* (Paris–The Hague; Mouton, 1963); and P. Bourdieu, *Algeria 1960* (Cambridge University Press and Paris, Editions de la Maison des Sciences de l'Homme, 1979).

18 The relationship between workers and union or political organizations could be described in terms of the same logic. Here, too, the present is the encounter of two pasts which are themselves partly the product of their past interaction. (For example, when one measures empirically the awareness workers in a given society have of the class structure, their image of work or their awareness of their rights – regarding industrial accidents, dismissal, etc. – one is recording the effect of the past action of the unions and parties, and it may be supposed that a different history would have produced different images and – in an area in which images play a large part in shaping reality – different realities.) In other words, their image of their position depends on the relationship between the traditions offered by the organizations (with the divisions between them, for example) and their dispositions.

Index of names

Index of subjects

action theory, 161ff
aggregate data, 2
aggregation hypothesis, 25ff, 59, 76f, 81ff
apparatchik, 313f
apparatus, 22, 305, 313f
associations, 283, 292

baboons, 281ff
black box, 285f, 298, 300
blood, 214ff
bureaucracy, 65f
bureaucratic field, 313f
bureaucratic institutions, 312ff

café-waiter, 309f
capability, 163ff
causal powers, 141
cells, 212ff
circulation, 213ff
coercion theory, 2
cognitive order, 2ff
cognitive processes, 3
cognitive psychology, 77
cognitive sciences, 44
cognitive sociology, 1, 5
cognitive turn, 2ff
collective, 2, 16f, 140ff, 155ff
communicative action, 262
communicative competence, 57
competence theory, 4ff, 152f
complexity, 19ff, 245, 265

conflict, 247ff
constatives, 178ff
construction, 6, 66f, 73ff, 85, 238f
context, 10ff, 55, 58ff, 153, 191ff
contract, 248, 278ff
conversation analysis, 54ff, 206f

descriptive epistemology, 5
de-thematization, 249ff
discourse, 52ff
dispositions, 304, 308ff
doctor-patient interaction, 68ff, 130ff
duality of structure, 168, 171ff

econometrics, 34f
economic structure, 266
educational institutions, 72ff
emergent properties, 142
empirical, 83ff
empiricism, 90
ethnography, 55, 60f, 63, 153
ethnography of speaking, 1
ethnomethodology, 1, 6f, 81ff
ethnoscience, 1, 4f
ethogenics, 1, 5, 151f
evolutionary learning, 259ff

face-to-face interaction, 11, 173
field, 308ff
field work, 61
fluid matrix, 213ff
function, 209f